FAMILIES
IN
PAIN

CHILDREN, SIBLINGS, SPOUSES, AND PARENTS OF THE MENTALLY ILL SPEAK OUT

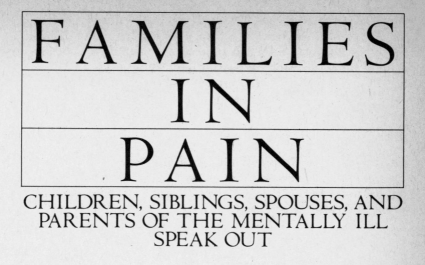

FAMILIES IN PAIN

CHILDREN, SIBLINGS, SPOUSES, AND PARENTS OF THE MENTALLY ILL SPEAK OUT

PHYLLIS VINE

FOREWORD BY
C. CHRISTIAN BEELS, M.D., M.S.

PANTHEON BOOKS   NEW YORK

Phyllis Vine received her B.A. from the University of California at Los Angeles and her Ph.D. from the University of Michigan. Since 1975, she has been a member of the faculty at Sarah Lawrence College, teaching courses on the history of the family and the history of health care. She is also on the faculty of Sarah Lawrence's graduate program in health advocacy. Phyllis Vine is a co-author of *Household and Kin: Families in Flux.* A member of her family is mentally ill.

Dr. C. Christian Beels is Director of the Fellowship in Public Psychiatry at the New York State Psychiatric Institute, and Assistant Professor in Psychiatry at the College of Physicians and Surgeons at Columbia University.

All rights reserved under International and Pan-American Copyright Conventions. Published in the United States by Pantheon Books, a division of Random House, Inc., New York, and simultaneously in Canada by Random House of Canada Limited, Toronto. Hardcover edition originally published by Pantheon Books, a division of Random House, Inc., in 1982.

Library of Congress Cataloging in Publication Data

Vine, Phyllis, 1945–
Families in pain.

Includes bibliographical references and index.
1. Mentally ill—Family relationships. 2. Mental health services. 3. Mentally ill—Rehabilitation. I. Title.
RC455.4.F3V56   1983   362.2   82-22539
ISBN 0-394-71418-0 (pbk.)

Since this copyright page cannot accommodate all permissions acknowledgments, they are to be found on the following page.

Text design by Dana Kasarsky Design

Manufactured in the United States of America

First Paperback Edition

For my family

Burn, glare, old sun, so long unseen,
That time may find its sound again, and cleanse
Whatever it is that a wound remembers
After the healing ends.

Weldon Kees—"Small Prayer"

Contents

CONTENTS

CONTENTS

CONTENTS

Acknowledgments

There are few things which give me as much pleasure as the opportunity to thank the many people who have offered their support and encouragement while I was working on this book. Among them are the mental health professionals who agreed that families of the mentally ill have a story worth telling. For their time and encouragement I want to thank: Carol M. Anderson, Ph.D., Associate Professor of Psychiatry and Director of Family Therapy, University of Pittsburgh; Ernie Drucker, Ph.D., Montefiore Hospital, Bronx, New York; Gerard E. Hogarty, M.S.W., Associate Professor of Psychiatry, University of Pittsburgh; Loren R. Mosher, M.D., National Institute of Mental Health, Washington, D.C.; Louis Ormont, Ph.D., New York City; Joan Speck, Ph.D., Ross Speck, M.D., Philadelphia; and Lois Staffin, A.C.S.W., Beth Israel Hospital, Newark, New Jersey. A special thanks goes to C. Christian Beels, M.D., Director, Fellowship in Public Psychiatry, New York State Psychiatric Institute, who sent me scurrying after references, answered countless questions, gave a trenchant criticism of the first draft, and graciously agreed to write an introduction.

Many people explained their involvement in particular aspects of mental health care, or their organization's activities. I am grateful to: John Beard, Fountain House, New York; Paul Friedman, the Mental Health Law Project, Washington, D.C.; Agnes B. Hatfield, Threshold, Montgomery County, Maryland, and the National Alliance for the Mentally Ill; Fran Hoffman and Tony Hoffman, Parents of Adult Schizophrenics, San Mateo County, California; Shirley Starr, National Alliance of the Mentally Ill.

Friends and colleagues, without whose support this would have been a lonely experience, have my appreciation. Otis Cavrell suggested that I write this after hearing about an episode with Joanna. Shortly after that, Frank and Jinx Roosevelt and Joan Kavanaugh listened to the ideas and helped me believe that it could be done. Fred Goldman and Joyce Riegelhaupt forced me to refine the focus, and Wendy McKenna and Lois Staffin criticized the first draft of the manuscript. Other friends who were available at important times include: Susan Cole, Pyser Edelsack, Benjamin Hollombe, Joan Kelly, Suzanne Kessler, Joan Marks, David Muchnick, Ruth Ozarow, Judy Papachristou, and Amy Swerdlow.

Sarah Lawrence College was an especially important source of support, first with a small grant and then with a generous leave which allowed me to reduce my teaching responsibilities while finishing the manuscript. To Alison Baker and Ilja Wachs, my thanks. Also to Phyllis Byan and the entire staff of the Esther Raushenbush Library for the ever cheerful search for obscure references—which I always needed in a hurry! Preparation of the manuscript was supported in part by an Alcohol Abuse and Mental Health Administration grant from the National Institute of Mental Health (MH 34325-01).

Marilyn Young introduced me to Jim Peck and Susan Gyarmati at Pantheon. Each showed interest and confidence when the project was little more than a few rough pages. When it was a few hundred, Susan posed the critical questions that forced me to clarify and sharpen the work. Her belief in the project and intelligent criticisms offered guidance and support. Finally, Nan Graham ushered me through the final stages with cheerful regard.

Of all of the people whose encouragement and confidence propelled me in this project, however, none were more important

ACKNOWLEDGMENTS

than the families to whom I spoke. Not all of them could be presented in these pages, and those who do appear are under disguise and pseudonym. I wish I could thank them by name, but for obvious reasons that is not possible.* But without their generosity and trust, their willingness to take a chance, and their desire to help others, this book would not have been possible. To all of them I owe a great debt, and I hope they know how deep is my gratitude.

Phyllis Vine
New York City, August 1981

*The episodes which appear in this book are the actual stories recounted by family members, and not composites. In order to guarantee privacy, however, it has been necessary to change the names of families, therapists, and hospitals. Because each appears under a pseudonym, any resemblance to actual individuals with the same name is purely coincidental.

Foreword

I was delighted to be asked to write an introduction to this book, because as a psychiatrist I want to recommend it to my colleagues. It will, of course, be an important book for a variety of lay people. It will have special importance for the relatives of the mentally ill because it is their story, and because sharing it will help them to feel less alone and lead to a better understanding of the situation that faces them. I hope as well that the book will convince legislators and others who make decisions about the organization of psychiatric care that the consequences of their decisions go far beyond the patients to another group of constituents.

But in particular I want to say why psychiatrists should read this book. It will remind them of things many of them have not thought about since they were young residents in training, when they had their first and only sustained contact with the victims of recurrent psychosis and their families. Most psychiatrists find that encounter as distressing as do the patients and families, and they quickly move on to specialize in another kind of work—psychotherapy with neurotics, for example. They prefer the office treatment of stable, solvent people whose interests are a little like their own. The treatment of psychosis, by contrast, has required that psychiatrists remain attached to relatively low-paying institutions, master a very difficult literature, participate in frustrating organizational politics, and spend a lot of time listening to the raving, or enduring the silent rejection, of patients in the grip of various kinds of madness. For these and many other reasons, psychiatrists turn their backs on the scenes described by the families in this book.

But since the book is written from the point of view of the relatives, it will give psychiatrists an opportunity to think the problem through again and to realize that by failing to organize the care and promote better understanding of the mentally ill in the United States, we have left the families to fend for themselves. They must deal with the state hospitals, which have the most poorly trained psychiatrists; or the nursing homes, which have no psychiatrists; often they find no place at all to turn to. The stories here are about the initial shock and then, over the years, the fatigue and disillusionment families experience as they come to know what is involved in the care of a mentally ill relative and slowly learn the courage to deal with that responsibility.

What about the patients themselves? They suffer from illnesses whose essential social characteristic is the inability to organize one's life effectively. Schizophrenia, and to a lesser extent other major psychoses, produce defects in the individual's ability to inspire the confidence of others, either in the short run, in daily conversations, or over longer periods. Promises are not kept, and mutual disappointment between the patient and others is the rule. Schizophrenia is, among other things, a failure of the kind of effective social initiative required in our society to keep other people interested in helping a person in need. In this the mentally ill are different from the victims of blindness, seizure disorders, paraplegia, and other chronic illnesses, who have begun to form effective self-help groups and lobbies to influence the organizing and funding of services. The chronically mentally ill are an interest group who are by definition un-organized, and the improvement of their lot requires a very special kind of social organization on the part of *others*. The question is, can the psychiatric profession take the lead in building and maintaining this kind of organization in the community?

Where have the psychiatrists been all these years while the families who talked to Phyllis Vine have had to struggle toward their own solutions? That is perhaps the part of the story I can tell briefly. The psychiatric profession in the 1950s was full of confidence in its ability to solve a great range of problems, from the conflict of nations to writer's block. To some of us, psychoanalysis was the universal solution; what problems it could not solve, those of us who had gone into social psychiatry were ready to tackle with general systems theory, family therapy, community psychiatry, and so on. In the 1960s the federal government responded to our optimism by giving us an enormous amount of money, which President Kennedy told us was to be spent on a "bold new approach" to the care of the severely mentally ill in the community. We spent it instead on psychotherapy, basic biological research, and social psychiatry. The last was for the most part an attempt somehow to make the community healthier, an indirect approach to serious mental illness by way of "prevention" rather than treatment. We avoided the problem of treating the chronically ill for two reasons in addition to the emotional ones mentioned above. One, we had not really learned much about how to do it. Two, the chronically ill were already in the hands of the small minority of us who were settled in the state hospital establishment—a comfortable arrangement for the rest of us.

Then, for a number of historical reasons, the patients began to be released from the state hospitals, and we found ourselves presiding over a new "shame of the cities" called the de-institutionalization of the mentally ill. By the 1970s our money had been spent and our reputation as the caretakers of this population discredited. Much as some of us would like to deny it, we must all share a little in that discredit, because, though we like to think of ourselves as liberators of the human spirit, the public continues to charge us with the responsibility for taking care of crazy people. It is like the expectation that police catch burglars and doctors save lives.

Meanwhile, quietly and in the background, several things were happening from which we may derive some hope for the future. First, a small amount of that federal money was actually spent on experimental social programs for the seriously ill. From careful evaluative research, especially in the last decade, we have learned how to design the kinds of programs of community care for patients that are described in chapters five and six.

Second, the development of anti-psychotic medication and the science of diagnosis for its accurate use have advanced to the point where most psychiatrists, especially the young and recently trained, feel confident that they know how to manage that aspect of care. Although fewer doctors are specializing in psychiatry now than in previous decades, those who do are learning a more eclectic kind of practice. With the passing of the era of idealistic social psychiatry, we realize that the work we had to do in the previous centuries of our profession's history is still there to do, and that as a result of recent research it is becoming a discipline of distinct intellectual and personal satisfaction.

As social programs for mental patients prove more effective, a shift in the role of the psychiatrist is becoming possible. Under the tutelage of psychoanalysis, psychiatrists used to think that the only respectable role open to them, commensurate with their years of special training, was that of psychotherapist. With very sick patients psychotherapy was notoriously unrewarding, both as an experience for doctor and patient and as an effective enterprise. Now doctors who work in good social programs for the chronically and recurrently psychotic can play a number of roles: diagnostician, family therapy consultant, program organizer, emergency team leader, educator, research consultant. It is clear that we do not need armies of psychotherapists to treat chronic patients; what we need is a much smaller number of really able psychiatrists to coordinate these social programs, and we need the space, clear of bureaucratic red tape, for them to work in.

As Phyllis Vine describes in her final chapter, the relatives of the mentally ill are getting organized. This may be the most important development, because only the relatives seem in a position to call with a single voice for housing, employment, and well-organized treatment programs. The psychiatrists and other mental health professionals who appear at government hearings still tend to be divided among themselves and against other professions. They are only slowly coming to realize they are in some ways public servants in search of a constituency. In times like these, when money is short, we need to simplify and focus our objectives. I hope this book helps to re-introduce psychiatrists to the relatives of the mentally ill, as it introduces the relatives to each other. Together, those two groups could make a coalition of great mutual benefit, and one of decisive importance to the patients whose care is their joint responsibility.

C. CHRISTIAN BEELS, M.D., M.S.
Director, Fellowship in Public Psychiatry
New York State Psychiatric Institute

List of Families

ADAMSON: Ellie Adamson is the mother of four adult daughters. She has been in and out of psychiatric hospitals, halfway houses, and rehabilitation centers for almost a decade. She needs independent housing and a job.

AMATO: Helen and Lou Amato's adult son, Joseph, lives at home, receives medicine as an outpatient, and has just started a job.

ANTHONY: Roger Anthony's sudden break forced his parents, Jim and Grace, into quick action one morning. Under the guidance of Dr. Golden, they cared for their teenage son at home for one month before having him admitted to a general hospital and then a long-term treatment center. He returned to live with his parents and younger sister.

BLOOMBERG: Linda Bloomberg's brother, Mark, has been in dozens of hospitals for emergency treatment over the last decade. Now in his thirties, Mark has never had sustained employment or continuous housing, and he is dependent on Supplemental Security Income. Linda and Mark live in different cities.

CONNELLY: Eventually Art Connelly had to hospitalize his wife, Ruth, whose behavior at first seemed little more than an exaggeration of some of her personality traits. Over several years she has been hospitalized for treatment for varying lengths of time. Today she and Art live in separate cities, though they are still married. They have three grown daughters.

FLYNN: Rosanne Flynn is a single parent to Emily, who was a teenager attending her first year of college when she became depressed. After two suicide attempts and having tried several psychiatrists and psychologists, Emily entered treatment in a psychiatric hospital, where she stayed for eighteen months. She now lives with her mother.

GOLDSTEIN: Natalie Goldstein has become estranged from her parents because of their differing beliefs about how to help Janet, who was in her twenties when her first break occurred.

GREENE: Selma Greene was institutionalized more than thirty years ago. At the time she had two small children. Carolyn, her daughter, went to live with an aunt and uncle. Marvin, her son, went to live with Uncle Harold and Aunt Eileen.

HARRISON: Fay and Stanley Harrison's son, Jonah, has lived in a state hospital since he tried to kill his father. Prior to that he had three years of unsuccessful treatment in various hospitals.

KANE: When Rebecca Kane was only a child, her father, Morris, was hospitalized following World War II. He was discharged after his wife, Claire, insisted that the Veterans Administration try Lithium to see if it would help. Soon thereafter Morris was being prepared to return home after five years of treatment.

KAPLAN: Donald Kaplan continues to be responsible for his former wife, Arlene. They have two young children—a boy and a girl—and she has custody of them.

MARTINS: Frank and Merle Martins divorced after more than twenty years. Arguments about how to help Alex, their mentally disabled son, spilled over into every part of the marriage and affected not only them but their younger daughter.

MCCOY: Scott McCoy's problems became apparent when he was away at college. He returned home to live with his mother, Berenice, and in between efforts to live independently in halfway houses or his own apartments, he has had a few hospitalizations. He would like to work but has had difficulty finding a job.

POLLACK: Nancy Pollack's daughter, Shelly, received treatment in many hospitals as well as through private therapy and as an outpatient in a day hospital. In the time between our interview and the publication of this book, Shelly died after an overdose.

STANWICK: Stella and Lloyd Stanwick's grown son, Christopher, has lived at home his entire life. Though he has been hospitalized only once, he is unable to work and spends most of the time in the basement recreation room.

VANN: Thomas Vann's wife, Evelyn, continues to be responsible for him, even though they remain married in name only. Because of his diabetes, Evelyn has had to commit Tom, and their three teenage children refused to allow him to return home when he was discharged from the hospital.

YOUNG: Dora and Thomas Young have cared for James at home. With three other children in the family, James's behavior provoked tensions with his brothers and sister when they were younger. Now that all the children are between the ages of twenty-two and thirty-five, they are anticipating how to care for James when Dora and Thomas no longer can.

Mental Health Professionals

DR. CHESTER: Roger Anthony's psychiatrist at Neartown Hospital, where he received long-term treatment.

DR. FUSTENBERG: Roger Anthony's psychiatrist at Alpha General Hospital, where he received treatment after an emergency admission.

DR. GOLDEN: The private psychiatrist who guided Jim and Grace Anthony before, during, and after Roger's hospitalization.

DR. HAMPSTER: The psychiatrist with whom Rosanne Flynn consulted before Emily's admission to Circlesville Psychiatric Institute and who eventually joined its staff.

LORRAINE HOWARD: A social worker who directs a day hospital program.

MRS. KAHN: Roger Anthony's psychiatric social worker at Neartown Hospital.

DR. MACINTER: The first psychiatrist Fay and Stanley Harrison consulted about Jonah.

MS. MARKOVE: The social worker who worked with Jim and Grace Anthony when Roger was in Alpha General Hospital.

DR. NGU: Jonah Harrison's psychiatrist and chief of the ward in a state psychiatric hospital.

MR. OLIVETTI: The social worker who tried to help Mark Bloomberg petition for Supplemental Security Insurance.

DR. SWEET: Mark Bloomberg's psychologist, whom he saw as an outpatient while living at the board-and-care facility.

FAMILIES
IN
PAIN

CHILDREN, SIBLINGS, SPOUSES, AND
PARENTS OF THE MENTALLY ILL
SPEAK OUT

Things fall apart; the centre cannot hold;
Mere anarchy is loosed upon the world,
The blood-dimmed tide is loosed, and everywhere
The ceremony of innocence is drowned. . . .

William Butler Yeats—"The Second Coming"

PART

I

THE SETTING

I

Living with Symptoms

A PERSONAL NOTE

"If I had thought there were others who had this problem," he said, "I would have been less troubled, knowing that I was not unique." That's how Harold Greene began to describe how his sister's mental illness has affected his life over the past thirty years. Harold, like most people who have a relative with a mental disability, dealt with the problem in social isolation. Whether it is because mental illness remains a stigma, or because its course is treated through a private medical route, the focus of attention has been on the patient and his or her needs. Yet for most people who are mentally ill there is a larger family: parents and children, brothers and sisters, husbands and wives, and grandparents who care. This book is about us—the families of those who are diagnosed as mentally ill. It is about how we have coped and fought, been overwhelmed and saddened, and struggled to understand the meaning that our relative's illness has for us.

I am not a stranger to this book's themes. At the time I decided to write it, I had already gone through the cycle in which family members, observing behavior in a relative that confuses and frightens them, begin to seek the kinds of professional help that have been recommended. I was then in the middle of a disturbing situation: my younger cousin, Joanna, who had been in a hospital for only three days, was being prepared for discharge.

"Three days isn't long enough," I said to the psychiatrist. "That's no help. How can you release her in such a short time?" The psychiatrist did not challenge my statements. It was obvious that three days' treatment was not much help to someone whose babble slowed only after she had received an anti-psychotic drug. Also, it was apparent that her medical needs were greater than she was willing to admit. But the young psychiatrist, who was still in his residency, offered no explanation. He just turned the pages of her chart, rereading some of the entries, while I stood there thinking about the previous weekend. It had been a marathon; I had listened to Joanna, walked with her up and down the streets of New York, and pleaded with her to get some help so she could straighten herself out. The steady changes I had seen over the last few years were getting worse. She insisted that ancient peoples were sending cryptic messages only she could decipher. Her inability to budget money left her in perpetual debt and me in the role of banker. And I was irritated by her requests, which felt more like demands, to find her a "good" job through my friends. She had proved untrustworthy in the past, and I didn't want to be embarrassed in the future.

Joanna and I had always been close. After her parents were killed in an accident, she came to live with my family, and we were raised as sisters. When my own parents died, there was never any question but that our bonds would strengthen. We had been a close family, and we remained so with our aunts, uncles, and cousins. Over the years these relatives witnessed Joanna's increasing "craziness," and each tried to help in his or her own way. But Joanna was resolute in insisting that whatever difficulties she had were either temporary or the result of an idiosyncratic situation. Whatever *we* thought about her delusions, to *her* they were real, and she spent many hours describing the details of encounters we considered preposterous. Nobody could help her. She didn't need any help, she claimed. A few years later, our lives and careers as adults took us to different parts of the country. We spoke often, and whenever Joanna was in town she would stay with me, and we would talk into the early-morning hours. In recent years many of these conversations addressed her recurrent difficulties in keeping the right job, using her talents to further her ambitions, and trying to understand those who were "out to get her."

By the time she was ready to leave the hospital I was confused and exhausted. I was also angry. I could not understand how a person who had talked of receiving messages from radios just the previous week, and had been living in streets and in the shadows of buildings, could simply be discharged without further help. I warned the psychiatrist that she would not return, as he suggested, for the recommended outpatient treatment. Over the previous decade she had been adamant that she did not need counseling or therapy. "I don't see what makes you think she will suddenly see the point," I said loudly, and with little regard for those who were standing nearby. "She is stabilized now," he responded. As an adult who was neither homicidal nor suicidal, she was free to leave.

I was utterly powerless to change the situation. How could I get her help? I wondered, while feeling responsible. I could not understand the realities of the 1970s which seemed to treat people with little of the compassion that was the promise of the 1960s. I was speechless at the apparent disregard for how she was to be helped, and my anger was ignited at the additional burden I was made to feel as the "next of kin," who the psychiatrist assumed would be her caretaker. It felt like a struggle for survival, and after the previous weekend I wasn't sure who would win. I had to know what it was about the system of mental health care that permitted someone like Joanna to return to the streets, as unprotected from the winter snow as she was from herself.

There was no question but that Joanna would spend the first few days with me after she left the hospital. When that became intolerable, as I knew it would, what would I do with her? When my patience with her demanding requests ran out, how would I respond? In the preceding months I had tried to meet her bizarre needs for a special diet and unusual artifacts with compassion in the hope of getting her to psychiatric help. Things *felt* different now. Professional help required her assent and cooperation. Without it I could not imagine what would sustain me as I

7

tried to help her. It felt like defeat, and I wasn't sure for whom.

As a historian with a specialty in the history of health and health care, I already knew about the medical and social conditions of the nineteenth and twentieth centuries which incarcerated the mentally ill. The horrors seen by Dorothea Dix, when she visited asylums a century ago, were common knowledge. But I knew nothing about contemporary practices. I was determined to learn. I started to read and discovered that while there are not precise figures, estimates for the incidence of mental illness may be as high as 10 percent of the population. Most of these people do not require hospitalization, but even for those who do, social, medical, and legal practices in the 1960s and 1970s altered the profile of treatment for people with chronic mental illness. I began to understand the background of the news reports about "de-institution-alization" of the large mental hospitals. Somehow, neither the headlines about these people nor seeing the "bag ladies" on the subways or even those living in the SROs that populate my neighborhood had made an impression until I imagined Joanna as one of them.* It was sobering.

I started to talk with friends. "Did you know . . ." I began. To whatever it was that I was saying with outrage and indignation, they would respond yes. The conversations often turned around. From my account of a frustrating experience I had trying to help Joanna, they would pick up the thread with a similar episode they had encountered. As we talked, I heard about a sister-in-law, a son, a father, a former wife, a neighbor's daughter. It seemed that everyone with whom I spoke had some firsthand experience. Whether it was a relative whose illness had bankrupted the family or a psychotherapist who was dismissive and ignored their alarm, many voiced anger or frustration because of relatives with psychotic problems. Even those who had greater success than I did in navigating the crisis shared painful anecdotes with compassion about the similarity of our situations.

---

*"Bag ladies" refers to those women who are often seen on New York City streets carrying all their belongings in tattered shopping bags. An SRO is a single-room occupancy hotel, into which many welfare recipients (including former mental patients) are directed. Such structures have been the target of criticism in response to objections that former mental patients are "dumped." Many are located on the Upper West Side of Manhattan, but they can be found throughout the country under different names.

I could scarcely believe that all these people had knowledge of what I was just discovering. While no two stories were identical, many were alike. It did not matter whether their relative had been diagnosed as having one form or another of schizophrenia or whether it was a manic-depressive problem. The technicalities of the diagnosis mattered less than the ways in which the families perceived their social and emotional obligations. Many families had lived through episodes in which a relative was diagnosed first as having one problem, later another, and sometimes no diagnosis was made at all. For this reason I have made no effort to define, describe, or specify the particular aspects of the numerous classifications of disability within the group of major psychotic problems. It became apparent that whatever the technical diagnosis, families who have coped with a relative's mental disability requiring hospitalization have undergone cycles of despair, hope, anguish, ignorance, frustration, anger, and gratitude. Each person's circumstances have brought a unique element to the situation. Taken as a whole, however, their experiences reflect a widespread social phenomenon.

The society-wide treatment for chronic mental illness affects members of different classes unevenly. This book looks at the experience of a primarily white middle-class population. The decision to focus on one particular segment of the population must not be read as an assumption that coping with chronic mental illness is easier among other social, racial, or occupational groups. Among families on welfare, or those dependent on the earnings of every family member, the financial problems carry a different urgency. The loss of food stamp coupons when a relative is hospitalized imposes a burden the middle class does not know and can't begin to imagine. Among elites, being able to meet the costs of hospitalization and knowing where the funds will be found reflects a security which those dependent on insurance payments do not know.

How middle-class individuals, many of them salaried and almost all of advanced education, coped with the tangible responsibilities of having a chronically mentally disabled relative is the focus of this book. It was not so much by theoretical design as it was by actual necessity that I had to understand how those, like myself, managed. I thought of the historical trends about which I have taught and lectured: changing patterns of kinship organization and household composition that have spread families from one end of the country to the other. These structural changes have occurred at the same time that the numbers of people living in a household have declined, making available fewer brothers and sisters or aunts and uncles to share some of the tasks which would have fallen on a larger pool in earlier times. The organization of work, which requires people to labor in offices and leaves homes empty during the daytime, has affected the structures within which caring for a dependent person occurs. Now, faced with the problem of what to do for Joanna, I romanticized the past while I damned the present. Yet I needed to know, and I learned from others in a similar situation.

Because Joanna was released from the hospital with little guidance in how to pull herself together, I feared she would deteriorate further. Thinking of my father's maxim about the importance of family, I let guilt compound my dilemma. Periodically, and especially at large family gatherings, I heard my father say, "You have only two things in this world which you cannot do without: your health and your family. Respect them both!" I thought of his words and wondered how they applied to me. Could I respect somebody who looked and acted the way Joanna did? Was it more "respectful" to force her into help or to give her the choice I believe people should have over their own decisions? Entrapped, I became obsessed with the question of what I was prepared to do for her. If she weren't my cousin, with whom so much of my life had been intertwined, what obligations would I feel? The friends to whom I spoke mentioned similar problems. To what degree could they provide, or should they arrange for, the housing which would be necessary for an adult son who lived across the continent? Where did one person's responsibility stop and another's start when Vocational Rehabilitation Services could not help a grown person find a job? Who would house the husband of one woman whose family had been shattered over the previous decade and whose children wanted only to be rescued from the tyrannical presence of their sick father?

It became increasingly evident that we shared a set of common concerns—for ourselves and for our relatives. Yet as I continued to read, I found only scant information and a few books which would help me understand the immensity of the dilemma I was in at that moment. After I spoke with friends and acquaintances who knew I intended to write this book, the names of other people who might be willing to talk to me were suggested. This book is based on these conversations—with individuals who were strangers to me when this process began. Since then, dozens of people have been interviewed for an average of three hours each. Some of them were interviewed twice. Several referred me to another member of the same family. Most interviews were arranged for me through a third party. This procedure, I believe, allowed people the opportunity to refuse to participate with the least amount of intrusion.

Only two people who were recommended preferred not to be interviewed. Some were initially reluctant, though they agreed to talk with some prompting. A few were enthusiastic enough that they called me before I could call them. Over eighteen months, in their homes or mine, in restaurants and offices, and in several cities and states, I spoke with family members of the chronically mentally ill. I began to understand how, on an individual and personal level, their relatives' predicaments affected their lives and those of other members of their family. The hopes and disappointments, the fears and fantasies that became concrete realities for daily living were a lens through which life was seen. Whether the person lived with them or not, the circumstances changed for families when the fear of chronic mental illness became a feature of life.

At some point in the interviews most people told me that the reason they agreed to dredge up painful memories, or discuss episodes they preferred to forget, was the desire to help others going through similar trials. It is widely believed that few people —clinicians as well as the lay public—appreciate what it means to a mother or daughter, a husband or son, to have a relative who is chronically mentally ill. Some of this was verified through my own experience. Some was confirmed when I talked to clinicians, an idea I abandoned early in the project. I quickly concluded that most of the psychiatrists and psychologists whose experience was based on a private practice did not understand the question I asked of them: Can you describe the impact mental illness makes on a family? Instead of viewing the problem from the family's point of view, many repeated the professional slogans and clichés about "the family's needs to have a dependent person." Or they explained theories of "scapegoating," or the "double bind." These were the assumptions with which they worked. This is what they wanted me to understand. One clinician went so far as to ask me,

"What makes the suffering of these people different from the suffering of others? Of those who lost relatives in concentration camps, in automobile accidents, or any other tragic way? Why should they be entitled to special pain?" I was dumbfounded that a therapist would deny the legitimacy of pain which is felt by millions of people. I also found it hard to believe how little she appreciated the importance of having a sympathetic community of people with whom to share such burdens.

My anger over this kind of response deepened my conviction that it was important for families who have been through the experience to tell what coping with mental illness requires. It is not a story that therapists can report; nor is it one that those who are or have been afflicted with mental illness can convey. While each has his or her own view, to understand what families have experienced, it is necessary to hear the story from them. The following pages attempt to portray that. Because the stories are told in retrospect, they have a clarity which distance encourages. It might not be the way someone in the midst of a crisis would describe events. It might not be the way someone on the edge of the situation would perceive it. In my own case, I suspect there was much more hysteria and less reason than I now recall. I also suspect that those living with or near me might describe the same events with more emphasis on one part, less on another. But what I have said about myself and Joanna is the way I remember the events unfolding, just as others in this book remember their particular experiences. And what has struck me continually, as I have worked on this over the past three years, is just how much we all share. For that reason, each of the people in this book says something which is in my heart.

RUTH CONNELLY

"When I was younger, I was convinced that my own life would be hell as long as my mother was alive," Maggie Connelly recalled. But when this twenty-five-year-old dark-haired woman was younger, she did not know that Ruth Connelly was behaving strangely because she was mentally ill. Yet even before Maggie thought of her mother as mentally ill, she knew that Ruth was different. Maggie also thought of her mother as "among the most delightful and charming people I know in the world. At least, she used to be," Maggie said as she began to tell of her contradictory feelings. While anger and hurt predominated when her mother's behavior confused and embarrassed Maggie and her sisters, she speaks now with compassion and understanding as she talks about how Ruth's illness affected the Connelly household.

Maggie admits that her compassion was slow to develop. It took years to outgrow the hostility she harbored when her mother's behavior was less clearly understood. Even now, more than seven years after Ruth's first hospitalization, Maggie was not sure that she wanted to be interviewed. Could she go through the story one more time? she wondered. Why not try to forget the old hurts while she was struggling to understand the present and plan for the future?

As we talked about her childhood and growing up in the suburbs, Maggie's apprehension slowly lifted. She described the behavior which she now recognizes was a symptom of mental illness and which, when it first appeared twenty years earlier, seemed little more than irritating or quixotic aspects of her mother's personality. As for others whose relative's illness begins slowly and builds gradually, it took a long time for the Connellys to recognize that Ruth's problems were out of control. Before that, when Maggie and her older sisters were still children, Ruth appeared idiosyncratic. Mental illness was alien to their world.

Maggie started by discussing her mother's strengths. She remembered Ruth's alternating periods of high spirits and sullen lethargy, her striking beauty, and the charm which captivated her daughters and their friends. Her charm had also captivated her husband, Art Connelly, who fell in love with Ruth forty years earlier when they met in college. As the youngest of the Connelly girls Maggie caught only glimpses of the person Art had courted. Art, however, remembered Ruth well before mental illness became part of the family's vocabulary. "She was always very sophisticated," he said. "And there was no question about it, she was a beautiful person. An unusually attractive woman."

In many ways Art thinks that their attraction to each other, and the strength of their marriage, were based on complementary temperaments. Ruth had, and still has, a wonderful sense of humor, which he continues to cherish. "It's like an Irish humor," he said. "The kind with a bite to it. And she is also a very sensitive and perceptive individual. She notices people and personalities and is interested in feelings. I'm much more pragmatic and, in most ways, even-tempered."

Ruth and Art dated through college, and they married six weeks before World War II. At the beginning of the war, when Art was sent overseas as a specialist in radio communications, they talked of her going abroad with the military so they could be closer together. Realizing, however, that they would be stationed in different wartime theaters, they decided simply to endure the separation as did hundreds of thousands of others. Art returned home only once in four years, and their oldest daughter, Irene, was born nine months later.

Art remembers worrying about his wife and daughter while he was overseas. He knew that Ruth's family would not be particularly helpful after Irene arrived, and he was mindful that it was a hardship for Ruth to care for an infant by herself. But she did manage alone, and as there was little else he could do, Art contented himself with the thought that thousands of others were in similar situations. When he returned home at the end of the war, they again faced a problem affecting all society: the widespread housing shortage. For a long time they looked for a place to live, and considered themselves among the lucky when they found even a tiny house way out of town.

The Connellys settled down for the first time in their marriage. Art commuted into town, where he was building a business in the burgeoning electronics industry. Ruth stayed home to care for Irene. They settled into the life-style of the post–World War II years: father at work; mother at home; peace and prosperity on the horizon; and the appearance of boundless opportunities before them.

Art and Ruth each labored during the day. He tended to his business; she, to the domestic tasks of being a housewife. The household chores, Art noticed, seemed to drain Ruth. "I would get home, and Ruth was tired after caring for this youngster all day. When I arrived, not much would have been done, even in this tiny house." But this didn't bother him. "I realized that she had been stuck in this house, which was far from everything, all day, and before that, she was alone with a child during the war. So I just

pitched in and fixed supper. Or sometimes we went ou
that she was fatigued, and I could understand that."

"My father has always been totally devoted to my r.
Maggie said. "He always was and always will be, even nov
added. Throughout my conversation with Art there was not a note
of bitterness or anger as he told how he returned home each night
and, though tired, was able to understand Ruth's frustration with
the domestic chores. That was life, and he is an accepting person.
Even as his business expanded along with his family, he continued
to participate actively in the household tasks. Another daughter,
Helene, was born three years after Irene, and they moved into a
larger house with more to do. It was a farmhouse in isolated
surroundings, which Art and Ruth quickly realized was "a marvelous place for two adults" but not ideal with young children. "With
rolling farmlands and lots of grounds it was a far distance between
the house and anything else. Every place the kids had to go, Ruth
had to drive them and then pick them up. They just couldn't run
out the back door to play with the other children," he noted. And
they were not there long because two years later they moved
again.

Art remembers that throughout these years there were
"times when things were pretty overwhelming for Ruth." Being
chauffeur and mother for two young children was a task made
more difficult by the isolation of their homes. But to him it seemed
no more serious than that "people get tired doing different things.
I wasn't concerned or worried," he noted. "You might even say
that I wasn't all that perceptive. I just accepted it as part of my
wife."

The business prospered, and for a short time Ruth helped Art
in the office, but she preferred to devote herself to the children.
She teased him about his work, calling it playing with electronic
gadgets. "She would tell me that if I wanted to play around with
these gadgets and a business, well, that was okay. But to her, the
important work was raising the children." And soon there was
another. Maggie, the youngest of the Connelly daughters, arrived
shortly after they moved from the farmhouse to another house,
which was located in a conventional suburb with neighbors and
children nearby.

From all appearances the Connellys lived a comfortable and
contented life. There were many successes and no major crises. Art

and Ruth enjoyed social relationships with their neighbors, gave and attended parties. Yet at the time when the external appearance of their lives seemed trouble-free, Ruth was increasingly overwhelmed and fatigued. She even thought it serious enough to want to visit a psychiatrist.

When, in the late 1950s, Ruth told her husband of her desire to see a psychiatrist, he was not enthusiastic. He didn't think she needed professional help just because she was exhausted from her domestic duties. To him the job of rearing three daughters was a reasonable source of fatigue. He is not sure why he was unenthusiastic about her plan. "Maybe it was the fact that we are Catholic and I thought this was not something we should do. But I guess if she had tried to speak with the priest about it, he would not have been much help. So I didn't discourage her either."

Ruth shopped for a psychiatrist, and when she found one she liked, and had seen him a few times, she asked Art to meet with him, too. He did. In retrospect Art thinks that the time Ruth was in treatment with this doctor was not fruitful and that despite his reputation, this doctor never appreciated his wife's strengths. "The psychiatrist told her that she would never be a good housewife. Maybe he even said a good mother." Art wasn't sure what the doctor said, but he did know that Ruth interpreted his remarks as critical of her mothering. Art thought "that was a mistake. Ruth was a very good mother. She was extremely concerned with the children. She always listened to their problems. In those ways she was a marvelous mother."

Whatever weakness either of them had as a parent or a person, Art is convinced the other compensated. "In a way I think the children had a balance. I was practical . . . the hard-work ethic . . . get it done. I get a lot of solace out of work. I'm also fairly organized. That's what I contributed," while Ruth shared her wit and warmth, her enthusiasm and her energy when she was feeling good. She conveyed to their children the value of humor and a taste for fine things. He thought they were a good team.

During the few months Ruth was in therapy, all Art remembered was that she felt "blue" much of the time. "But I would never think of the word 'depressed' at that time," he added. One day, when he picked his wife up after her appointment, she told him that she had "had it" with the psychiatrist. Art was not alarmed. "I thought we could handle it on our own. Maybe I emphasized that too much. But I thought we would just face it ourselves," he said of his lack of worry for the seriousness of "it."

Art was attentive and concerned about his wife, but not worried. Maggie, on the other hand, sensed something unusual in the family. She thinks the first clue she had was Art's involvement in the home. "My father always did a lot of things around the house," she said, adding how it embarrassed his daughters in the 1950s. The "typical family" in the suburbs, or at least those Maggie saw around her, followed a greater division of sex roles than did her family. Maggie couldn't understand why her father often got them ready for school, fed them breakfast before they left the house, or thought nothing of making dinner when he returned home.

While Maggie compared her parents with her friends' parents, Art was not in the least fazed by his participation in the household chores. After his own father had died, when he was still a youngster, he and his brother had pitched in to help their mother. "My brother and I always figured that it was part of what we should do to help out. So housework and chores were part of my life. I had no questions about doing them." But to Maggie and her sisters, her parents seemed odd. "My mother was overwhelmed by so many of the activities that were typically called mothering. Because of that, my father had to do all this stuff that other fathers didn't. I knew that was different from my friends. It was embarrassing. And I realized that my mother did things differently from other mothers, too."

Maggie remembers her mother's projects caused embarrassment. When she was spirited, Ruth engulfed the family in large projects. Rearranging the cabinets, cleaning shelves, emptying years of accumulated debris from the basement or the attic were among the things she started. But she never finished them. Ruth got as far as taking things off the shelves and piling them into boxes. Maggie remembers the house in perpetual disorder because she never put things back and wouldn't let her daughters help. Eventually Art picked up the mess and put everything back together. "My mother always resented this," Maggie said. "She claimed that she was going to get to that job." In the meantime, they lived in upset.

The energy Ruth expended in beginning new projects was coupled with pensive moods. Her wonderful humor and spirited enthusiasm sometimes turned to quiet observation and hours of inactivity. The Connellys accepted Ruth's moodiness and idiosyncrasies as being simply her. Like other families in which mental illness later forces a reconsideration of what everybody has taken for granted, they were not unduly disturbed by foibles and traits of a familiar person. Everybody develops ways of responding to particular personality traits in those they love. Some of the traits that doctors later called sickness, Art still believed were simply Ruth's character and had nothing to do with "being sick." They would have been present no matter what.

Art remembers those years as the time they lived like a "typical" American family. The Connellys enjoyed a good life. Their children attended excellent private schools and were blessed with friends and activities. For several summers the family went to a seaside resort and enjoyed themselves as they swam, hiked, sailed, and had barbecues. This seemed like a good way to vacation with children ranging in age between five and twelve. "I thought she liked the seashore," Art said. "But apparently, when we were all having a good time, she wasn't. I thought if I had fun swimming, so did she. But she didn't enjoy any of it. She remembers the summers as hard times. And even now she is still surprised that we all enjoyed it so much."

When the girls were older and it was easier for them to travel alone, Ruth and Art occasionally went abroad, where he was developing further business. There was even one summer that the entire family spent in Ireland. Art remembers Ruth's enthusiasm for horseback riding, which she was able to do there. In the afternoons, rain or shine, she would go riding. And when she returned, she would have a drink or two to relax and get warm. After returning to their home in the United States, Ruth continued to drink. After several episodes, Art wondered whether she was an alcoholic. "I never thought she was. Maybe it was my high opinion and respect for her. But I suspected that she was not. When she was in another mood, she wouldn't drink at all. There was nothing progressive about her drinking."

Yet Art noticed that the intensity of Ruth's moods was heightened. Her feeling of being overwhelmed was more exaggerated than it had been in earlier years. This put a strain on the children, and he wondered how much stress they were placing on her. He thought about ways of reducing the tensions in the household and wondered whether it would be better for everybody if the girls went to boarding school. So first Irene went, then Helene started boarding school, too. Maggie stayed at home. As the eleven-year-old "baby" of the family Maggie felt that she was almost an only child, with her sisters returning for occasional weekends and holidays.

Art was right in sensing the added pressures Ruth felt during those years. "I didn't know it at the time, or what to call it, but she was depressed. She now claims that she had always been depressed from childhood. Tracing it back, however, I see there were times when she was feeling good—really enjoying life. And there were times when she wasn't—very long periods." It was during these low points that Maggie became distressed by what she had earlier dismissed with a casual "That's my mother." With her older sisters away, Maggie was the focus of her mother's attention, and she saw Ruth's frustrations in coping with life with greater intensity than she had before.

At this point Art was working on a project which kept him traveling, sometimes for as long as a week at a time. Maggie remembers: "My mother was drinking. I now understand it was a form of self-medication. And when she was drinking quite heavily, she would fall on the floor or want to go for a drive. I remember hiding the keys to the car and telling my father about it when he returned home." Ruth, however, always sobered up before Art got home. Maggie tried to save "evidence," such as empty bottles. But Ruth managed to dispose of it all, and Maggie never did convince her father that Ruth went on binges during his absence.

During these moments, along with the love and admiration Maggie had for her mother's warmth and gregariousness, other less affectionate feelings grew. She remembers hostility because she thought Ruth was keeping her hostage while drinking; she was frustrated and angry with her father for his inability to acknowledge Ruth's problems; she was mad at herself for not convincing him. Ruth's daily behavior began to frighten Maggie in ways which still evoke pain. "She would be so depressed that she couldn't speak," Maggie said as she recalled the times when her mother asked her to sit nearby so she could stroke her head "for hours and hours. I think it was her way of trying to relate to me in ways that were not verbal. There were other times, however, that she wanted to talk." Maggie sat in one chair; Ruth, across the room in another. "She wanted to talk for hours. She expected me to sit still and listen. Maybe it would be for six hours at a time. It was very difficult, and I would often say, 'I can't listen anymore.' Or I couldn't sit there physically."

By the time Maggie herself went to boarding school she had developed a battery of responses to cope with her mother, but still she left with relief. "I thought it was my only chance to get away," she acknowledged. Even later, when Maggie began college and Ruth's problems intensified, the teenager thought her mother's behavior simply duplicated the earlier pattern. Ruth would call and demand that Maggie run an errand, or instruct her daughter about a particular task. During her manic moods "she would call every fifteen minutes, twenty-four hours a day. Literally around the clock." This upset Maggie. "When I returned from the library, there would be this list: Your mother called; your mother called; your mother called—all the way down the page, taped to the outside of my dormitory room." Embarrassed in front of her friends, she told them, "That's my mother," and offered no explanation to her curious roommates. For this reason it was quite a shock to Maggie the day her father said that he was taking Ruth to a hospital.

Art had realized that his wife's appearance was no longer characteristic of her. She looked disheveled and unkempt more often than not, and she made unreasonable demands more frequently. This was not the spirited and beautiful woman he had married who had occasional "blue days," but somebody else. Art decided that he had to take her to a psychiatrist and arranged an appointment. After one consultation during which Ruth was in the high phase of her manic-depressive cycle, the doctor recommended hospitalization.

Before we come to the realization that a relative is mentally ill, we all develop special ways of responding to the events that form the mosaic of our relationship. The behavior that is a clue to mental disability becomes part of the way we understand that person. Later there may be countless hours of discussion about the past as we try to piece together the whens, the whys, and the hows. The need to understand the origins of a person's difficulties leads to microscopic examination of events. Like other families with a mentally disabled relative, Art and his daughters replayed the different episodes and events in their own minds. What could, or should, have been done differently? What did it mean that Ruth's projects never got finished? That one day she would be the center of attention, telling wonderful stories and jokes, and the next day feel withdrawn and sullen? Could they have guessed something before her increasingly unkempt appearance deteriorated into wearing clothes that didn't match? And who in the family could have been more alert or taken action that they overlooked because Ruth Connelly's "symptoms" were part of the way they all had learned to understand her personality?

Such questions, and this process, engulf families as they try to identify the events which lead them to recognize mental illness in someone they love. Because the initial symptoms occurred within a familiar context, their significance was obscure or even invisible. Only in retrospect does a pattern form. But at the time they occurred, the events and actions were met with complacence, understanding, bewilderment, frustration, disappointment, or irritation.

Having lived with her mother's "nutty" behavior for her entire life, Maggie was stunned. She always thought her mother somewhat "crazy." But she had never thought her *crazy.* Until they took Ruth to a psychiatrist, nobody understood the significance of her depressions—for her or for themselves. Afterwards, according to Maggie, "it was as if someone had told us something that seemed bizarre. But it also explained so many questions about my whole life. It was liberating and horrible at the same time." The psychiatrist who saw Ruth couldn't understand how the family had been living with what Art described. "You are not doing her a service," the doctor informed Ruth's husband.

Despite having taken his wife to a psychiatrist, Art had not expected the diagnosis to be mental illness or the recommendation that she be hospitalized. He knew that she needed something, but he was shocked to be told that what they had coped with for years by themselves, and contained within a supportive family, urgently required treatment. They had protected Ruth, and themselves from her, for such a long time that now they were not prepared to reorganize their lives and hopes instantly to deal with the demands of understanding Ruth as mentally ill. Art wanted to think about it for a day or two before taking his wife to a hospital.

MARK BLOOMBERG

Though the Connellys and the Bloombergs lived in entirely differ-ent parts of the country, they could have been neighbors if they had lived in the same town. Like Art Connelly, Marvin Bloomberg was an independent businessman who began a family during World War II. As a child of the Depression, memories of hardship affected Marvin throughout his life, and he wanted only the best for his wife and two children. By the early 1950s it was clear that he was headed for success and the financial security with which to ease memories of the poverty of his youth in a Jewish ghetto.

Marvin Bloomberg provided comfortably for his wife, Rita, and two children, Linda and Mark: fine clothes, excellent schools, and a home with every modern convenience. Rita Bloomberg helped her husband build his business, and when it was estab-lished, she considered herself a housewife and spent her days in leisure. One day a week she went to the beauty shop, another found her playing cards with women friends, and a third was devoted to charity work. Always she returned home in time to fix dinner before her children and husband arrived. Because their growing up was so uneventful, Linda Bloomberg had difficulty pinpointing the specific problems which made her younger brother, Mark, stand out from his friends. Nor could she say how his childhood led to what was eventually diagnosed as "chronic schizophrenia" when he was twenty-five.

By the time Linda and I talked she had told the story many times over the last decade. "I've gotten so that I can reduce it to the bare essentials," said the thirty-eight-year-old sociologist, who has had to repeat her family's history to different physicians as they call long distance. "Over the past few years every social worker or psychiatrist makes me start from the beginning. 'What was his childhood like? How long has he been this way? How does he live? Did he have friends? Has he ever been in a hospital before? Do others in your family . . .' What boxes do they fill on his chart with this information?" she asked. "I wonder if it is supposed to help."

Linda's set of responses includes the story of their childhood in a comfortable suburb. She spoke about the summers they spent in the backyard swimming pool or at the tennis court where round-robin competitions were held. "There didn't seem to be any visible signs," she began. "Well, maybe now that I know what I should have known then—if in fact it would have helped to know it then—his stubbornness and inflexibility, and I guess he had a few psychosomatic problems. But who knew then that those were latent symptoms? Not all kids with them grow up to be crazy," she said. "I didn't."

In a group Mark and his friends had looked pretty much alike as they raced into the house for a snack in the late afternoon or spent hours on their bikes circling the neighborhood. As Mark grew older, spending more time with one or another friend, he talked of girls and sports. "Ours was not an intellectual family. I remember conversations at the dinner table were pretty ordinary . . . what each of us did that day, whom we saw, or news of relatives and friends. After dinner my brother and I did our homework; my father read a paper in the living room; sometimes my parents watched TV or they went out." Nothing extraordinary happened in their lives as individuals or as a family. Nothing, that is, until the year Marvin Bloomberg died.

"Mark had a pretty rough time the year my father died," Linda explained. "Dad's death was unexpected. He had a heart attack, and six weeks later he was dead." Mark and his father had been close. In addition to the baseball and basketball games they went to on weekends, Linda described her father and brother attending synagogue together. "My father helped build the temple, and so he was kind of a big shot there. Going with him was always an event because he was well liked. And Judaism was one of the things which gave great meaning to his life, so he was always happy there." Linda remembered the particular year that Mark prepared for his Bar Mitzvah and what joy it gave Marvin. "Each night after dinner they would go into a separate room, and Dad would help Mark learn the Haftorah." Rehearsing that part of the ceremony which Mark would be called upon to recite, Marvin and his son sang the passage until each knew it by heart. "Night after night they would go over it. And while Mark memorized it, he got into the habit of playing with a yo-yo." After a while it became a family joke. "We told Mark that he knew the passage only with his yo-yo. And we asked if he would remember this passage on the day of his Bar Mitzvah without it. He kept saying he was the only Bar Mitzvah boy who had so many talents!"

An observant Jew, Marvin passed on to his son traditions which his own father had taught him. "Centuries of Jews have done it this way," he told his children at the different holiday meals. "And one day you kids will be teaching your children how to do it. That's what it means to be a Jew," Marvin said with pride. Year after year Marvin taught Mark the meaning of manhood within Judaism so that he was well prepared when he was called to the Torah at the age of thirteen. He was also well prepared to observe the period of mourning, the year his father died, by attending religious services twice a day, the way he had seen his father carry out the tradition before him.

There were many times during that year when Mark's observance of the mourning rituals tried the nerves of his sister and mother. "He became very rigid," Linda said. "It was almost as if the whole purpose of his life were to attend those services. And there were times when it threw the family—my mother and me —into chaos." Linda remembered when her mother wanted to take them away for a long holiday weekend. Mark wanted to go. "But we couldn't arrange the traveling to guarantee that he could get to a temple before sunset. Still, he wouldn't stay at home either. I remember huge fights and accusations about who cared about whom and what each person thought my father would have wanted." Arguments also occurred around other events, where scheduling Mark's attendance conflicted with other people's needs. "Sometimes they got pretty fierce," Linda mentioned. "But we knew what a loss he had suffered, and we wanted to cushion it any way we could. Most of the time we tried to be agreeable, but I'm sure there were times we simply indulged him or gave in because it was easier. And Mark carried out this tradition with impassioned rigidity."

In retrospect, Linda thinks she sees part of her brother's mental illness, which sometimes took the form of thinking himself a religious mystic with telephonic communications to ancient tribes of Israel, in the strictness of his religious devotion that year. "At the time we had no idea it was part of a sickness. And I'm not sure that I would have given it more thought were it not for this compulsion to understand how he got to be the way he is today," she remarked.

The year Marvin died Mark was finishing high school and Linda was attending college. She started noticing that the family fought almost all the time. Mark was contentious. He seemed to pick a fight over everything from the way his socks were folded to what other people watched on television. "Meals were the most impossible," Linda remembered. "Instead of the easy conversations we had before, now everything was a battle. I couldn't stand being home, and my mother was hurt by almost every comment that Mark made in anger. I'm sure I played some role in the arguments but can't really say how. What I do remember is that it got pretty nasty." Linda was concerned. She saw Mark's personality become wrapped up in anger, and she decided to talk to a psychologist she knew from school. "I was most worried about Mark, but I was concerned about my mother, too. I didn't know what the tension was doing to her. Since she had a heart condition, I was afraid of all the strain."

Linda made an appointment with the psychologist. She went to his office at the university's medical center. She told him the story of Mark's persistent and stubborn focus on the mourning period. She added details about the conflicts in their house. She reported her concern about Mark's inability to express any emotion other than anger. "Even when he was told that my father died, he showed only anger. I thought that a sixteen-year-old should have shown something else, too . . . maybe sadness or maybe he should have cried. But he never did. He just got mad and stayed that way all year."

When Linda finished her story, the psychologist told her that very often people who express concern about their family are really talking about their own problems. Was there something worrisome about Mark? Perhaps it was Linda who was having the difficulties? Though Linda did not think that she was misrepresenting the situation, she agreed to think about it. When she returned for another appointment, two weeks later, she did so with the conviction that she had not misperceived. "Mark's report card came out. He had always been an above-average student. Well, the report card was a catastrophe. His teachers said he couldn't concentrate, and they were worried about him, too," she told the therapist.

The therapist agreed that Linda, Mark, and Rita Bloomberg should come for an appointment the following week. Though Rita disapproved of the idea, she agreed because it might help Mark. Mark thought his sister troubled, difficult, and spiteful, so he agreed only because he wanted to help her. And Linda thought Mark needed help and her mother needed guidance. Nobody thought he or she would profit from the sessions, but everybody thought it was a good idea for the others. They went.

There were three difficult sessions, during which Mark and his mother went after each other and Linda sat back with calculated aloofness; Rita Bloomberg accurately perceived that the situation was getting worse instead of better, and she disregarded the therapist's assurance that this was normal. Instead, Rita decided that she had had enough and the family was going to stop. "There was one last session with each of us individually," Linda recalled. "I don't remember much about it and don't know whether the psychologist predicted how things would turn out. But as far as I was concerned, these sessions were not successful, and my mother was convinced that the whole thing was a disaster."

Linda isn't sure how they managed to live out the year under the same roof. At the end of it, however, when she was graduated from college, Linda moved to another state to start graduate school. What happened at home remains somewhat of a mystery, though she remembers her mother's complaints about Mark's disagreeable nature and lack of consideration. Linda tried to appease Rita by suggesting that most teenage boys need to rebel and that part of the difficulty in their situation was that Rita Bloomberg was the only target for Mark.

It really was not until three years later that Linda began to sense the difficult personality patterns which later crystallized into a disability. By then Linda was finishing graduate course-work in sociology and Mark was a sophomore in college. He still lived at home, and Rita had taken a job to occupy her days. Before she finished her graduate work, Linda planned a trip abroad. Mark met her for two weeks of that trip. "The trip was a nightmare," Linda remembered. "It was horrible. Mark was demanding, arrogant, petty, and argumentative. He seemed to pick a fight every ten minutes. None of it seemed to be over major things; yet he was a terrible traveler, so inflexible. I couldn't wait until we parted." While Mark had always betrayed some of the qualities that touched off fights—a concern for meticulously planned arrangements, a fastidiousness about his appearance—she attributed his behavior to his having never traveled outside the country and certainly not to areas of poverty where his standards of cleanliness had to bend. Also, she thought it might have been her own perceptions. "After all, we hadn't lived under the same roof for more than a few days in several years. Then suddenly we were thrown together for two whole weeks. I felt bad," she recalled, "because I kept thinking maybe I should have been more patient. I was older, and I should have been more responsible. But he wasn't exactly a child either," she said of the brother who was then in his early twenties.

When Mark was graduated from college, five years after the death of their father, Linda began to see the troublesome pattern she would be called upon to recite. Having just finished school herself, she took a job another 1,500 miles away from home. "During those years Mark came to visit. But his visits were always a total surprise. Sometimes he would just appear at the front door, and half the time he had no baggage. When he popped in on those occasions, he always left after an argument. There were a lot of them at the time, and I remember my mother kept telling me he was 'just finding himself.'"

Linda was more angry than worried about the behavior that seemed so disrespectful of others. She remembers talking to friends about how his demands failed to take into account that he was a visitor, and an unexpected one at that. "He went through these stages when he had all sorts of rigid diets—vegetarianism or macrobiotics. He always expected to find my house stocked with unbleached walnuts and whole-grain noodles. And he was a big slob, too. He would take records out of the jacket and leave them lying around the floor and things would get piled on top of them, and I remember a huge argument because some of my favorite albums got ruined." Mark's arrogance and carelessness were an irritant. Linda tried to be patient, yet she started to smolder when Mark ignored repeated requests. When she could control it no longer, the arguments flared. "We would fight like cats and dogs, and then Mark would just leave. I would walk into the kitchen, and there would be this nasty note saying he had left. It was very upsetting."

Friends began to tell Linda about cousins or brothers who, like Mark, just "hung out" during these years when the youthful counterculture made family conflict practically a rite of passage. Why should he be different, they asked her, from others his age who were challenging what they considered bourgeois culture? But their remarks didn't help. Mark had never participated in the anarchistic aspects of the counterculture, and whatever ideological positions he espoused, he had intended to take his place within the liberal establishment after going to law school. So Linda worried about the suddenness of his different plans and his frequent traveling. He would set upon one course of action, to find the perfect job or a place to live. "The internal logic of each plan made sense. What didn't was how frequently he changed his mind," Linda said as she listed the plans Mark had for the future: law school was postponed until he took the LSAT exam; business school quickly faded when he missed the deadline for applying; working as a copy editor for a small-town newspaper was abandoned in a few short weeks because he didn't like the social life in the town.

"There were so many things he intended to do that I can't even remember them all. But I remember that he seemed in such good spirits the day he got on the bus to go to Chicago. He was chipper and enthusiastic about seeing college friends. I even thought this made sense—his plan to work in the Art Institute while he tried to support himself as an artist. He had tremendous ability. But now I realize that the expectations of a fruitful life in Chicago, or the plans he had for Detroit, San Francisco, Rome, London, or Los Angeles, masked the problems," she said regretfully.

When Mark's efforts reaped continued frustration and disappointment, his mother suggested that he try something new: a year on a kibbutz in Israel. Not since the two weeks when he traveled with Linda had he been abroad. An unpressured atmosphere and the chance to think things through made sense to them all. "I know Mom was hoping this would be what he needed. Perhaps he would decide to go to graduate school in the meantime or do something. So we sort of had a family powwow and thought this might help him feel there was no urgency to making a decision."

Mark rejoiced in the idea and was eager to go. Once in Israel he wrote cheerfully of picking oranges and grapefruits, learning a new language, and meeting wonderful people. He looked up distant relatives and dined with visiting family friends from the United States. When he returned, he seemed like a new and different person. "I remember it vividly," Linda began. "The night he got back we sat and talked and joked, and I heard about his different experiences. He was in great shape, and he looked rested and handsome. When we phoned Mom, I remember telling her that he looked grown-up and had the same twinkle in his eye that my dad had had. We all felt great about his homecoming."

During the three days of Mark's visit after returning to the United States, he spoke about his adventures abroad. Dwelling on a theme which would reappear in the future, he reported being followed by the CIA during a stopover in London. During the ten days that he was there he had attended a rally against the war in Vietnam. Mark told of being followed to pubs, to the theater, and even back from museums. Linda was a sympathetic listener. She had been active in civil rights activities in the early sixties and later in the anti-war movement.

As for many people who develop paranoia, the first stages of Mark's illness produced stories which fell within the range of normal experience. Because his suspicions seemed to contain a glimmer of reality, Linda never doubted them. And because the other things he did reflected exaggerated tendencies of his personality, nobody viewed them as symptoms of illness. Because his words and behavior were familiar, neither Linda nor her mother was alarmed. If anything, they searched for ways to understand better what he said and did. The gradual erosion of his ability to stick to any pursuit, to separate himself from the religious figures he studied, or to identify real from imagined dangers occurred over a decade. And only then, after they had fitted all the pieces together, did it appear that the stories to which Linda and Rita listened so closely were probably constructions of Mark's mind.

When Mark first discussed the CIA's interest in his overseas activities, it seemed plausible to Linda. She even wondered aloud if he was still being followed upon his return. It wasn't until much later, when she began to receive letters which sounded preposterous, that she started to wonder about Mark's statements. "I remember it was about six weeks after he returned from Israel. He had gone home to visit Mom and then decided to look for a job. Several months later I got this letter saying he had lost a job prospect with the Speaker of the House." It didn't seem particularly odd that he would seek such a job since he had been a political science major, but Linda remembers wondering whether the Speaker would hire anybody who wasn't a resident of his state. "The next letter mentioned the most bizarre turn of events. It was postmarked from Nevada, and Mark said that he had been beaten up one night by Elvis Presley's bodyguards because of his powerful connection with Howard Hughes. Well, that was absurd. And in the meantime, he started to travel again. By the next time he dropped in he was a mess."

When Linda saw Mark sitting on the curb outside her apartment building, she knew he was not well. "Mental illness still hadn't crossed my mind. Well, nothing like 'chronic schizophrenia.' I thought he was strange, undisciplined, erratic. He looked physically sick, too. Drawn and tired. And I had this sinking feeling that there was something terribly wrong. It was all over his face. I didn't know what I was going to do."

In Mark's case, as in Ruth Connelly's, psychiatric intervention came at the end of several years of symptoms. Mark Bloomberg's behavior was interwoven with the social choices of the sixties, and interpretations placed on his actions were understood in those terms. Some of his symptoms had always been a part of his personality: stubbornness, argumentativeness, being opinionated. It took considerable deterioration to make his family recognize that his problems were not the isolated events he portrayed, but a way of life. Because he was lucid and articulate and spoke with clarity and determination, none suspected that he had begun what has been called the "insidious decline" in some cases of chronic schizophrenia. Since he was relatively energetic during his various pursuits, the lethargy or physical deterioration which often accompanies illness was slow to appear. Only after many different episodes had begun to build on one another was it apparent that a self-destructive life-style was being perpetuated. That was when Linda started to look for help.

ROGER ANTHONY

The symptoms of illness which had escaped Mark Bloomberg's and Ruth Connelly's families did not pass unnoticed by Roger Anthony's parents. For Jim and Grace Anthony, the onset of mental illness for their fifteen-year-old son occurred suddenly during an unmistakable psychotic episode. His mother described it this way: "Roger came into our bedroom one morning at six. He had been reading Einstein's theory of relativity for school. When he came in, we could see he was quite agitated. He started to talk about mathematics." Grace could not say exactly what Roger said, though she remembered that "some of it sounded like a real intellectual breakthrough. There was a lot of insight. But he just kept going on and on and on. He was pacing around. Jim finally got up to be with him." Roger, however, wanted to go back into his room and read some more. He left for a few minutes. Then it started again, and Grace recalled the sequence: "He came back into our room; then he took a bath; then he went into the kitchen. Jim sat with him at the kitchen table talking Einstein. All the time Roger just went on and on and on. He was talking so fast it was so hard to follow. It was as if everything were on this one train of thought. It didn't seem to be keyed into anything he was saying. And I remember the word 'deranged' came into my head. I wondered if this is what 'deranged' means."

Grace and Jim were stunned. Their son had shown no previous signs of a flight from reality such as this experience suggested. The hour-long and frightful monologue, the uncharacteristic bath in the middle of the night, the nervous pacing in the kitchen as he spoke were clearly not normal behavior. That was apparent immediately.

The Anthonys have always been family-centered. Even today, with Roger almost twenty and Karee eighteen, it is not uncommon for Grace's sisters, brothers-in-law, nieces and nephews, or Jim's entire family to picnic together or take vacations near one another. When Roger and Karee were small, these family get-togethers were one of the high points of the year, with Grace's family gathering at her parents' ranch, where three generations of almost twenty people spent two weeks each summer. With more than ten children playing together, Roger and his "best-friend cousin" Vicki were practically inseparable. Each year at these reunions the children formed teams and groups, gangs and pairs, in various outdoor activities from breakfast to bedtime.

Not only did the children flourish during the summer months, but Jim Anthony reveled in spending uninterrupted time with his own kids as well as his nieces and nephews. Jim, an architect by training, is a tinkerer by temperament. These weeks afforded him the opportunity to build things for and with the children. One year he built a tree house which became the youngsters' headquarters. Another year he rigged up bicycles in a special way which made for a rider and passenger, and the kids raced in five teams of two.

Jim Anthony found pleasure in these activities. Vacations were not the only times he could be found busily engaged with the children. From the time that Roger and Karee were infants, Jim built toys for them and showed his children how to work them. When Roger was older, Jim taught him how to use building equipment, such as drills, saws, planes, and all kinds of wrenches. In the basement, which had been converted into a workshop, Roger and Jim spent many hours building electric trains and bunk beds, or they fixed car engines or bicycles. After Grace's parents sold the ranch, the basement became the center of activity. There Jim built a houseboat, and there he and Roger made an electric car, rebuilt a motorcycle, made a sailboat, and built a darkroom and an enlarger.

Grace talked of these times with delight. She and Jim had fun with their children, with each other, and with the activities in their neighborhood. Grace remembered it as a time when "we didn't have to lock doors. We couldn't. There was always a troop of children coming in and out." It was fortunate that they lived in a neighborhood where on either side of them lived children the same ages as Roger and Karee. Roger and these boys were close-knit. As a child, Grace recalled, Roger did not move into new situations with ease. He was "a bit standoffish and somewhat of a nonconformist," and his mother does not know if it would have been more or less valuable for him to have had to seek friends more aggressively than he did. As it worked out, there was an abundance of them, practically in his own backyard, and from the time he was a young child his neighbors were his closest friends.

Roger was also quite intense, Grace noted as she sketched his complex personality. "You would describe him as a willful person . . . someone with his own sense of what he wanted." The intensity of his drive and his keen intelligence, however, produced frustrations for him very early in school because he had a reading difficulty that went undiagnosed for several years. When he was eleven, Jim and Grace had him tested by two learning specialists. This was not the first time they had sought help for Roger, whose unhappiness at school contrasted sharply with the moods that sustained his numerous activities outside. And when the learning specialists saw the classic signs of dyslexia, they were appalled that the school psychologist with whom Jim and Grace spoke when Roger was in the second grade, and the many teachers in between, had not recognized this major obstacle to his ability to read. No wonder this child was frustrated, they noted. But however horrified those specialists were at the failure of the schools to recognize Roger's problem, it did not solve the problem which had vexed the boy for so long and which contributed to increasing disappointment as he judged himself harshly.

Grace and Jim were not as worried about Roger's actual learning difficulty as they were about the pressure he placed on himself because of it. "We tried to help him learn to live with the frustration and be satisfied with different stages of the learning process," Grace recalled. They also knew that their son had many talents and skills. Whether it was as a natural compensation for his reading difficulties or whether it was an innate talent, Roger had a good eye for photography. Jim taught him how to shoot, develop, and print photographs, and Grace thought he used this skill with imagination. She remembered an assignment he did in the fourth grade. The students were asked to describe their neighborhoods. Even before there was a technical term for his problem with deciphering letters and words, Roger instinctively knew he would rather photograph his neighborhood than write about it. He spent many hours taking pictures and developing them, and he edited a photographic essay with the pictures keyed to a map he had drawn. Not long after that, along with his friends, Roger started making animated movies. So his parents were confident that he had imagination, ability, and talent, and they hoped he could temper his urges toward perfectionism and become more content with himself.

By the time Roger was twelve and Karee ten each had several after-school activities which occupied their respective afternoons. Grace decided that it might be time to resume the career in journalism which she had interrupted when the children were infants. She had occasionally taken free-lance assignments, and now an opportunity was presented to join the staff of a magazine she had long admired. For the next few years Grace and Jim enjoyed professional success in their respective fields and commuted to their offices, while the kids continued their zestful activities.

Roger's life, outside school, was indistinguishable from that of other teenagers growing up in the 1970s. Along with his friends, he was moved by the fads that have a corner on the adolescent market. When skateboards were the center of attention, Roger made and rode them. When battalions of kids went to rock concerts, he went with them. When ten-speed bikes became the rage, he and his father rebuilt one so he could join his friends on day-long outings. And by the time he was fifteen, the fad that captured his attention was drugs.

Along with the others in his high school, Roger experimented with LSD. When school officials told the Anthonys that Roger and several other boys had been caught with the drug, Jim and Grace acted at once. They knew they were dealing with an issue in which the cultural tide conflicted with the law, and they decided to seek the guidance of a psychiatrist with a specialty in family therapy. Perhaps Jim and Grace would not have looked for psychiatric help had other parts of Roger's behavior been more normal at that time. But the same year he was discovered with LSD, Jim and Grace noticed that their son was less predictable and more inconsistent than he had been in the past. For the teenager whose behavior included erratic hours around dinner and bedtime, Jim and Grace tried to set boundaries. They thought he was at the age where they had to help him navigate between dependency and childhood, independence and increasing responsibilities. When drugs were added to the list of issues they were trying to handle, they decided to get help.

The year prior to Roger's psychotic episode, Grace and Jim met regularly with Dr. Golden, a highly respected psychiatrist. Because it was the drug adventure that had caused them to seek assistance, they wanted Roger to participate also. And because they didn't want Roger to feel that he was being isolated, they wanted Karee to join them. Roger, however, after one session, did not want to be a part of the family therapy; he "was adamant that he didn't have any problems." According to Grace, it then became a question of whether to force him to come to the meetings. They concluded, and Dr. Golden agreed, that Roger should not be forced to participate; if he did not, Karee should also be excused. But Jim and Grace knew that they still wanted guidance in understanding what was going on in their son's life and how it was affecting them.

In some aspects, the Anthony household seemed like any other for the remainder of the year. Sometimes Jim and Roger worked together on a building project; other times the family visited with friends or relatives; frequently Roger or Karee spent days with their own friends. Grace remembers that the children were at an age—fifteen and thirteen, respectively—when they seemed to move in large groups. If one of them wasn't having dinner at someone else's house, a friend or two would be dining at theirs. Though Jim and Grace enjoyed an occasional dinner by themselves, mealtime was always a special time in their household, and more people around the table simply made it merrier and enlivened the conversation. Nothing was ever so structured that more tomatoes could not be added to a salad or additional vegetables prepared to expand the offerings.

The normal course of events in their lives contrasted sharply with the concern and alarm which began the morning that Roger unexpectedly started to spout Einstein. Grace remembered how he was "going on and on and on," as if he had a point to make and would reach it momentarily. A person who behaves the way Roger did makes others feel that they are suffocating, almost as if the words were choking them. Listeners become impatient and irritated, want to interrupt, scream, or walk away. Under the barrage of words conversation ceases, and there is only a "talker" and a "listener." This pattern sometimes indicates a psychotic break. It needs immediate and professional attention.

Grace called Dr. Golden and described the morning's events. He did not think that the criteria for hospitalizing somebody applied. Roger was not harmful to himself, nor was he dangerous to others. Therefore, after seeing Roger, Dr. Golden encouraged the Anthonys to try to manage at home. He told them how to keep Roger safe and observe his behavior under the prescribed medication. Under Dr. Golden's guidance, Jim and Grace took turns staying home with Roger to give him the special care and attention that might prevent his having to enter the psychiatric unit of a nearby hospital. They settled into a routine that provided the safety and structure in which he was going to be all right.

"We just kept things going one day to the next," Grace said as she described the month. At first Roger was cooperative. He was frightened by his own behavior and wanted to be helped. He welcomed Dr. Golden's suggestions and readily agreed to take his medicine and accept his parents' efforts. Then, as he improved somewhat under medication, he became more resistant. "He interpreted our efforts as an infringement of his freedom," Grace explained. "And indeed, it was! But he didn't have a great deal of judgment at the time. He wanted to do things like ride his skateboard to the shopping center for magazines. He would have traveled one street which was almost like a superhighway." It wasn't like the cul-de-sac in front of their house; it was a six-lane road. They obviously could not permit that. Their exhaustion from round-the-clock supervision intensified their fears that his poor judgment would result in a crippling injury. "That would have been too much even to contemplate. We really felt we had to keep him safe to help him get better," Grace explained.

After one month it was apparent that Roger's psychosis had not abated. He still talked of imaginary enemies, was unable to organize his thoughts coherently, and needed constant supervision. Though medicine reduced his anxiety while he was taking it, he soon stopped taking his medicine and started smoking pot once again. The Anthonys consulted Dr. Golden, and after a session with Roger he concluded that hospitalization was necessary. In fact, it had become urgent.

At this stage the idea of mental illness was just as foreign to Jim and Grace as it was to the families of Ruth Connelly and Mark Bloomberg. Each family knew that their relative needed help, but each assumed that whatever help was necessary would be a temporary interruption in their normal life pattern. Even if the interlude lasted months, each believed that the period represented a hiatus with an end in sight rather than the beginning of their entire family's reorganization around mental illness. At the time these families sought professional advice, none anticipated what lay ahead, either for their relative or for themselves.

2

Entering the System

The psychiatrist whom the Connellys at last went to see recommended immediate hospitalization. Ruth was taken to a hospital, and after a considerable effort at persuasion she signed herself in for treatment. The family, in the presence of a psychiatrist, had to convince her that she should admit herself voluntarily. Maggie remembers the scene with a mixture of horror and shame and describes her own ambivalence during the process. After having spent two nights at home with Ruth while Art looked for a hospital, Maggie was furious about her mother's destructive behavior, yet felt protective toward a woman whose sickness was no longer invisible.

At the hospital the entire family was asked to participate in the initial intake interview. "The psychiatrist asked me what happened in the previous day or two," Maggie began. "I felt like I was turning state's evidence," said the young woman, who had then described for the psychiatrist the previous days when Ruth tried to run away, did not sleep for two nights, cried and screamed in her room, and threatened to have the local newspaper investigate her husband and children. "It was as if my mother were sitting there and I were sending her to jail. And that side of me felt that I had gotten my revenge. But it was horrible. She couldn't believe that this was happening to her and that every one of us was citing yet another crazy incident." Her mismatched clothes, the mess in the house, the frequent car trips when she told nobody where she was going or when she would return—and more. Each of the Connellys told part of the story of the previous eight years of Ruth's disintegration. While they sat there, telling of these events, Ruth broke into what sounded like a string of accusations and turned to her youngest daughter, crying, "Maggie, how can you do this to me?" Maggie was "simply undone by it."

Maggie did not understand why the psychiatrist asked each person to describe one or more aspects of Ruth's bizarre behavior. "Perhaps he felt that he was making it real for my mother," Maggie mused. "But it was a profound experience. I felt trapped. If I didn't tell him, she wouldn't get help. And in a way, my mother was having a great time," Maggie said. "She was high as a kite. And that's what was so hard to understand. I would ask, 'How can she be living the life she is?' I would think, she is not aware of what is happening. But in reality, *we needed help. We* couldn't take it any more," she concluded.

At first Ruth refused to agree to admission. Maggie was proud of her, watching her spirited mother put up a fight. "You are standing up for your rights," she thought with pride. In the next moment she thought, "I wish they would commit you." She said, "It was great that my mother was responding the way she was, but I kept thinking, 'Now you are going.'"

After great effort and much persuasion Ruth finally admitted herself to the hospital for observation. Had she not, Art would have had to go to court to obtain a legal commitment. That would have been the only other way to get her into treatment. He might not have succeeded, however, because the use of courts as a vehicle to force people into treatment has been widely curtailed in the past decade. Legally it is difficult to have somebody like Ruth involuntarily committed, and families are often in the position of cajoling, persuading, or arguing with a person whom they want to help.

The changed legal circumstances which require families aggressively to convince their relatives to sign themselves into a hospital, rather than commit them, as would have happened a decade ago, dates from the 1970s. Lawyers who examined public mental institutions began to question the civil commitment procedure in instances where patients had received inadequate or negligent treatment after they were admitted to a hospital. And the civil liberties lawyers discovered other shortcomings, among which was the notorious institutionalization syndrome, which was a condition of passivity and dependency fostered by being in a hospital. In the cases of children who were retarded, ample evidence existed that they actually became less functional after hospitalization, losing skills such as toilet training. Those who studied these patterns wondered if the patients were not harmed by living in hospitals. Instead of helping patients acquire skills to cope with the pressures of real life, the oversized and understaffed state and county mental hospitals seemed to curtail rehabilitation and to diminish their ability to function outside the institution.

Several legal cases were presented in the 1970s to curb abuses of the commitment process. Citing the cruel and unusual punishment clause of the Eighth Amendment and the due process clause of the Fourteenth Amendment, lawyers presented cases on behalf of patients whose civil liberties had been denied. One of the landmark cases of this period involved the life of Kenneth Donaldson and is often referred to as *O'Connor* v. *Donaldson*. The circumstances which were revealed in the unfolding of this case, argued by Bruce J. Ennis, dated from 1957. The elderly and infirm parents of forty-eight-year-old Donaldson had committed their son to Chattahoochee, a Florida state hospital, for "care, maintenance and treatment." Donaldson's account, poignantly told in *Insanity Inside Out,* illustrates a paradox in the law as well as the shameful disregard he suffered in the name of psychiatric rehabilitation. For fifteen years Donaldson tried to have himself discharged, applying for writs of habeas corpus and telling his doctors that he was not insane. The more he challenged them, the more they were convinced that he was sick. His stubbornness fueled their recalcitrance for more than a decade. At the same time, he was confronted by a legal system which refused to grant him a hearing because he was in a mental hospital. Most important, however, Donaldson received no therapeutic treatment, which he claimed, and the court confirmed, was his right.

Despite his own efforts to secure a discharge, Donaldson was not released from Chattahoochee until 1971, a few weeks before Ennis was scheduled to present the case in a federal district court. Four years later, in 1975, the United States Supreme Court (having previously refused) heard this case and established a precedent by concluding: "A state cannot constitutionally confine without more a non-dangerous individual who is capable of surviving safely in freedom by himself or with the help of willing and responsible family or friends."[1]

Following the Donaldson case, and building on others which had already ruled that patients have a "right to treatment within humane physical and psychological environments" *(Wyatt* v. *Stickney),* lawyers pressed state legislatures to enact several reforms. One goal was to create less restrictive settings in which treatment could be obtained for the mentally ill. The advocates argued for the establishment of facilities, outside hospitals, where rehabilitation would be more speedy and where people were not "warehoused" and forced to live in exile.

Another campaign in their advocacy efforts addressed the circumstances under which a person could be involuntarily hospitalized or committed through civil procedures. As a result, the extraordinary powers of the civil commitment system were circumscribed. The widely used *parens patriae* powers, which date from feudal times, were modified. *Parens patriae* had permitted the institutionalization of a person who seemed menacing. It allowed the court to order his or her detention to protect society from the deviance and social discomfort of someone whose peculiarities were evident. Legal procedures have changed. Many states now require that the person whose hospitalization is being sought manifest a clear danger to self or to others. In some states a danger to oneself may include the inability to attend to basic physical needs such as food, shelter, or clothing. Other states are more vague. But simply displaying symptoms such as delusional thinking, hallucinations, or other forms of disordered thought is not sufficient.

Involuntary admissions occur under state jurisdiction. States differ in their criteria for commitment as well as in the length of time they will permit the detention of someone who is hospitalized involuntarily. In Colorado, for example, the police or a mental health professional can initiate somebody's emergency hospitalization for no more than seventy-two hours. At the end of seventy-two hours, a discharge is mandatory if the person is found to need no further treatment. If, on the other hand, he or she is thought to need additional treatment, the least restrictive setting is mandated. In the case of Colorado that treatment may be imposed for no more than six months. In other states a psychiatrist or other doctor can facilitate an emergency admission whereby a person will be held for different lengths of time. But at the end of the specified time civil commitment is required for additional involuntary hospitalization.*

Today's legal codes make it more difficult to have somebody hospitalized than it was ten or twenty years ago. Safeguarding the civil liberties of patients, the courts have restricted families' and doctors' use of the law as a vehicle for having people with mental health disorders admitted to hospitals. Because of this, psychiatrists often find their hands tied when families implore them to help a relative, and many decry a situation which blocks access to treatment to scores of people because of the need to show that a person is dangerous.

MARK BLOOMBERG'S "PNEUMONIA"

Other situations which make it difficult for families when a relative requires hospitalization in an emergency arise from the bureaucratic red tape of hospitals, which appears to conflict with the basic purpose of dispensing services to those who need them in emergencies.

Linda Bloomberg discovered in how many ways procedures can become obstacles when she tried to help Mark the evening he arrived and waited for her on the curb outside her apartment, making no sense, talking of being pursued, and sounding fearful and hostile at the same time. He had a real problem, and it was now on her hands. "I know it sounds silly, but I now understand

*For a state-by-state list, see the Appendix, pp. 240–45.

how clichés come into our vocabulary," Linda said. "I thought to myself, 'He's blown a fuse.' " Linda tried to persuade Mark that he needed immediate attention, and she hoped he would agree. He said he had just been discharged from a hospital where he had been admitted for three days of psychiatric observation. At the time Linda didn't know whether it was true or not; so much of what he said made no sense that evening. After a night of discussion which ran well into the next day, Mark consented to let Linda help him.

"When he complained of radio messages causing him pain, I told him that a doctor would help alleviate the pain. That was the only thing I could do," she said. And when Mark agreed to see a doctor, Linda realized that "it was one thing to say it and another to arrange it. I didn't know what to do, where to turn, whom to call. Do you call a 'crisis line,' a friend for his therapist, or just start going down the list in the phone book? I was lost!" Whatever she did, Linda knew it would have to be done quickly before Mark changed his mind. She called a psychologist who worked at the same college she did. He was able to recommend somebody. That's how the list began. To each person to whom she spoke she described Mark's sullen, downcast appearance. She told doctors about Mark's stories of religious leaders sending signals through radios, of television sets directing him as a special messenger. She told them how once he started talking he wouldn't stop. "It was weird. I felt strange, and I must have sounded half-crazed myself as I repeated this story in a semi-hysterical voice," she remembered. "Some said to come in the next day, but that didn't seem to be very helpful," she said as she listed the kinds of advice she received. "Others gave me more names, saying their practice was full. One said he didn't work with psychotic patients." That was the first time Linda heard a name for Mark's behavior. "Finally, one said that the only way to get him help soon was to take him to a particular hospital which had an emergency room with psychiatrists."

Accompanying a relative to a community hospital's emergency room is among the more common ways people first encounter mental health workers. When police are called to assist a family, or when one does not have a private psychiatrist who is affiliated with a hospital with a psychiatric unit, the emergency room becomes the first step. When Linda took Mark to the emergency room of the hospital to which she was directed, she had no idea how many people do the exact same thing.

When they got there, Linda was not sure what she expected to happen, how long it would take, or what information would be needed. As an adult, and one who was not covered by her insurance, Mark would become a Medicaid patient. Despite her concern over the finances, Linda could think of no other way to proceed. If necessary, she would use the small inheritance which Rita Bloomberg, Linda's mother, had left when she died earlier that year. "But I knew that psychiatric care was expensive—hundreds of dollars a day—so I thought it best to try to have him go in on his own. That would have to be as an indigent," she said of the initial plan.

Having had no experience with emergency rooms, Linda remembers being depressed when they arrived at around four in the afternoon and saw a roomful of people. Some were family or friends who accompanied sick people; others were hospital personnel who had come down to use the food machines which were near the lobby entrance. "And then there were the people who were brought in by ambulance. It was horrible. They were listless on stretchers and looked more dead than alive."

Mark gave his name to the nurse on duty and said he didn't feel well. "Then he walked to the back, past the No Smoking sign, and lit a cigarette. I decided I should tell the nurse that I was there also," Linda elaborated. "I strolled up and identified myself as his sister and said he needed to see a doctor, probably a psychiatrist, as soon as possible. I told her about his radio messages and all the things I told the different doctors." Linda also remembered her own embarrassment, which was beginning to settle as she watched her brother. "I wanted the nurse to know that I had not caught whatever he had, so my demeanor and attire conveyed both distance and concern," Linda admitted.

Linda grew anxious waiting in the emergency room. "The psychiatrist was busy with another case. We could hear all sorts of yelling in the back. And then the shifts changed, so I had to go back to the nurse who just came on duty and let her know that we were there. And all that time Mark was pacing up and down. He was ignoring the No Smoking sign, and the guard ignored him. So I figured it was okay. But Mark ran out of matches, and he was so nervous that he started chain-smoking, lighting one cigarette with the butt of another. And he was pacing all the time and wearing a stocking cap that he hadn't taken off. I remember thinking how strange he looked and how hot the room was."

Informed that the psychiatrist would be at least another forty-five minutes, they went to a restaurant for a snack. "I wasn't particularly hungry, but I had to get out of there," Linda said. She remembered being "glad that there were no familiar faces—nobody I knew. I wouldn't have known how to explain or what to say. When we ordered coffee, Mark asked for a straw." Surprised at this, Linda asked him why. "The sores in my mouth hurt when I eat something hot," he said. "And I remembered the signs of malnutrition. I was sick. He ordered a piece of baklava, and when he picked it up with his fingers, I saw how bony his hands were, and I couldn't even look at him eat."

They watched the clock so they would be sure to return to the hospital in forty-five minutes. Linda didn't want to be late. "We respectfully told the nurse of our return," Linda said. "She motioned us to have a seat. We waited for fifteen, twenty, thirty minutes. It seemed like an eternity, and I couldn't believe how busy that place was. I wished I had something to read because I couldn't stand watching Mark pace. He was so nervous that people moved away and formed a circle around him. I was getting more and more anxious. Finally, at eight o'clock, I went back to the nurse and reminded her of our problem. She said the doctor was someplace upstairs. Then I started to yell. 'Doesn't the doctor realize there is a sick person out here?'" At that point Linda's self-control dissolved, and her fear grew. "I was afraid that this nurse would become a hindrance when we needed her—this stranger who was going to help."

Self-conscious about her own behavior and fearful of having alienated the nurse on duty, Linda tried to sit still and wait. She noticed the time; they had been there for more than four hours. "By the time the psychiatrist arrived, after eight, we were all angry," she said. Linda asked for, and received, permission to accompany Mark for his interview. "We entered a barren office which is probably only used for this kind of thing. Mark was asked to tell his story, and the psychiatrist interrupted him with questions as he rambled. She asked him why he wanted to be admitted. He said something about wanting to learn how to take care of himself. She already had the basic information about his age, his travels, his work experience. Then the doctor turned to me and asked, 'What's in it for you?' " Linda was shocked. "I think I mumbled something about my concern as his sister. Whatever I said, I know it was feeble. I was really shaken by this 'guardian of mercy.' I had to explain that I was the only relative and that my mother had died recently and all of the things which would help her see that I was all that Mark had."

Linda remembers how Mark stumbled over the answers. "I felt numb when he had difficulty remembering my father's name." When the psychiatrist asked if he had ever tried to kill himself, Mark answered, "No," emphatically. "But he said something strange after that. He said it wasn't his idea; it was that of the person who lived with him. Apparently the psychiatrist was confused. She asked if he hadn't said he lived alone. He nodded yes. She then got angry and asked me if I thought he was trying to be humorous." All this baffled Linda until somebody later told her that the blank and far-off look on his face was a clear sign that Mark was in trouble. His answer about suicide and living alone should have alerted her to something. But Linda didn't know what it meant at the time and tried to contain her frustration. "I tried to behave with respect simply because I was too frightened to do anything else," she said.

After a few more questions the psychiatrist said she didn't think Mark needed hospitalization. She claimed that there were no beds, but Linda distinctly remembers hearing the same psychiatrist try to admit a person who refused to stay. For whatever reason, the doctor then informed Linda that she thought Mark probably had epilepsy . . . that it was a more likely diagnosis than psychosis or related mental illness. "She recommended that we wait to see an internist. And then she did two things. The first was to give him liquid Haldol, but I didn't know what it was at the time. Then she said, 'We are on a triage system.' " After more than four hours of a runaround Linda decided she had nothing to lose by telling the psychiatrist that she thought the diagnosis wrong. "I told her about my conversations earlier with all the doctors I called. I started to yell. I reminded her that it was a public hospital, that I paid taxes, and I promised her that she would hear more about this."

But what could be done? Mark had been refused admission through the emergency room. Linda was frustrated, angry, and completely confused about what to do. Mark, who was under considerable strain, wanted to stay at the hospital and see an internist. He knew that he could not stay at Linda's apartment and also knew that his chances for warm shelter were greater in the hospital than outside. They stayed.

When an internist saw Mark, later in the evening, he said that it was not epilepsy. He would not challenge but did not understand the psychiatrist's recommendation. However, Mark's stubborn cough, lingering from a cold of the previous week, might provide an avenue through which he could be admitted and later transferred to psychiatry. This resident told Linda he clearly needed psychiatric care. Once he was admitted to a non-psychiatric medical unit, they would give him medicine to reduce the disordered thoughts. Then they would move him to the psychiatric unit later in the week.

At 11:00 P.M. Linda left the hospital. She was grateful that this young doctor was sensitive to the situation, furious with the psychiatric resident who had refused to admit Mark, and saddened by the evening's events. Linda Bloomberg's encounter with the emergency room raised questions in her mind about the services available in the community and left her embittered by the initial dealings with a mental health professional. More important, it alerted her to the reality that Mark's problems were more severe than anyone had realized previously. "It was clear that these problems were no longer his alone," she said. "Now they were mine, too, and I kept having this sinking feeling that I had to do something and could no longer just hope that he would pull himself together."

During the next few days Mark was treated for "walking pneumonia" on the medical unit; he was also treated for his mental disorganization. A psychiatrist saw him, prescribed a tranquilizer, and agreed to transfer him to the psychiatric unit when his chest was clear. Mark consented. During consultations with Linda the psychiatrist asked questions about Mark's history, their family. He showed compassion for her dilemma. Together they outlined a program whereby Mark would remain in the medical unit for several days to determine what the next step would be. In the meantime, he would prepare Mark for the transfer. This psychiatrist was certainly different from the one in the emergency room, she thought. Linda was heartened as she saw Mark gain weight and take more interest in his grooming.

The day before Mark was to be transferred to the psychiatric unit, Linda arrived for visiting hours with the usual assortment of pads of paper Mark asked her to bring daily so he could scribble the indecipherable figures he claimed carried profound messages. She also brought a chocolate bar, some magazines, and a new pair of slippers to substitute for the throwaway pair from the hospital. Cheerful when she arrived with the bagful of treats, she was surprised when Mark said that his regular doctor had not visited that day. A new set of physicians had been to see him instead. "I went out to the nurse's station and asked to speak to his doctor. They said he was no longer on that floor but I could speak to the chief resident. But he was busy. At the time I did not know that he was busy with an entirely new rotation of medical personnel and that the doctors who had been working with Mark were transferred to obstetrics or something equally implausible."

When Linda finally spoke to the chief resident late that afternoon, he said that Mark's transfer could not take place the next day as planned. Nobody who was still on the unit had followed Mark's case, and the necessary arrangements with social services were still pending. Mark would be able to remain on the medical unit for another few days, and in the meantime, they would try to arrange for the transfer.

Linda was furious. She felt betrayed again. It was the second time the hospital seemed plagued by an inconsistent bureaucracy and doctors who appeared to work in isolation. She didn't know what to do, to whom to appeal. But then it didn't matter anyway. Upon seeing an entirely new crew of doctors, and not having seen the psychiatrist whom he was growing to trust, Mark decided that the move would be unnecessary. His cold and cough had improved, and unaware that his delusions and hallucinations had disappeared as a result of medication, he decided that he was fully prepared to leave the hospital and begin another adventure. This time he discussed rabbinical school.

"I tried to persuade him that he needed more time to recuperate and that he also needed some guidance—the kind which a psychiatrist or psychologist could offer," Linda said. She pleaded and bargained, cajoled and reasoned with her brother. "He wouldn't hear of it. Mark insisted that his bad luck was turning and that this would be the last time in a hospital." Linda was gradually beginning to hear of other hospitalizations prior to his recent arrival, and each story she heard convinced her that he needed longer treatment. But always stubborn, Mark was even more so now. He claimed to know what was best for him and saw no reason to change his lifelong ambition of becoming a rabbi.

After a while Linda turned to one of the new interns who had been assigned his case. She made an appointment and told this young physician the story as best she could piece it together; Linda also inquired about forcing Mark into treatment for a few months through commitment proceedings. The doctor was puzzled. "Is he hurting anybody?" he asked. "Is he hurting himself?" The answer to each question was technically no. Mark was not suicidal; he was not homicidal. "Then there is really nothing we can do," responded the physician. "We have to just wait and see."

"Why do we have to just wait and see?" Linda asked. "For what? Why does a life have to be wasted? I really don't believe it has to be this way . . . but somebody says there's nothing they can do. What are *we* supposed to do, and for what are we supposed to wait?" she asked, in disbelief that her brother could so easily be discharged from what she began to appreciate was yet *another* hospital.

ROGER ANTHONY'S EMERGENCY

Roger Anthony's parents had more legal power over their fifteen-year-old son than Linda Bloomberg did over her brother, who was in his twenties. And the Anthonys were more successful in having Roger admitted through emergency-room procedures than was Linda. Perhaps it was because Roger was unmistakably psychotic or maybe it was because Dr. Golden called ahead to alert the hospital of his arrival. For whatever reason, the Anthonys succeeded in having Roger treated at Alpha General Hospital.

Grace and Jim remember the long wait—seven hours—in the emergency room before Roger was taken to a room. But following that stressful day, Roger stayed in the hospital for the next two months. At the time of admission he required the management and protection that could be offered only in a hospital specifically oriented toward treating crises, diagnosing symptoms, and making recommendations for future consideration.

As Jim and Grace went home, they began a new phase of coping with Roger's mental illness. Like others who are just beginning the cycle, they were filled with questions about their son's condition, anxious to understand the prognosis, the implications for his future, and saddened by events which had led them to a psychiatric ward. As they tried to understand what had led to it, how to help in the future, and what the hospital's recommendations would be, their lives were changed. The clarity of the past and the structure of their household were transformed by the phone calls to and from the hospital, the social worker and staff which worked with Roger. In one week they were inducted into the ranks of families in which a relative has had a psychotic break.

Within days of Roger's admission, Jim and Grace began attending the battery of meetings which the staff needs and families want in order to plan the next step. Because Alpha General Hospital is not designed for long-term rehabilitation, its goal is to work with the patient and family to identify and obtain appropriate care after discharge from Alpha. The Anthonys knew this and were therefore anxious to participate in the steps along the way which would help the hospital understand Roger's past. They assumed that together—parents and psychiatrists—they would develop a program for restoring him.

Grace remembers these early conversations very well. Inexperienced with hospital procedures and exhausted by the previous week's ordeal when Roger had been at home, she wanted to be helpful in giving the staff information to help Roger. But almost from the first evening, Grace recalled, the hospital assumed that Roger had always been a manipulative child and his parents easy targets. Grace found it difficult to convey to them what his behavior had been like before the psychotic break because questions were asked in a presumptuous tone. "Has he manipulated you like this for long?" asked one social worker when she saw a list of items Roger wanted his parents to bring to the hospital. In addition to books and magazines, Roger asked for supplies with which to finish a skateboard he was then making.

Disarmed by the tone of this inquiry, Grace did not know

how to respond except to say no. But the impact of several insensitive queries which felt like accusations took its toll. The Anthonys began to feel the effects of the labeling process which occurs when textbook formulations are made about families of the mentally ill. When she responded that Roger had not been a manipulative child, the social worker simply concluded that the Anthonys were blinded by denial. "Denial" is a technical term which suggests that families ignore, sometimes willfully, the obvious symptoms.

Among the things Grace thought it important to tell the social worker and psychiatrist was the history of Roger's learning disability. On several occasions she tried to bring it up, to describe how it affected him and produced frustration in his efforts to achieve his ambitions. On each occasion, Grace remembers, the information she tried to give was treated as irrelevant and dismissed. Instead, "they inquired about the crazy parts of Roger's personality." But prior to this experience there had been no "crazy parts" which Grace could tell about. She did not know how to give them what they wanted. After consulting with Dr. Golden, Grace read a number of books and articles about symptoms of psychosis and learning disorders. As an informed consumer she tried to convey Roger's entire personality—and the parts of his life which worked well along with those which didn't. She told them of his vast circle of friends and the activities in which they engaged as a group. Grace thought it telling that even during his most extreme psychotic period his friends remained loyal. She again raised the problems associated with his learning disorder which may have affected his ability to perceive situations and reason them through.

Grace remembers that Ms. Markove, Roger's social worker, did not want to hear about these parts of his life. She dismissed the information. So, although they, as parents, thought it pertinent, for a while they went along with the professional opinion. "Who were we to argue with any conviction?" Grace asked. "We had our feelings, but we were also quite bewildered."

While the social worker and psychiatrist were in the early stages of assessing the situation, Grace and Jim were called to a meeting. This was just the second meeting with Ms. Markove and Dr. Fustenberg, Roger's psychiatrist. The Anthonys met in the lobby of the hospital, arriving separately from their respective offices. They joined Ms. Markove and Dr. Fustenberg in the conference room, and the doctor began with his impression of Roger's needs, current status, and level of functioning. While the Anthonys were still trying to absorb this information, Grace remembers the Alpha staff was already recommending dispositions. "Alpha is really a short-term hospital, and they felt that long-term psychiatric treatment was necessary. And they told us what they recommended." On Dr. Fustenberg's list of treatment centers were places like the Austen Riggs Center, The Menninger Foundation, Chestnut Lodge, the Sheppard and Enoch Pratt Hospital. The Anthonys were troubled. "They were saying this without saying anything about the diagnosis. We didn't know why they were recommending these places," Grace said. The choices which were offered to these parents of a troubled teenager appeared in a vacuum. Grace and Jim did not know why long-term elite psychiatric centers were being presented or what Dr. Fustenberg had determined Roger's problem was. So they began to ask questions about the diagnosis.

The Anthonys wanted to know what it was, why Dr. Fustenberg and Ms. Markove thought one of the facilities which provided two- or three-year programs was necessary for their son. Grace questioned them about the nature of his problem. Jim asked how they recommended treating it. The Anthonys had a list of questions, which grew longer as each inquiry yielded less information than they thought they needed. Basically they wanted to know what was wrong with Roger. And they wanted to participate in planning his rehabilitation.

Dr. Fustenberg refused to speak about the diagnosis. Ms. Markove did not contradict, challenge, or add to the information he provided. "They spoke euphemistically," Grace recalled. Dr. Fustenberg said that Roger was at an age where it was good to be away from home anyway. "You are really too close to him," began the resident psychiatrist. Looking first at Grace and then at Jim, he added that they "should learn how to separate themselves." He concluded, "This will be good for all of you." "Okay," thought Grace, "maybe we are too close, but if that's all it is, we could have put him in boarding school." Dr. Fustenberg agreed. "You know, it's sort of like being at boarding school." Jim and Grace became impatient. They were on the psychiatric ward of a general hospital trying to understand the seriousness of their son's problems. They were not at a PTA meeting or preparing for college entrance examinations. Grace reminded them that "there's something about it which is not quite like sending your child to boarding school" as she worked to dislodge the explanation, which was slow in coming.

Dr. Fustenberg and Ms. Markove were unyielding. "Boarding schools allow teenagers to learn to live in the world with their peers and not be totally dependent on their parents. The time away from home permits parents to view their children as midway between childhood and adulthood. Actually, how different was Roger from other fifteen-year-old boys in live-away schools?" "A lot different," thought Grace. As indefatigable in their efforts to understand as the two staff members seemed to be to withhold information, Jim Anthony began to press them about his son. He got as far as pointing out that they must think that Roger was very sick if they were recommending something as drastic as treatment for the next two years when Roger had been in the hospital for less than a week. Dr. Fustenberg switched to another example. By way of an analogy, despite his efforts to avoid it, he stumbled over the word "schizophrenia." Without his intending to use the word in the presence of these educated, intelligent, and concerned parents, "schizophrenia" was introduced into the discussion.

Dr. Fustenberg was somewhat embarrassed that he had used this word, which he refused to explain or amplify. Jim and Grace sat there feeling emptied by what they heard. After only two visits with his parents, schizophrenia was what the team of psychotherapists had concluded was Roger's problem. Schizophrenia was what they thought required a long-term facility. And schizophrenia was thought to be so frighteningly complex that the only explanation they could offer these parents had to be as opaque as "Schizophrenia means nothing. It's really a wastebasket term," Dr. Fustenberg's reason for his refusal to provide them with a working definition.

The picture was slowly being filled in. Grace understood pieces of the argument which had occurred just minutes before about boarding schools being no different from long-term facilities. That was why they were recommending the places they did. Yet without helping Jim and Grace to understand what he recommended, Dr. Fustenberg expected the Anthonys to accept his presentation. The faith Dr. Fustenberg and Ms. Markove expected Jim and Grace to place in them did not develop. Grace explained why: "Until we understood what Roger's problems were thought to be, it was hard for us to take that leap. We knew that Roger had had a breakdown. We knew that the last year had been really impossible. But on the other hand, it was hard just instantly to accept the fact that your fifteen-year-old son would be in a hospital for the next two or three years without knowing a little bit more about it."

Whatever Jim and Grace wanted to know about schizophrenia or other treatment centers, they were not going to find it out from Dr. Fustenberg or Ms. Markove. Throughout all their consultations Grace had the feeling that these people viewed them as an unfortunate nuisance and an impediment to planning for Roger's future. While Alpha Hospital wanted to place Roger in a long-term facility, Jim and Grace were hesitant. They wanted to think about alternatives, and if they decided upon hospitalization, they wanted to investigate different facilities. They were unhappy about the prospects of sending Roger to a hospital which was a thousand miles away, and they were apprehensive about launching him on a journey that would last two or three years and be located in a psychiatric hospital. Before they took that step, they wanted to think about alternatives to hospital treatment as the core of their son's rehabilitation.

When the Connellys, Bloombergs, and Anthonys took their relatives to hospitals, the situation with which each had coped had deteriorated to the point where it could no longer be managed at home. Each family agreed to hospitalization to keep their relative safe for the duration of the episode, and none knew what the next step would be. Their principal concern was the moment. The future, with its choices for further treatment and social management of their relative's problem, was too distant even to contemplate. Care for an emergency was what each needed, and it was through an emergency room that two families sought help.

Ruth Connelly was admitted after lengthy and arduous efforts to persuade her to sign herself in voluntarily. This saved her family the ugly decision whether or not to have her committed. The situation for Mark Bloomberg was more complicated. Linda never anticipated that he would not be admitted through the emergency room. Then she was frustrated to see that he had come so close to getting help while he was being treated for a mild case of pneumonia but slipped through the hospital machinery when arrangements became unglued. And Roger Anthony's treatment, which did provide the care he needed for the acute period of his psychosis, turned the hospital into a battleground between his parents and the staff. Grace and Jim wanted to participate in decisions about what would be best for him. Instead, they were treated as incidental at this important first stage.

Each of these families entered the system in a different way. None was aware that when they sought the initial help, they were just beginning what would become a perpetual concern and a new kind of preoccupation with their relative's welfare along with their own. The short-term treatments are only the first step; the next is to decide if further treatment will be required and how it will be obtained within the available choices. This, however, is predicated on the diagnosis.

3

The Dilemma of Diagnosis

When a relative is taken to a hospital for the first time, families are anxious to learn the diagnosis. Not only do they wait to hear "what the problem is," but they want to know what can be done about it. How long will the person be there? When can relatives visit? What does it mean that the family has been asked to remain at home until the person has been calmed—perhaps for as long as two or three days? Which doctor will be in charge? And how do they speak to her or him? Stunned by their relative's presence on a psychiatric ward, parents and children, spouses and siblings do not know where to begin to alleviate their fear and confusion.

"Do you know what it is?" frequently tumbles out in the early moments while they wait for the admission. A name for "it" —the set of erratic disruptions which the family has seen and felt in the previous days or months. For many, knowing that a term can be attached to behavior not otherwise understood offers reassurance. Perhaps it means that the doctors know what to do and how to restore their relative. For others, it is frightening; the idea of mental illness conjures up unpleasant images and stereotypes.

But for most families, it is the first time that the issue is discussed in terms of an illness rather than somebody's peculiar personality. Even if they challenge the doctors later on, hearing a name for the behavior is a powerful instrument in reorganizing the families' image of themselves. It is also the first step in facing what lies ahead, in understanding duties, responsibilities, and obligations.

In the course of reaching a diagnosis, several members of the hospital staff will work with the person who has just been admitted. A psychiatrist heads the team, though many other people are involved. A psychiatric social worker will participate in some hospitals as he or she gathers information from the family and forwards observations of the patient's behavior to the doctors. Clinical psychologists may administer personality or intelligence tests. There are nurses with special training to work with psychiatric problems, and along with the aides on the unit, nurses probably have the most contact with any patient. Nurses and aides take charge of many details of the patient's daily care, especially if somebody has been placed on maximum observation. In these circumstances the patient is not permitted to go any place without the supervision of one of the hospital staff. An aide will not only observe the person through a window but will walk him or her down the hall, to the bathroom, or wherever is necessary. Finally, there might be another social worker who is not trained to do therapy as is the psychiatric social worker. The other social worker might process the paperwork which insurance or Medicaid involves.

This team of individuals, then, is involved in the early stages of figuring out what is wrong and what can be done. They consult with each other, and sometimes the psychiatrist and the psychiatric social worker present the case for discussion and advice during staff meetings of the entire unit. Before they arrive at a diagnosis, there are many questions they need answered. They may ask the family about the patient's earlier behavior to understand what he or she was like when functioning at peak levels. They are likely to ask if other relatives have been mentally ill, if the hospitalized person has good "social relationships," what kind of job he or she has and whether it has been a success. Families are asked when they first noticed peculiar behavior in the person and what events preceded it: Was there a death or divorce which brought about the departure of an important person? Was a different kind of trauma

—the loss of a job or a move to a new house—experienced?[1] If the person has been hallucinating, the staff wants to know how long this has gone on and how the family dealt with it; and if he or she is delusional, they want to know the nature of the delusions, when they began, how they affected behavior. This information is needed to enable doctors to classify the symptoms, one of the first steps in the diagnostic process.

The first time families answer these questions in a harried emergency, facts become confused, recollection fails, and the reasons they are being probed may seem strange. It is hard to remember some of the information. Answers may be garbled, and the narration of events contradictory. Later they learn which of the facts are relevant, which can be skipped over lightly, and when the background traumas and previous episodes need to be explained in detail. But during the first emergency they don't know. Yet how the intake interview flows, whether the parent or spouse cries or is matter-of-fact, or the number of questions they anticipate, affects the staff's first impression of the family.

Whatever their response, families are conscious that somebody is evaluating the way they handle that first interview. In some instances staff and family form erroneous impressions, and judgments follow throughout the patient's treatment. For the family that has never before accompanied a relative to a hospital for psychiatric treatment, the "experts" whom it encounters at that time imprint boldly.

While families are asked questions about the individual's appearance, eating habits, finances, grooming, and sexuality, they are also asked information about themselves. Because those asking the questions do not always explain their purpose, the interviews can feel intrusive and impertinent. The social worker or psychiatrist who needs this information often fails to recognize that the entire family is affected by the situation and feels it is being placed under a microscope. While it is important to gather facts that will help in the treatment of the hospitalized individual, it should be remembered that the rest of the family is shocked by what has happened and unsure of itself when suddenly forced to answer questions that may feel like an assault.

One reason why the initial interviews with a treatment team can be disconcerting is that the professional vocabulary contains words which connote scorn or disapproval. When families explain how they tried to understand the bizarre behavior with compassion and empathy, mental health professionals may accuse them of "denial." This telegraphs the opinion that something must have been terribly inadequate in those who "failed to see" the symptoms earlier. Family members are sometimes made to feel stupid or inadequate, or the deliberate agents of malevolence and sadism. Many are told that they want a relative to "remain dependent" when they report how they have tried to help the person. Some families with a mentally disabled relative even report that professionals accuse them of "resisting" help when they ask why a question is pertinent or what purpose the information will serve.

The initial interviews with the family provide essential information for diagnosing the situation since patients are difficult to read when they are most agitated. Also, given the fact that the main reason for going to a psychiatric unit in an emergency is the person's safety, often tranquilizers are prescribed right away. Replacing older forms of restraint, such as straitjackets, tranquilizers help modify hallucinations, calm a wild agitation, and consequently allow a first glimpse of the person's basic responses.

In any event, reaching the correct diagnosis is a complicated matter, for unlike other branches of medicine, psychiatry is still imprecise despite its being one of the older medical subspecialties. It emerged as a distinct field in the latter part of the nineteenth century and grew out of neurology. Each generation of psychiatry, between 1880 and 1970, has added a different explanation for the cause of mental illness, while basically treating it the same way: institutionalization of the disabled. At the turn of the century a German psychiatrist named Emil Kraepelin first observed that there were two outcomes for patients in the insane asylum where he worked. On the basis of the person's likelihood of returning to society, Kraepelin offered two classifications of disease. The first, a group of disorders he called dementia praecox, which was characterized by a gradual and steady deterioration, was renamed schizophrenia by Eugen Bleuler in 1911. The second was the group of manic-depressive psychoses, which reflected wide swings in mood and which Kraepelin thought was not as debilitating as dementia praecox. This category is called affective disorders today.

Despite the considerable attention that he paid to trying to understand the relationship between symptoms, causes, and eventual outcomes, even someone as skilled and innovative as Harry Stack Sullivan, who is known for his work with schizophrenics, observed in 1946 that psychiatry, as it was currently practiced, was "not science nor art but confusion."[2] Since the end of World War II, and especially after drugs became widely used in the 1960s, the field has swelled with research. Still, the sophisticated diagnostic aids that physicians rely on for other illnesses are just being developed in psychiatry. Blood tests, X rays, urinalyses, and other biological evaluations used routinely in the diagnosis of other diseases are of limited and uncertain help to diagnose, or predict, subtypes of the schizophrenic or manic-depressive disorders.

While other branches of medicine have long and rich traditions in laboratory research, psychiatry has been plagued by internal debate and conflict over whether the practice is an art or a science and by a preoccupation with the characteristics considered essential in the person of the therapist, who has been viewed as the instrument for cure. Also, the allocation of research funds for mental illness has lagged behind grants for other diseases. While in 1976 schizophrenic disorders cost society about $20 billion a year, which was the same estimated cost as that for cancer, research monies for schizophrenic disorders ranged between $10 and $12 million, while funds for cancer approached $700 million.[3]

Despite the relatively new emphasis on laboratory research in the field of psychiatry, there have been some promising findings that may contribute to diagnosing mental illness at a future time. One of these discoveries is what appears to be a decreased amount of a particular enzyme, MAO, in schizophrenics. As of 1979 there were thirty-two studies to test the level of this enzyme, and the deficiency was documented in twenty-six of them. Further studies indicate that another substance, PEA, which can be detected through urinalysis, is found in higher amounts in paranoid schizophrenics than in chronic schizophrenics. And it has been learned that another chemical, norepinephrine, is found in elevated levels in the spinal fluid of schizophrenics.[4]

These findings, which are beginning to grow, offer hope to researchers that at some future point there will be greater precision in diagnosing and treating mental disabilities. At this point, however, not enough is known to make accurate predictions or measurements. If a tranquilizer calmed someone in the early days of a psychotic episode, then at least one part of the puzzle temporarily may be filled in. If it did not, then another might be prescribed while the staff waits for the patient to respond and react. It is known that in a given number of cases some people respond well to something while it has no effect on others. When a medicine is effective, there is a tendency to assume that it is working on a particular disability. Hence, in contrast with other illnesses, research findings are only vaguely linked to treatment plans and a diagnosis often follows therapy rather than precedes it.

Reaching a diagnosis can be a very slow process. Many drugs require a few weeks before their effects can be measured. And unlike other drugs, which have standard dosages regularly administered for treatment of allergies or bacterial infections, there are none for the psychotropic drugs used to treat mental illness. A patient might be started on 300 milligrams of Thorazine, for example, by one doctor, and another could prescribe 1,000 milligrams. This contrasts with the way antibiotics are prescribed. If someone is taking tetracycline for an infection, the standard dose is 1 to 2 grams daily in divided doses.

If the prescribed psychotropic drug has not produced the desired results, a doctor might raise the dosage or try something else. Or in cases where there are extremely negative side effects, another might be substituted. But since most drugs have some side effect* (such as the muscular contractions known as tardive dyskinesia; weight gain; insomnia; inhibited ejaculation), psychiatrists will wait until the reactions are severe before they consider changing a prescription which works otherwise.

After enough information has been gathered to judge the symptoms and to evaluate the history and results of the different medicines, psychiatrists are ready to venture toward a diagnosis. But the diagnosis is based on interpretations and judgments, which may change if the symptoms do or if the patient's response to a particular situation introduces new information. Confusion often occurs when the symptoms of one illness are also those of another. At one time it was thought, for example, that delusions and hallucinations were found only among those suffering with problems in the family of schizophrenic disorders. But one recent

*For a list of side effects of different drugs, consult the Appendix, pp. 249–50.

study reports that "the mere presence of hallucinations or delusions in a patient does not spell out a diagnosis of schizophrenia, since these symptoms occur in more than 20 percent of affective psychoses."[5] Even the content of delusions is among the issues under debate.[6] Psychiatrists also disagree about whether a particular symptom is a phase of one illness or a separate one altogether. One example of this kind of disagreement may be seen in diagnosing the depressions which are known to follow acute psychotic episodes.[7]

Cultural and subjective criteria also influence professional opinion. It has long been known that doctors in the United States more often diagnose schizophrenia for hospitalized patients than do their colleagues in the United Kingdom. Though each country's physicians found schizophrenia among 20 to 30 percent of all admissions to hospitals in London and New York between 1930 and 1942, in the next decade almost 80 percent of the patients in New York were so classified, whereas the percentage did not change in the London hospital. The differences in diagnostic opinion are not only seen in different cultures and countries but are apparent on different wards of the same hospital.[8]

Clearly there are non-medical factors which influence the diagnosis. One expert believes that these subjective influences include race, sex, socioeconomic status, type of interview at the time of admission, and religious or political beliefs of the patient.[9] But for a family that brings a person into the hospital for the first or for a subsequent admission, these aspects of the process are not known. Nor are the confusion and lack of consensus in psychiatry.

Because a diagnosis provides guidance for treatment, psychiatrists want to be as precise as possible. Yet the field is far from the precision which would generate confidence. This is apparent when a person's symptoms do not fit the criteria for one category of illness to the exclusion of others. There is considerable overlap in symptoms, the course of the illness, and even treatment for some kinds of schizophrenia and manic-depressive psychoses.[10]

Families of hospitalized patients are generally not informed about the abundant contradictions, debates, disagreements, and various viewpoints within psychiatry. Yet it is exactly these areas of disagreement which make the process of diagnosis fraught with difficulties. It is also one of the reasons why families who have had several encounters with mental health professionals might hear one diagnosis from one and receive a different understanding from another.

Despite the confusion which surrounds diagnosis, many psychiatrists believe that it is important to have one. This is because a diagnosis is like a road map: it spells out how to proceed. It contains a theory about illness and health, and that becomes the basic framework guiding subsequent therapy. For this reason, the American Psychiatric Association pays strict attention to diagnostic categories and in 1980 was prompted to revise its edition of the *Diagnostic and Statistical Manual II* published only six years before. Between 1974 and 1980 a task force of mental health professionals worked to establish greater precision in identifying and classifying symptoms within discrete disorders with the least amount of overlap. What the previous *DSM* had simply called schizophrenia, for example, is now divided into seven subentities. Each subcategory takes into account the overt symptoms as well as the length of time they have persisted, how they erupted, and whether a "healthy" state of mind occurs between the onset of symptoms.

While many physicians and families alike believe that the accurate diagnosis of mental illness is the first step in treating someone, others believe these categories are little more than labels which are prejudicial to patients and their families. Mental illness is still regarded with fear and misconception in contemporary society. Along with open discussions about sex and death, acknowledging mental illness in one's family remains on the frontier of social conversation. Though the incidence of mental illness is higher than that of many other illnesses, it continues to carry a negative connotation, and hushed revelations are more common than open disclosures.

There is another reason why a diagnosis becomes important to the family. Without a diagnosis to place on the appropriate hospital form, families will not be entitled to benefits of their private insurance coverage or Medicaid payments. One social worker at a community hospital mentioned that there are times when she prefers "not to pin a label on somebody—especially a young person." Lorraine Howard, who has worked with families of patients brought into the emergency psychiatric unit, finds there is no alternative. "If you don't," she said, "they will not get funded."

Part of the silence that surrounds mental illness comes from ignorance about it. And this becomes a circular problem because the void is maintained when people hesitate to ask questions or seek information. Another element that promotes silence is the belief that mental illness is a blemish which cannot be erased, and that it contaminates all who are associated with the patient.

When mental illness was thought to be an instrument of the devil, many avoided the person whose faith was so tenuous that he or she allowed nefarious influences to dominate. Nobody wanted to be associated with that individual. In the sixteenth and seventeenth centuries witches were exiled or burned to rid society of them while punishing them for their sins. With changing theories about human nature, free will, and personal volition, the ideal of individual choice explained behavior in the eighteenth and nineteenth centuries. New theories emerged simultaneously to explain why some people who acted differently from others were a threat to the social order. By the twentieth century, when medical and scientific modes of explanation dominated social institutions, bureaucracy, and even efforts to reform, bizarre behavior was understood as an illness which had to be treated by physicians with special training. Yet there are many, psychiatrists among them, who argue that the mentally disabled are not "sick" but simply different, for which reason they are ill-served by being called "psychotic" or "schizophrenic," a label as ostracizing as was the earlier one of "witch."

The historical tendency has been to isolate the mentally ill. They have been exiled to hospitals with locked wards resembling prisons. Cartoonlike images of insane asylums wherein naked patients were shown caged or portrayed as having lost their senses added to the myth that they were ferocious. Because of the public disparagement of the mentally ill, families did not discuss their mentally ill relative. A book by John Neary called *Whom the Gods Destroy* [11] contains a moving account of one man's efforts to discover why his uncle had been institutionalized in the 1940s. Through conversations with his uncle's family, high school friends, and neighbors, he discovered how fearful the family was that knowledge of the breakdown might discredit it in the community. The family believed that it would be tarnished by such idiosyncratic and peculiar behavior and feared the consequences.

Some of the negative consequences of public disclosure of

mental illness have led Loren R. Mosher, M.D., to question whether diagnosis can be non-pejorative.[12] He notes that as soon as a diagnosis is attached to a patient, the hospital's staff tends to telescope its perception of that person's needs to correspond to an impression of what "schizophrenics" demand or require. Too, the families of patients can be stereotyped. Instead of being treated as the parents or spouse of somebody who has had a breakdown, family members are often treated according to preconceived notions about what they are supposed to feel, how they are supposed to act, and with what range of emotions they are likely to respond. This gets in the way of dealing with them as individuals or listening to what they say with objectivity. Grace's frustration with Alpha General Hospital is a case in point. She remembered that Ms. Markove wanted to hear only about the schizophrenic parts of Roger's personality.

Part of the frustration families encounter in the present system of mental health care is that many professionals behave in a way which is alienating. If the lay person does not have a usable framework for understanding how a diagnosis unfolds in concrete terms, then it is up to the professionals to provide one. But many do not. Moreover, the way in which families are treated when their relatives are diagnosed as having a problem of psychotic proportions often aggravates the situation. Disguised as well as open hostility often greets relatives who are presumed to be complicit in their relative's illness.[13]

Because the system of mental health care focuses on rehabilitating the patient, even when families are asked to participate in a therapeutic setting there is scant attention paid to the cultural surroundings that give meaning to terms such as "schizophrenia" and "psychotic episode." Too often the words still resonate with fear and apprehension. Since the families of individual patients are often no more enlightened than the culture of which they are a part, telling them that their relative has been diagnosed as schizophrenic requires that they also be offered a usable explanation to understand the implications. When they are not, they are kept on the periphery of their relative's problems. They are not helped to think about themselves in a way that reduces self-reproach and confusion or offers guidance.

Some family members resent hearing that their child or spouse has been diagnosed as schizophrenic or manic-depressive because the way the information is presented by the staff is not useful. The mother of one person who has been hospitalized a dozen times still does not know what is really wrong with her daughter. After years of alternating short and long hospitalizations she has not been able to get a consistent answer. The first time her daughter was in the hospital, the intern announced five minutes into the interview that she was "schizophrenic." Though the mother did not challenge his qualifications for making this assessment, she thought that "it was awfully fast for him to make that diagnosis. Also, I don't like labels. But after that, when I would ask doctors, 'Is my daughter schizophrenic?' they would say, 'Oh, no.' I've also heard 'borderline' and 'depressive.' I just don't know what she is," concluded this mother.

Other families hunger for a diagnosis because it is the only way they can begin to understand what has occurred. As Maggie Connelly noted when her mother was taken to the hospital and the family was told that Ruth was manic-depressive, "it was for *us.*" Giving the Connellys a name for Ruth's behavior helped them. Maggie readily admitted that prior to that she couldn't share her frustrations about her mother and couldn't fathom her behavior because she didn't know what to call it. "We had called it unusual behavior or just 'the way she is.' I hadn't called it mental illness. I didn't have a way to deal with it. And that was important . . . to have a name for it if nothing else."

When she knew that her mother was ill, relief settled in. Maggie understood aspects of her mother's behavior which had only stupefied her before. A diagnosis also helped Linda Bloomberg understand part of what was in store for Mark. Prior to hearing a doctor call it schizophrenia, she had no way of understanding why her younger brother seemed to be deteriorating when his childhood had been so full of promise. For the Anthonys, hearing that Roger had been diagnosed as having had an acute schizophrenic episode was not reassuring because Dr. Fustenberg refused to elaborate.

When Grace and Jim Anthony asked the doctor for a working explanation of Roger's schizophrenia, he responded that "schizophrenia is confusing to lay people." He was correct. It is a confusing concept for lay people to understand. That is because it is also confusing for psychiatrists. But when the family is kept ignorant, and the professional tries different things which may not work, frustration and anger grow. Uninformed of the professional staff's consensus on Roger's problems, Grace and Jim were at a disadvantage when they had to plan for his next step. Yet they did have to make decisions about a next move because Alpha was not a long-term psychiatric hospital. They had to decide where Roger's rehabilitation would take place, and they had to know what the choices were for that.

. . . the expensive delicate ship that must have seen
Something amazing, a boy falling out of the sky,
Had somewhere to get to and sailed calmly on.

W. H. Auden—"Musée des Beaux Arts"

PART

II

THE NEXT STEP: CHOOSING PROGRAMS

4

Psychiatric Hospitals

ROGER ANTHONY'S PARENTS TAKE CHARGE

When the Anthonys consulted with Dr. Golden after their meeting with Dr. Fustenberg and Ms. Markove, it was clear to Jim and Grace that their son needed more treatment. But what kind of treatment, and where, still had to be decided. Alpha General Hospital's staff concluded that Roger should be hospitalized for two or three years and suggested several places. Jim and Grace were hesitant, however. They wanted to make sure that a long-term psychiatric hospital was what was called for. Alternatives such as a day hospital program, a special school, or even private therapy were worth considering. Which of these programs, they wondered, would be best for their fifteen-year-old son who had experienced one acute psychotic episode?

While each family wants what is best for its relative, some choices are eliminated because of finances, age, or even the diagnosis. Roger, for example, was too young for a day hospital program. Though Jim and Grace would have preferred this option, whereby Roger would have had guidance during the day, come home in the evening, and received private therapy with a psychiatrist of his own, the minimum age for the day hospital programs in their community was sixteen years. If they could not have afforded a private hospital, and he still needed treatment, Roger might have gone to a state or county hospital, where, in 1970, slightly more than 6 percent of the patients were males under eighteen, and 18 percent of them were diagnosed as schizophrenic.[1] The Anthonys were lucky, however, in that their combined insurance policies afforded them the privilege of considering long-term psychiatric hospitalization. If it were not for this coverage, they would not have been able to afford the then current rate of $175 per day.

Again relying on Dr. Golden for guidance, Jim and Grace began to canvass psychiatric hospitals. Alpha's Dr. Fustenberg had sent Roger's records to the few centers where he thought Roger should be. Jim and Grace took time off from work to talk with the directors of the facilities that Alpha General recommended. The places they saw were pleasant enough. One adolescent center looked almost like a resort. The others lived up to their reputations with rolling hills, beautiful grounds, and impressive staffs with credentials from the best training institutions. But the Anthonys were distressed by the distance each hospital was from home. What would it mean for his treatment or visiting when Roger was more than a thousand miles away? Would it be possible to maintain any relationship when they could see their son only once or twice a year? What about their participation in his rehabilitation and in the family therapy programs that hospitals are promoting now? Jim and Grace worried. Was this the most sensible thing to do? Troubled and confused, they again turned to Dr. Golden, who had been honest with them in the past.

Dr. Golden told them about the vagaries in mental health care and disagreement among professionals. By giving them straightforward answers, he became an educator as well as a therapist. He suggested more material they might read. He told the Anthonys that the prognosis for any individual was complex and that Roger's situation was even more so because of his learning disability. He outlined the facts, and however gloomy they were, this was satisfactory for Grace and Jim, who needed to know.

Dr. Golden helped the Anthonys appreciate that each hospital would have a slightly different orientation. "There were no rights and wrongs," Grace remembered his saying. "He helped us see that each position was a point of view." Though treating mental illness can include an eclectic approach to therapies, most hospitals emphasize one form of treatment over another. The type of therapy a hospital emphasizes is based on what that particular institution believes is the source of a person's difficulty as well as the most effective way to help him or her restructure a life. And almost every long-term center stresses something slightly different, whether it is reliance on drugs, psychoanalysis, behavior modification, milieu therapy, or a combination of these.

For most of the history of psychology and psychiatry, the focus of therapy has been on the individual problems a patient presents. Therapy has been conducted in a one-to-one setting with a psychotherapist. Starting with Freud and continuing today, "talking therapy" aims to help individuals acquire an understanding of their behavior. This, it is believed, helps them gain control over it. Because they require a patient to participate actively in stating his or her frustrations and feelings, the different forms of "talking therapies" have not been as successful with problems of psychotic proportions as with the neurotic difficulties. They are, however, often used in conjunction with other modes.

In contrast with the individual or group "talking therapies," which unravel how the patient's difficulties result from his or her entire life's experience, are the behavioral therapies. These forms of treatment focus on specific problems and teach people new ways to behave by setting concrete goals that measure changes. Rewards often acknowledge the successful meeting of goals. Initially behavior therapy may focus on personal care to which a patient needs to attend, such as dressing in an appropriate manner or tending to grooming. After someone demonstrates the ability to care for his or her own body, more challenges are added to the list. These might include rewarding a passive individual who succeeds in asking for something on his or her behalf, or rewarding a chronic complainer who demonstrates that he can tolerate a minor inconvenience which might have upset him earlier. Praise or compliments, privileges on the ward, or "tokens" to be traded for goods constitute the rewards which theoretically serve as incentives. The rewards also mark achievement that the person can see in concrete terms on a frequent basis.

Another orientation one might find emphasized in a hospital is milieu therapy. This form of treatment addresses the entire surroundings in which a person lives. These can be interpreted widely, and an extreme application of milieu therapy seeks to involve the patient in the management and actual process of decision making about issues that are relevant to the ward or hospital. The hierarchical arrangements characteristic of the patient-doctor relationship carry less impact in milieu therapy, where collective decisions of the community and small group prevail. Just as behavior therapy tries to replicate an aspect of real society by offering rewards for appropriate action, milieu therapy is modeled on the notion that social people participate in their surroundings. Therefore, patients and staff meet in small groups to discuss problems involving the government of the ward, just as any other group of people who work together might meet to discuss a problem that affects their mutual interaction. By giving patients on the ward some responsibility for their own situation, this type of milieu therapy is designed to create an atmosphere in which the therapeutic process occurs in the context of a community, not just of patient and therapist.[2]

These are only three of the orientations which Dr. Golden outlined for Jim and Grace Anthony. Within each one there are special programs a hospital staff might emphasize in accord with the general outline of its approach. Jim and Grace are grateful that Dr. Golden believes families have a right to be informed about the differences in treating mental disabilities and should be consulted in deciding how a relative might be better served by one or the other. "He believes that the families have a right to know, and so do we," said Grace.

Dr. Golden's elaboration of the kinds of hospitals and their philosophical underpinnings helped the Anthonys appreciate that by choosing a particular hospital, a family implicitly accepts a philosophical view about the origins of mental illness, how to treat it, and what role the family ought to play in the process. He helped them understand that psychiatric hospitals not only concern themselves with treating patients but are also fertile training grounds for young psychiatrists who are still learning their craft. Because the younger doctors are tutored and supervised by a group of older, experienced practitioners who command status in their field based on their writings and publications, there are definite points of view being promoted. Most institutions work this way, though when families are concerned primarily with someone's rehabilitation and return to normal living, these important differences may go unexamined. Also important is the issue of how the hospital participates in outpatient programs, which are essential for today's treatment of mental illness. Although it is important for someone to receive quality care while in a hospital, it is equally necessary that there be some provisions for continued care so the patient and his or her family are not just abandoned at the time of discharge.

After looking at several places, Jim and Grace favored a hospital which was widely respected for its work with adolescents. And they discovered that Dr. Golden thought highly of the hospital and encouraged their decision. This was encouraging to the Anthonys, who were also pleased that the institute was closer to their home than any of the others. Heartened by this well-known hospital's interest in Roger, the Anthonys returned to Ms. Markove to discuss their findings.

Grace tried to explain their reasons for leaning toward Neartown Hospital and found it troublesome that Ms. Markove raised obstacles. She thought Jim and Grace were too involved in selecting the hospital where Roger would be treated. Grace resented this attitude. At one point Grace made an appointment with Dr. Fustenberg to discuss Neartown Hospital. Dr. Fustenberg agreed reluctantly to this meeting, and Grace resented his condescending and arrogant attitude. "I remember commenting on one aspect of Roger's appearance—how he looked better that day. Dr. Fustenberg told me, 'That was very well put, Mrs. Anthony.' Then he began to object to my reading about mental illness. He objected to my using the word 'schizophrenic,' saying he couldn't know what I meant when I used it. If a colleague used it, he said he knew. But he didn't ask what I meant, and he wouldn't explain what he or a colleague meant. He kept saying, 'Schizophrenia is confusing to lay people.' " Alpha General Hospital telegraphed the message that Jim and Grace should remain uninvolved in deciding where Roger's further treatment would take place, and that they should accept the staff's more enlightened recommendations.

Grace tried to explain to Dr. Fustenberg some of the reasons they preferred Neartown Hospital, such as its location, its record of working with adolescents, and the favorable impression the Anthonys had had when they visited the hospital and spoke with the staff. Dr. Fustenberg's patience wore thin, and he made it clear that it was unusual for him to speak with parents about such matters. He countered Grace's statements with recommendations from the hospitals to which he had sent Roger's records. Grace began to wonder, "Whose decision is this?" Whereas she and Jim felt their concerns warranted a respectful compassion in the midst of this trial, it seemed as if Dr. Fustenberg could treat their inquiries and requests only with imperious disregard. Grace concluded that Alpha's tone and purpose were designed to "expedite the disposition of the patient and to get the family to accept the recommendation." Grace and Jim now realize that they were too willful and full of questions to satisfy Alpha General Hospital, which preferred parents who remained passive and docile. But these parents held to their convictions and transferred Roger from Alpha General Hospital to Neartown Hospital.

The attitudes in the Alpha Hospital staff which Grace and Jim resented were evident throughout discussions of how Roger was going to be transferred to Neartown Hospital, forty-five miles away. When he was ready for discharge from Alpha, Grace and Jim expected to drive Roger to Neartown themselves. They disliked Ms. Markove's recommendation that their son be transported in an ambulance, sedated for the trip and accompanied by a guard. To them it seemed harsh and dehumanizing. Their preference for driving him to Neartown stemmed from their vision of parenting and sense of responsibility. Furthermore, they wanted to treat Roger with respect and allow him to participate in his therapy, as they were doing. Though Grace expressed her disapproval of Ms. Markove's plans, the social worker remained firm in her beliefs. She would not budge, but neither would Grace and Jim. As they tried to explain themselves, Ms. Markove responded that they were guilty of gross ignorance. She continued to insist on the conditions—ambulance, sedation, guard—as an essential aspect of Roger's transfer. And her insistence did not wane when she was told that Grace and Jim were legally responsible once they signed Roger out of the hospital.

At one point Ms. Markove proposed that Grace come to the hospital to discuss this problem. Wearied by her stubbornness and by the frequent discussions, yet anxious to have the matter settled,

Grace met with Roger's social worker. She was determined to explain their attitude about taking Roger to Neartown Hospital. Grace said that getting him to the hospital really fell into their laps as parents. After he was discharged from Alpha, they were ultimately responsible for his care. Halfway into her explanation, which was made with all the tact she could summon, Grace could see that Ms. Markove was becoming edgy as she sat behind her desk. She disagreed with everything Grace said. Ms. Markove could hardly keep the frowns and grimaces off her face as Grace was soft-spoken yet firm in her commitment to having the transfer take place in an atmosphere of trust. Finally, unable to contain herself any longer, Ms. Markove broke in, "What is it about you that makes you think you are so different from everybody else?" Stunned by the hostility of this rhetorical question, Grace did not even attempt to answer when Ms. Markove said to her, "By taking Roger there yourself, you are not letting him know how important this is to his therapy. I think you are doing this because you feel so guilty about what has happened to your child. You are feeling blamed. Everything you and your husband are doing is just to relieve your own feeling of blame."

Whatever feelings of blame or guilt Jim and Grace felt, Ms. Markove's remark was not helpful. It seemed like an assault, and the Anthonys concluded their association with Alpha General Hospital's psychiatric unit with this clash of viewpoints. At a moment of stress such as this, Grace thinks they needed support rather than disdain. After Roger's discharge from Alpha General Hospital, Grace remembered feeling "shame, failure, and blame. Alpha lacked respect for our opinions and wishes as parents." Neartown did not. At their first meeting with Mrs. Kahn, their new social worker, the Anthonys were asked how she could help. Mrs. Kahn outlined the ways in which she was available to them and then asked the Anthonys to suggest where she could start. Grace recalled waiting for "Mrs. Kahn to tell us what we *should* want from her." But Mrs. Kahn was silent on this matter. Instead, "she waited to hear what *we* wanted." Initially the Anthonys wanted only information about Roger's progress: that was all. "After our previous hospital ordeal I think we wanted to be left alone for a while. We were still vulnerable and felt judged," Grace said. She summarized it by saying, "I had battle scars."

During the first months of Roger's treatment at Neartown

Hospital, Jim and Grace were not permitted to visit their son. They spoke regularly to Mrs. Kahn, attended the hospital's family therapy sessions, and worked on restoring themselves. This period was certainly more peaceful than the months before. But the calm, which was ushered in with Roger's long-term hospitalization, proved elusive. He ran away from Neartown Hospital while on a field trip with other boys from his unit.

Roger disappeared after having written a long "organized letter presenting a case for coming home. He wanted treatment as an outpatient. It was a letter with convincing eloquence," his mother remembered. Roger's statement about wanting to be out of the hospital was prophetic, for he managed, for two weeks, to avoid his parents, the hospital staff, and even the police, with whom he was listed as a missing person. Grace remembered it was "awful and frustrating. We didn't know exactly where he was but knew his friends were sheltering him. In one instance a parent was even involved. All these people disapproved of hospitalization for treatment."

Grace described these two weeks as a time when Mrs. Kahn and Dr. Chester, Roger's psychiatrist, "were extraordinary in their support of us. Dr. Chester spoke to several of Roger's friends. He tried to help them understand, or at least see it in a different way." Roger needed treatment, and harboring him was not helpful. "But his friends were not easily swayed in their opinions," Grace knew. She and Jim spoke to the same people Dr. Chester and Mrs. Kahn contacted. The boys had been childhood friends with close ties to Roger. "They represented him with fierce loyalty. And they offered persuasive arguments on Roger's behalf. The force of their arguments, our own fatigue, and the many times we wondered if we were doing the right thing made us seriously question the hospital issue," Grace said.

Again the Anthonys had doubts about whether long-term hospitalization was the best form of rehabilitation. They spoke with Dr. Chester and Mrs. Kahn, weighing the alternatives and asking whether Roger's strong desires to leave the hospital should not be taken seriously. While they were in the midst of these discussions with Dr. Chester and Mrs. Kahn, Roger returned to the hospital and admitted himself voluntarily.

Jim and Grace believe that the discussions held with Neartown's staff prior to Roger's return were a pivotal point for them.

It was important for them, as parents, to work with people who showed respect. "I knew it was the way they listened to us. They thought about the questions as carefully as we did." They did not respond with absolutes when the Anthonys wondered about hospitalization, even though they disagreed with Jim and Grace. Dr. Chester and Mrs. Kahn both thought that Roger could be helped by further treatment and that he was just beginning to let himself be reached. Grace was particularly touched by Dr. Chester's willingness to have another psychiatrist offer an opinion. "Dr. Chester said he didn't feel that he could help Roger as an outpatient yet, but another doctor might feel differently." He encouraged these parents to get other opinions, recognizing that his approach was not the only way to treat Roger's problems. His openness evoked confidence in the Anthonys, unlike their dealings with Dr. Fustenberg. Grace and Jim were comforted by the dialogue in which Dr. Chester engaged willingly. And having already heard (from Dr. Golden) that psychiatry rests on opinions and judgments, they were reassured by Dr. Chester's flexibility and willingness to listen to the opinions of other professionals who might disagree with him but from whom he could learn.

Grace's reserve dissolved in Mrs. Kahn's warm concern during Roger's absence. "She called us every day for the entire two weeks. I found that tremendously helpful," Grace said. "She even gave us her home phone number, a rare thing for someone connected with a hospital to do. All this was a great support system and in the end helped us believe in the hospital and its staff. Their concern for us and for Roger was real." The Anthonys were further heartened by the way Neartown Hospital responded to Roger when he returned to sign himself in. "He was warmly welcomed back by everyone there. It was a very moving, touching thing to witness. After he settled back into things, everyone decided his 'elopement' had been of great therapeutic value." Seeing their son acknowledged and positively "inducted" back into the milieu from which he had fled gave them confidence in the hospital. The Anthonys rested easier because they "could see so clearly that Neartown cared about Roger as a person, not just as another sick patient. They were committed to him, and through him, to us."

Neartown Psychiatric Hospital has programs for the families of its hospitalized patients. The staff believes that when a person is in the hospital, the entire family suffers a shock and needs help in absorbing it as well as in learning how to manage and cope with future demands. Since an entire family is reorganized by the needs of a mentally ill relative, many psychiatrists and mental health professionals believe that attention has to be focused on how everybody will live with this fundamental change in his or her life. And the hospital is a place where people can begin redefining some of the expectations which arise after the patient is discharged.

Formerly treatment was intended only for the patient, and staff efforts were directed only at his or her problems. Today's health professional realizes that this is no longer adequate, especially when hospitalization is a short interlude and most patients return to live with their families, who bear the major responsibility for them. Studies have indicated that when patients are discharged and return home to cope with many of the same tensions which produced stressful situations before, the problems are exacerbated and there is a high incidence of readmission. Some of the tensions are perpetuated by family members who have been neglected or ignored while their relative was the focus of attention. Other sources of difficulty may stem from idiosyncratic communication within a family which produced turbulence and frustration for all, particularly for the individual who ended up in the hospital. Frequently there is a residue of hostility which surfaces only when a person is in the hospital and no longer making unreasonable demands that cannot be met. Whatever patterns occurred prior to someone's hospitalization, mental health professionals believe that the entire family needs attention, help, and support.

Hospitals which share this sense of responsibility to the entire family offer various programs for patients and their kin. What kinds of programs sometimes depend on whether the mentally ill person is a child or parent, brother or spouse. Often a single family will work with a therapist, and other times several families do. Whether or not the patient is included in these sessions depends on the program's purpose.

Recognizing that it does little good to ignore the family while salvaging the patient, many programs try to provide a forum for releasing the emotional turmoil that parents or children have sustained. However laudable and necessary the concern with the emotional well-being of the rest of the family, for Grace the techniques employed left much to be desired. She remembered that Alpha's Ms. Markove kept trying to force her to express her anger long before she felt it. "At the time I wasn't able to experience anger. I was just feeling sad. Ms. Markove was very impatient with that. She wanted me to recognize anger," Grace said. The social worker kept telling her that she was "really a very nice person," as if giving her permission for the hostile thoughts and feelings she might have had. Although Grace recalls growing angry much later, when she was meeting with Ms. Markove she had the sense that she was expected to have the feelings textbooks enumerate rather than the ones she did have. "I was sad that this had to happen to a fifteen-year-old boy and sad that it had happened to us," she said.

At Neartown Hospital Grace and Jim had a more successful experience. Concurrent with the private sessions, which included only them and Karee, they also participated in meetings with the parents of other hospitalized patients. For Jim and Grace the meetings with other parents were more helpful than the family sessions. As they talked of their common pains and similar circumstances, Grace had the sense that "we were the same. We shared the same hopes and fears, the same confusions and frustrations." Grace remembered one parent, a man whose daughter was on the same ward as Roger and who took a special liking to the Anthonys. They would talk of their children's progress and their hopes for them. The connection through the hospital helped establish a community which permitted a stranger to offer support and have it accepted. Grace was deeply touched when this man told her about special sacraments which could help Roger. "He told me how to pray, how to make an altar just for Roger, and to light a candle and keep it burning for him." Despite the cultural and religious differences, Grace felt "connected to this man, as I did to many of the others. They were our real world at this time."

The sharing of experiences helps make the pain socially concrete. It serves to remind families of the changes that are taking place. But despite the comfort she derived from being with other parents, Grace felt ambivalent about her own role in the sessions. Like many others who feel confused during a relative's hospitalization, Grace "was flattered when someone mistook me for the staff and asked me if I were one of the doctors." Not knowing what the parent of a mentally ill teenager acts or looks like, initially Grace believed that her quiet strength and unusually calm carriage meant that "I looked different from most of the mothers of mentally ill patients. It was important for me to think that," she added with awareness that she secretly feared stigmatization. The questions about how one compares to others do not cease, even when all are thrown in the same boat. Grace admitted having had "difficulty accepting myself in the role of the parent of a psychotic son."

Whatever educational value these sessions have, participating with other parents or siblings, spouses or children, is also a reminder that one's particular burden exists in a larger context. More than two million people and an equal number of families are burdened by schizophrenia. For some families these sessions address nagging questions of self-incrimination. Hearing how others have coped, what mechanisms they have drawn upon, what responsibilities they have faced, and who has helped them conquer particular problems allows families to place their own experience in a perspective that is comforting and useful.

Roger was ready for discharge from Neartown Psychiatric Hospital one year after he entered. It was spring, and his family prepared for his return with care. Making plans for his weekend passes, talking weekly with Dr. Golden, and feeling delighted that he was showing enough progress to continue treatment as an outpatient, Grace and Jim found themselves in studied awareness prior to his return. "We wanted Roger to be able to come home," Grace remembered. "He definitely wanted to be home. But I was afraid. . . ." Grace and Jim wondered, "Would it be the way it was before? Could we stand that again? The previous months had been terrible," she said about the time immediately preceding his treatment. "I wondered if I could go through it any longer."

When Roger was in the hospital, family life, though far from uncomplicated, returned to normal in many ways. "Jim, Karee, and I made a very simple life, and we enjoyed each other's company. We got along easily," Grace said. The easy moments of Roger's absence contrasted sharply with those in his presence. Arguments which had occurred during his turbulent moods and filled everybody with conflict and tension were gone. The quality of attention that he demanded and required and the urgent worries over his physical and emotional safety diminished. Roger's presence had imposed an erratic life-style based on episodic crisis, and when that lifted while he was in the hospital, the family resumed a normal routine. Karee, who had hesitated to bring friends home the year before, felt comfortable inviting them to the house again. When his behavior was at its worst, she hadn't done this. "It wasn't that I was ashamed that he was having problems," she noted. "It was that I was ashamed of the way he acted when he was having them. He embarrassed me," she told her mother. For Karee there was tension in not knowing how he would act when Grace took them and their friends on different outings. Roger's unpredictability had left Karee anxious.

The year Roger was in the hospital, predictability returned and structure became more certain. The moments of certainty, however, were mixed with apprehension. While they knew they wanted Roger home, "we had to struggle with ourselves and our feelings. That took time," Grace remembered. "And distance, too."

Roger started coming home on weekend passes for a few months before his discharge. Grace remembered the first ones "were sheer delight. His whole face had lifted. His eyes were shining. There was a childlike joy to him," she said of these short reunions. Prior to Roger's discharge there had been discussions about how to continue his therapy. Once he left that hospital, his parents would be required to make plans for his rehabilitation. With the guidance of Dr. Golden, they began to understand what would be asked of them and how to cope with the demands Roger would make. The choices he would have to make would be of concern to the entire family: Would he return to school? Find a job? With whom would he be in therapy? These and other concrete decisions required adjustment to Roger's situation, and Jim and Grace needed to deal with the current realities rather than an earlier hope or dream.

ELLIE ADAMSON'S DAUGHTERS NEGOTIATE THE SYSTEM

Jeanne Adamson is a veteran when it comes to coping with Ellie, her mentally ill mother. Along with her sisters, Nancy, Sandra, and Kate, she has seen her mother in several hospitals. Ellie's problems are heightened by alcoholism, which is similarly found in many others her age. Of the men and women between the ages of forty-five and sixty-four who were admitted to state and county hospitals for mental disorders in 1976, 40 percent were admitted for alcoholism. Another 12 percent were admitted for depression.[3] And like thousands of other children, Jeanne and her sisters have watched Ellie go through alcoholic binges and stupors and witnessed the aftermath of de-toxication programs; they have been called to hospitals to which the police brought Ellie after dish-breaking rampages; and Jeanne has brought her mother home after she signed herself out against medical advice. The daughters have seen their mother in so many different stages of exhaustion, medication, and agitation that they have acquired considerable knowledge about what medicines have worked in the past and how she responds.

Because of the frequency of Ellie's hospitalizations, Jeanne was dispirited and disappointed, though not surprised, when she received a phone call from a hospital in a neighboring state. The social worker at the other end of the line said that Ellie had been treated after being brought in through the emergency room. But the hospital could not hold her, and was summoning Jeanne to pick Ellie up and arrange for her transfer to another hospital for continued treatment.

Jeanne called two of her sisters, and they rented a car for the seven-hour trip. When they got to the hospital and saw their mother, Jeanne was horrified because she couldn't walk. "She was being given Thorazine," said her daughter, "because the staff knew she was aggressive. She was also in pretty bad shape." Ellie's arms were trembling, and were curled stiffly in a position that looked as if she were straining to carry logs. She had to be moved in a wheelchair, and she was so disoriented that she didn't even know where her clothes were.

Jeanne's first instinct was to remove her mother as quickly as possible. On the basis of previous experiences she believed that Ellie had been given too much Thorazine. "I recognized the side effects," Jeanne said. "When I asked, they said they were giving her eight injections a day. I couldn't believe it, and that's why they wanted her to go to another facility. She needed restraint, and they didn't have the special rooms."

84

The people with whom Jeanne spoke gave her the impression that the arrangements had been made for Ellie's transfer to a long-term facility in her home state where she had been once before. "They said they had already arranged for her to go to Nouveau Psychiatric Hospital. We were just sort of the drivers." Jeanne, Sandra, and Nancy now realize that they should have hired an ambulance to take their mother to Nouveau Hospital. But without money to pay for one and anxious to have her under medical care, they drove her back to Nouveau Hospital that same day in their rented car.

Because Ellie was heavily medicated, her mouth was cotton-dry, and her daughters gave her sips of ginger ale as she lay on the back seat, which was covered with a sheet. When they arrived, worn out from the tense and unpleasant ride, the person to whom they had been sent knew nothing about the transfer. "Nobody had told them anything at all. There was no record of the phone calls which the other hospital said it made. And Nouveau doesn't just take admissions upon arrival. You have to arrange it in advance," Jeanne noted. In addition, by the time they arrived doctors were gone for the day, and Jeanne remembers her mother had to be admitted as an involuntary emergency case.

Jeanne and her sisters found themselves in conflict. "Having to admit her involuntarily put me in an awful situation," said the woman with a deep commitment to civil liberties. "Here I was trying to force the hospital to admit my mother when I am so strongly opposed to that kind of thing. It was a draining contradiction," she reported as she described what happened that evening. First they went to the emergency admitting room, where Ellie was given the mental exam. "My mother's answers to some of the questions were strange." The doctor who administered the mental exam asked the standard questions: What day of the month is it? Who is the president? Subtract 3 and count back from 100. Ellie failed all parts of the test. Jeanne remembered that "this was a nightmare. While we were there, she had to go to the bathroom. But they didn't want to let her go to the bathroom because she wasn't admitted yet. They didn't have insurance, and if she fell and hurt herself in the bathroom and wasn't admitted, it was a problem for them. But they didn't want to admit her because she was in such bad physical shape. They didn't want to take the risk. They said she should go to a general hospital. But we didn't want her to go to a general hospital because then she could discharge herself and sign out as soon as the drugs wore off."

They also encountered a language problem with a foreign-trained psychiatrist who was not fluent in English. In 1975 one-half of all staff psychiatrists in state and county mental hospitals and almost two-thirds of psychiatric residents in these hospitals were born and trained in foreign countries. Of the total 3,691 reported foreign medical graduates employed in these institutions, the largest percentage were educated in the Far East (43 percent), followed by 28 percent in Europe, 19 percent in Latin America, and 10 percent in the Near and Middle East.[4]

For Jeanne and her sisters, the language barrier was enormous and confusing as they negotiated with the psychiatrist. The doctor was unable to convey the status of Ellie's admission; many things were hard to understand and had to be asked over again. "Someone would come with a message, and we thought it meant that she could be admitted. The aide would say all right. And I would look at Nancy with relief. Then the psychiatrist said, no, that wasn't the case. In fact, she couldn't be admitted." Jeanne and her sisters tried to ask about the regulations defining admission. "The psychiatrist didn't know what the regulations were," Jeanne recalled. "It was a real problem, and nobody else explained them." Unclear about what to do, how to proceed, or even who understood what, Jeanne and her sisters were confused.

Ellie was admitted after two hours. But her daughters were uncomfortable with the situation. "They said she was in such bad shape that they couldn't give her a room." Her daughters were told "she would have to sleep on a pull-away cot in the hallway because there wasn't enough staff to give her a single room." Ellie was put near the aide's station, a glassed-in room from which staff members could glance out to monitor her through the night. Jeanne remembered "all sorts of people walking around in pajamas or half-dressed. Bearded aides tried to be compassionate yet were busy with their own routine, and they didn't want to have to deal with still another hysterical family that wanted the best care for someone. I tried to pay them off," Jeanne explained, "to have them take care of her. I wanted to make sure she didn't get hurt and that she got a room. But they wouldn't do that." Seeing their mother lying in the hall, Jeanne and her sisters were afraid that someone might harm her inadvertently. "It was very difficult to leave when it was time for us to go," Jeanne concluded.

Jeanne realized that after two weeks in the state hospital her mother would have to be transferred to another facility where the emphasis was on rehabilitation rather than on maintenance. They arranged for Ellie's admission to a private psychiatric center. Like many hospitals, this one required the entire family's participation in a therapy program. Though the Adamson daughters had not found such sessions helpful in previous hospitalizations, they agreed to participate in the weekly sessions.

"The whole family had to go to these meetings," Jeanne began matter-of-factly. Because Jeanne lived almost two hours from the hospital and could visit only once a week, she resented her time being spent in this fashion rather than visiting privately with her mother. This expensive private hospital in which Ellie Adamson was being treated was primarily an adolescent center. With thick pile rugs and more social workers and psychiatrists than patients, it was considerably more attractive than the state hospital from which she had been transferred. However, Ellie felt out of step with so many young people whose problems and lives differed dramatically from her own struggles with alcoholism and recurrent hospitalizations. In the therapy sessions the Adamsons attended, Ellie raised this as a problem. Jeanne shared her mother's perspective. "But the social worker kept asking about 'the family responsibility' and where the problems were." Ellie said, "My problem is that this place depresses me with all of these rich adolescents. There is nothing for an older woman to do here." The psychiatric social worker disagreed that Ellie's problems, past or present, had anything to do with needing more companionship than the youngsters at the hospital provided. The social worker asked again about "the family responsibility," and Jeanne would say, "Well, she's the problem; she's it," from which the social worker "concluded that I was the 'difficult' family member," Jeanne reported. "My sister Kate kept pushing my mother to resolve her problems. The social worker liked that. I responded, 'How do you work out your problems if you are in here?' And my mother would say, 'I agree with Jeanne.' "

Each person had strong viewpoints. The social worker tried

to delve into the deeper psychodynamics of Ellie's character and personality structure. But Jeanne was puzzled, knowing that the immediate problem was how to arrange for Ellie to find housing after she left the hospital. That is what she needed, a place to live, not psychotherapy or continued treatment. She could not live with any of her daughters. Jeanne had an infant and lived in an already overcrowded one-bedroom apartment. Sandra was still in school and lived in a student apartment with several college friends. Nancy's husband would not permit Ellie in the house overnight. Kate used her home as an office and did not want the intrusion.

The daughters would not abandon their mother any more than they would turn their back on one another. A strong bond had tied them together through years of difficulties, including Ellie's wild behavior, their parents' divorce, and the efforts of one parent to turn the daughters against the other. Jeanne told of one episode which occurred five years earlier. Shortly after she went off to college, though she was estranged from her mother for several months, she spoke frequently with Sandra, who was still in high school. During the periods of Ellie's hospitalizations Sandra was remanded to foster-home care, which upset everybody. Jeanne felt responsible for her younger sister while their mother was in and out of institutions. Over the previous two years thirteen-year-old Sandra had already lived in several homes. This, thought Jeanne, was too much for any youngster to sustain.

"I very much wanted to help my sister and provide her with a stable environment where things were more normal. I wanted her to grow up where there wasn't a problem all the time. I wanted to be able to help give some structure to her life," Jeanne explained. So, rather than have her sister returned to a foster home, Jeanne decided that she would interrupt her college education, move out of the dormitory, and provide a home for Sandra. But it didn't work out very well, Jeanne noted. Her devotion and concern were greater than her maturity as a college junior. In retrospect she realizes why it became a problem: "I was young, and it ended up with me doing all the work to begin that family," which consisted of the two sisters. "It just didn't work. We were living with no money, I was going by myself to do all the chores, and I had no support from friends because I had a little sister living with me."

Their social existence in a college town without friends or

networks of support was barren. The activities in which Jeanne had taken part as a student were not suitable for her sister, and Jeanne herself was being excluded. "I wasn't included in student activities at all," she said. "Nobody let me know that any were going on, and they knew that I had no money, so I couldn't do those things that required any." Even close boyfriends stopped calling. "They just dropped out because I wouldn't have them stay over." Those who were available "gave me pity, which I didn't want. I needed support, and I wanted regular friends, and I wanted my sister to have regular friends. I wanted her to develop a network so that she would feel comfortable. In doing that, I became estranged from my own network." Jeanne knows she erred by assuming that "it could be the same for Sandra. But she was just too young to participate in a college student environment." After realizing this, Jeanne tried to find scholarships which would allow Sandra to attend boarding school. She borrowed a car and had a friend drive them to the different places where Sandra could be interviewed. But in the end, Sandra wanted to go back to where she had friends. She ended up going back to a family in her hometown before her mother was discharged again.

Jeanne's determination to help her sister sprang from the same source of strength as her later efforts to help her mother when Ellie needed a place to live after the hospital. But throughout, the social worker froze discussion by pressing them all to focus on Ellie's personality. Jeanne continued to object because Ellie found the social worker's questions insulting. "My mother kept saying that she saw nothing wrong with her personality. She wanted the social worker to be more specific about what her personality problems were. But the social worker wasn't," Jeanne said. Throughout their several sessions the predominant theme that emerged was Ellie's discomfort in a hospital where she was the only person in her age group. She missed people with whom she could have had conversations appropriate to her life's experience as a mother and grandmother. She was not interested in the world of adolescents, their music or drug experiences, their idols and culture.

Jeanne Adamson still believes that one of the major problems throughout Ellie's illness was the limited range of alternatives available after she left a hospital. Ellie's work experience included employment as a maid, a dishwasher, and part of a cleaning crew.

It pains Jeanne to think of her mother working in one of these jobs when she recalls her childhood in an affluent upper-middle-class suburb. Yet it distresses her even more when she thinks of Ellie's being unable to work because she is in a hospital. For Ellie, employment bolsters self-esteem, which drops with each hospital readmission. Whenever she is able to find work as a live-in housekeeper, the problems of shelter and food take care of themselves. She also has a little spending money, which makes her feel less dependent on her daughters, and they do not resent her other requests as much. During the interludes when she is unable to find employment or has a job that does not provide housing, the issue of where Ellie will live remains a major problem. It causes her to fret about her existence and future. It troubles her daughters, too.

Jeanne and her sisters are bitter that in their opinion, "not one of the social workers helped facilitate aftercare arrangements." Though the staff members made some suggestions, Ellie, Jeanne, Kate, Sandra, and Nancy each felt that their recommendations were inappropriate. "The social work staff in the private psychiatric hospital wanted her to go to a long-term state facility," remembered Jeanne about the early conversations. "It was a recommendation based on complicated reasoning." The idea of a long-term facility seemed unnecessary for this woman in her fifties who functioned adequately between psychotic episodes and alcoholic binges. Because Ellie took care of herself with a minimum of difficulty between hospitalizations, the daughters wanted something that would permit her the greatest movement rather than a restrictive alternative. But "when we turned down the long-term facility, they didn't offer other alternatives. One of the ways the social services could have been more responsible," Jeanne reasoned with controlled anger, "would have been for them to offer more than one suggestion. Just because one of the things they suggested was turned down didn't mean we were going to reject everything they offered." Throughout the conversations Jeanne thought "it was like a battle of power. They would say one thing. My mother would reject it. Then it would become a fight over why she rejected it. Instead, they should have suggested something else. They never moved to other alternatives."

One of the choices that is less restrictive than a hospital and designed to offer shelter for patients in transition is a halfway house. These facilities have mushroomed since the 1970s, when hospitals began discharging the mentally disabled in the shortest possible time. Halfway houses vary in quality as well as in the services they provide. Many are no more than boardinghouses with expensive rents managed with little orientation toward the needs of their residents. Others require residents to participate in housekeeping duties as a form of rehabilitation; still others are connected to counseling services, job rehabilitation programs, or psychotherapeutic agencies. Halfway houses are among the alternatives which were expanded to meet the judicial mandate for treatment in the "least restrictive setting." By the attachment of services to halfway houses through formal or informal arrangements, the letter of the law is approached.

From her previous experience, Ellie knew that halfway houses might answer her housing problems. Having lived in them before her admission to Nouveau Hospital, however, she had definite ideas about which ones would suit her. "My mother didn't want to go to the kind of halfway house that was generally full of kids," Jeanne said. "She wanted to work, and she wanted to live in a halfway house where that would be possible." The social worker continued to insist that Ellie wasn't ready for work, but Ellie countered that she was insecure when she had no income. The discussion was then escalated when the social worker reminded Ellie of her previous work experience—many jobs for no more than a year at a time—and concluded that Ellie was still not ready for a job. "My mother disagreed vehemently," Jeanne said. She remembered her own pain when Ellie told the social worker, "Working is the only thing that gives me any purpose . . . any activity at all," in a voice that was barely audible.

Jeanne was torn during these discussions about where Ellie would go after the hospital. She wasn't convinced that living in a halfway house was the best solution for her mother, but she could not think of a better one. Trying to be supportive of her mother, and having difficulty controlling her anger toward the social worker, Jeanne argued that Ellie ought to be given a chance. At least she should be placed in a halfway house and helped to find a job rather than discouraged from becoming self-sufficient. After all, how many other people change jobs frequently, and wasn't it a healthier sign for her mother to want a daytime activity than for her to have no goals at all?

Jeanne was growing cynical. She knew the existing system of

mental health care is supposed to help people adjust to society, yet the social worker encouraged the idea of sending Ellie to a long-term hospital. Jeanne was told there are higher rates of rehospitalization for people who do not have supportive networks, but Ellie was discouraged from thinking about work as a way of feeling useful and connected to a larger world. Irritated that nothing seemed to fall into place, Jeanne decided to bypass the social worker and take matters into her own hands. She went to the library and found a book which listed community residences within a two- or three-hour drive from her house. "I selected the places which claimed to be residential and said that they accepted people with histories of alcoholism and repeated mental hospitalizations. And I called everyone that I found on the list. I went through it all from *a* to *z*. And all of them, each of the twenty-five or thirty facilities which stated in writing that they took somebody with her problems, or someone like her, said they would *not* take her. A couple said they would look her over. But we couldn't go on something so tentative. We couldn't take the chance of going to a place and having her think she had somewhere to live and then have her be rejected. It would have been too much for her to have to take."

In retrospect, Jeanne knows that many of the facilities listed in official directories already have waiting lists, or have restrictions that effectively disqualify the families of mentally ill people from using them. While they were listed in public sources and advertised as such, for practical purposes they were not available to her mother. Jeanne did not believe the paucity of choices when she first started to call. Afterwards, she conceded that the social workers are limited by what they have to offer. "I didn't believe it at the time," she said, "but I think the social worker would have encountered the same difficulties if she had done the same thing I did. I don't think she would have been able to get my mother into any of those places either. What my mother needed was a place where she wouldn't be the only person who was middle-aged. She is too independent and too old to be confined by restrictive rules. And she needed a place out of which she could work." These requirements, which the facilities could not meet even if they had agreed to take her, would have permitted Ellie the companionship which she sought and which her daughters knew would be therapeutic.

Jeanne thinks that some of their difficulty was also rooted in the idiosyncratic nature of Ellie's personality. Her upper-middle-class background and her occasional pretenses to style mean that she objects to conditions she thinks beneath her. Ellie expects qualities of cleanliness which are not standard in many halfway houses. To complicate matters further, Ellie doesn't consider herself crazy. Despite the decade during which she was in several institutions for short periods of time, according to Jeanne, "When she's not in the hospital, she doesn't think of herself as an ex-patient. Therefore, she doesn't want to live with 'crazy' people. There is a total change in her sense of her own status; when she's out, that's it—she doesn't expect to go back in." Jeanne remarked that Ellie "functions well between hospitalizations. And she complains about living in places where people do not function normally."

The criteria for admission to halfway houses vary, and proprietors do not always determine a person's ability to care for himself or herself before accepting a resident. For this reason people like Ellie often feel alienated in the midst of those whose level of functioning is under less control than their own. In efforts to help place their mother, Jeanne and her sisters encountered many of the frustrations social workers voice. While a social worker is supposed to arrange for aftercare, he or she can only rely upon what is available.

In some instances families can sustain a relative's chronic demands only when the person does not live with them. One form of assistance that families need most is access to residential housing they can rely upon. Parents, children, spouses, and siblings actively join the social work staff in the search. Relatives are fully aware of what the mental health professional can only guess: living with that particular individual would drive others crazy.

By the time we spoke Ellie Adamson had been out of the hospital for three months, and Jeanne was hopeful that her mother's current situation would continue. Though the hospital had not succeeded in placing Ellie in a job or a halfway house, a former employer helped her find a job as housekeeper on an estate. Whether Ellie will remain in this job is still uncertain. Jeanne no longer assumes that today's situation will be tomorrow's reality. But for the time being she is content, knowing that her mother is temporarily out of a hospital.

EMILY FLYNN'S MOTHER GROWS CYNICAL

By the time Rosanne Flynn took her twenty-year-old daughter, Emily, to Circlesville Psychiatric Institute, she had lived through almost three years of her daughter's bizarre and disruptive behavior. It was damaging both of them. The hospitalization at Circlesville Psychiatric, which lasted eighteen months, was Emily's fourth in two years. Having been admitted to general hospitals through emergency rooms on two occasions when she overdosed with drugs, Emily was discharged from each in a matter of days. The third hospitalization, which lasted four months, ended when her doctors concluded that they had accomplished as much as they could with their therapeutic emphasis on stabilizing and maintaining a patient with drugs. The hospital recommended that Emily receive additional rehabilitative therapy lasting for at least one year in another place. It recommended either private psychiatric counseling or a psychiatric institute.

When Rosanne heard the choices the hospital offered for her daughter, she was convinced that she would never forgive herself if she did not try a psychiatric hospital for rehabilitation. By then Emily had already been in private therapy with several different people, and Rosanne had not seen progress, which left her discouraged. By the time she was presented with these two choices Rosanne was convinced that she had to try a long-term psychiatric hospital in the hope that it would succeed in restoring Emily.

Like other parents whose children develop a mental disability in their teens, Rosanne Flynn finds it difficult to pinpoint childhood problems that led to the situation with which she and her daughter now contend. Reared in a family that was always fast-paced, from an early age Emily Flynn moved in a world of intellectual and cultural distinction. Gerald Flynn, Emily's father, was an accomplished musicologist whose work is well known and widely respected. Her mother combines part-time teaching with a position as the head of a research division in a pharmaceutical laboratory. I had some intimation of the busy schedule Rosanne kept when I had to call several times and speak with different secretaries in order to make an appointment for an interview. My expectations were confirmed when I arrived for a three-hour interview that she graciously gave me, while colleagues, phone calls, and scheduling rearrangements interrupted us. Yet the contrast was evident between the finality of decisions she makes dozens of times each day in her professional life and the lack of clarity in her personal life as the parent of a troubled youngster.

Rosanne's office, in a twentieth-century amalgam of concrete and steel, was decorated with overgrown hanging plants and colorful tapestries to soften the brick-walled room. After pouring coffee, Rosanne recounted the sequence of events which led to Emily's increasing dependency and the mental disability that affects both their lives. For the past six years, in addition to a divorce and the death of her former husband, Emily's condition has been her major preoccupation. Rosanne spoke with little prompting.

The problems started when Emily was almost seventeen, after she had just been graduated from a demanding high school for highly motivated students. During her last year of school Emily was using drugs, which Rosanne did not know at the time. "I even found it hard to believe when I did find out," she added. "But because Emily was growing up in the 1960s and 1970s, of course, I was always worried and frightened." As a research biologist, working with different synthesized drugs as part of her profession, Rosanne worried about the increasing availability of illegal drugs among teenagers. She was familiar with too many studies discussing side effects of LSD, knew too many students who appeared dazed and without motivation, and understood exactly how dangerous the "street scene" could be. "I knew she used pot," Rosanne continued, "but even that upset me a great deal. I'm enough older that I thought people should not. As far as I was concerned, pot was as bad as anything else," she said.

The summer between graduating high school and beginning college, Emily managed to conceal her use of drugs from her parents. It was later that they learned she had been using them that entire summer. Yet without being aware of this at the time, Rosanne and her husband, Gerald, suspected that their daughter needed help. They noticed that she was sleeping long hours, aimlessly staying around the house, and gaining so much weight that she grew from a size 9 to a tight 11 in a few months. This behavior was not characteristic of Emily, who had previously been a self-starter—someone with lots of energy, a person with a project under way all the time and preoccupied with her appearance, as are many seventeen-year-old girls. They were concerned, but Emily was loath to discuss these changes in her behavior with her parents. They, however, thought she might be helped by therapy during the summer before she went off to college.

Rosanne scouted around and asked friends to recommend someone. When she located a therapist for her daughter, Emily protested initially, but eventually agreed to see this psychiatrist in order to placate her parents for the remaining time before she left home. The psychotherapist whom Emily saw for these few weeks concluded that she was experiencing adolescent anxieties. Like other teens he had seen, she did not want to be in therapy. He concurred with her wishes to stop, and Rosanne and Gerald accepted this as Emily was about ready to pack and take the day-long trip to her new school.

Rosanne remembers that Emily moved with ease and grace in social situations. As a child she always seemed self-confident. She made friends easily, adapted well in new situations, and generally gave Rosanne and Gerald little to worry about. The maturity and self-reliance, which were apparent to all, dissolved the day her parents drove her to school, the same way they had taken her older sister, Carole, five years before. The comparison stops after the pleasant ride and discussions of what the next four years would be like—of roommates and college courses, of dormitory living and research in the library. After helping her get settled and then having dinner, Gerald and Rosanne returned with Emily to her dormitory room to say good night on the eve of their daughter's enrollment. It was then that Emily first indicated how nervous she was, and Rosanne remembers the scene where her daughter protested their departure. "She didn't want me to go," she recalled. "It was frightening. It was like leaving a child in nursery school. I couldn't believe it was happening. This child, who had gone off to camps and embraced the world as if she were eighteen at the age of twelve, at the age of seventeen seemed like she was eight."

With mixed emotions, Rosanne and Gerald left. They reminded Emily that she was not off in Siberia but just a short trip from home; she would be able to return for visits. Confident that the weeks between Labor Day and Thanksgiving would evaporate as she became immersed in her time-consuming work, they told her that she would be home before she had a chance to miss them.

That was not far from the truth. The first semester away at college Emily came home frequently and several times before Thanksgiving. She would arrive after her last class of the week and stay the weekend, sleeping all the time. This concerned Gerald and Rosanne, who thought their daughter was not behaving the way first-year college students do. But their only clues were her marathon sleeping and the frequent trips home. Emily refused to discuss school, her exhaustion, her new friends, or what was on her mind. She hardly said a word, spent most of the time in bed, and "in order to just wake her in the morning when she was supposed to return to school, I actually had to scream at her to get up," Rosanne said.

Whatever value there was in the previous summer's therapy, Rosanne thought Emily needed more. Relying on friends who lived near the college, she asked for help in locating a good therapist for her daughter. "Emily went to one person who was in a clinic. She didn't like the clinic. He used a tape recorder, and that didn't work for Emily." Emily asked to find a therapist on her own, and she saw a new person for the rest of the school year. Her parents still did not know it, but "Emily was very heavily on drugs. And apparently the reason she spent so much time sleeping when she came home for weekends was that she was just sleeping them off," her mother figured out later. But whatever was going on, Emily camouflaged it well enough that her grades did not show it. Her final grades for the year were not outstanding, but neither were they a disaster.

Emily saw her therapist regularly during the year, as Rosanne and Gerald knew because they paid the bills. Then, at the end of the first year of college, and without any warning, the therapist whom Emily was seeing and whom her parents had never met told Emily that she should not continue with school full-time. He said she should go to a halfway house. Rosanne and Gerald were shocked, and they were opposed to the idea. "This came like a bolt out of the blue!" Rosanne said. "I had no idea, and I was very much against it." She called the therapist to discuss this. "Essentially he did not want to talk to me. And he didn't." Rosanne now thinks that was quite foolish. "In retrospect I know how stupid that was. If he had made some effort to talk to me, I think I would have known earlier the magnitude of the problem

I was dealing with. I would not have thought I was just dealing with some unmotivated kid who could be made to toe the line, grow up, and act her age."

Kept in the dark, Rosanne responded to Emily's lethargy and the psychotherapist's recommendation with irritation. Though Emily had not shown growth or maturity that year, short of a therapist's saying that she needed to be in a halfway house, there was nothing to indicate mental disability. Having been around college students through her work and the teaching positions she held, Rosanne knew that some students have difficulty adjusting to school. Emily's lethargy often angered her parents because they expected their daughter to continue with her characteristically high motivation. But Rosanne didn't believe that mediocre grades were sufficient reason for Emily to drop out of school and enter a halfway house. So at the end of the year, in addition to being extremely disappointed and frustrated by the therapist who refused to consult with her, Rosanne assumed that in the fall Emily would return to the Ivy League coeducational college where she had completed her freshman year.

"Emily worked that summer as a camp counselor," Rosanne continued. "Then she came home and just told me that she would not go back to college." There were arguments, but Emily had already made up her mind. "I was furious. I screamed and yelled, but there was nothing I could do. Emily came home to Circlesville to live and moved back in with us." And she was depressed. "She gained a tremendous amount of weight and was struggling with all the problems which strike during this adolescent period. Gerald and I talked and decided to put her in therapy again. I called somebody I thought was respected. This person told me about somebody else. Emily went to this psychiatrist for several months. And all the time she hated him. She just loathed him, and she kept telling me that she didn't want to go. I kept saying she had to go, and her father kept saying that she had to go. We wouldn't budge. One day Emily came home from seeing this psychiatrist, and she had a report with her. He had sent her for tests, and she was bringing the results home. The report said that she had a very low IQ, which might be attributable to the drugs she had taken. And the psychiatrist told Emily that he didn't know if she was permanently brain-damaged." Dismayed and frightened, Emily now worried that the LSD and speed had damaged her irreparably.

Rosanne and Gerald were equally alarmed learning of Emily's drug use. But despite their alarm, they still did not appreciate the severity of her emotional problems.

Because she had lost confidence in the psychiatrist for showing Emily the report, Rosanne found another therapist for her daughter, who was now almost nineteen and gaining more weight while showing less energy. Again the pattern was repeated: Emily was not enthusiastic about the new psychiatrist, this one a highly recommended psychoanalyst. Still, she stayed in therapy with this woman for two years, but these seemed to be years of only minor progress. Though Emily did not like her doctor very much, Rosanne had the feeling that the psychoanalyst was very interested in Emily. "She cared a lot, and perhaps she was more involved than competent." Rosanne also noted that Emily was probably not an easy analytic patient. "But the therapist just couldn't deal with her." Emily continued to act in self-destructive ways. While Rosanne was gone during the day, Emily began pawning some of the household silver; she smoked constantly, and her parents later found cigarette burns in sheets, table linens, and other materials which could have gone up in flame.

Without violating patient-doctor confidentiality, Emily's psychoanalyst spoke with Rosanne and willingly made herself available to the mother, whose concerns were as deep as the daughter's troubles. For her compassion and concern about Emily, Rosanne is grateful. She felt that "at least this doctor didn't shut me out; she didn't refuse to talk to me; she was very concerned about my daughter."

Despite the therapist's concern, Emily was not improving. She quit a temporary job. "She wouldn't get up in the morning to go to work. Finally, though, the therapist was able to help her start back to school." To Rosanne and Gerald, whose lives for two years were punctuated by arguments with Emily over getting up in the morning, getting herself to work on time, and finding something to do when she quit work, returning to school seemed to be a step in the right direction. She went back gradually, part-time in the spring and full-time in the fall. She lived in a dormitory and continued in treatment for the first half of that year. "I was still not fully aware of the magnitude of the difficulty," Rosanne admits, "even though during the year there was a moment when the therapist said she might have to hospitalize Emily because she was displaying 'suicidal ideation.' She didn't want to hospitalize Emily, however, and I don't think my daughter ever knew it was an issue. Then Emily quit the therapist in the middle of the semester and continued in school."

The accumulated burden, the constant strain, and the frequent arguments over Emily's progress, her problems, and how everything was going to be handled were too much for Gerald. At the end of Emily's year back in college he and Rosanne separated. When summer vacation began, Emily returned home to live with her mother, and because she was going to attend summer school, Rosanne thought it was okay. Yet that period of her life she now regards as "a mess. My marriage was breaking up, and I was breaking up." Her other daughter, five years older than Emily, was out west in a doctoral program. In the meantime, Rosanne was scheduled to participate in a week-long international conference which was taking place in Europe. So, with Emily attending summer school and beginning treatment with yet another psychologist, whom she had found for herself, Rosanne went abroad for a conference she had been planning to attend for more than a year. "I felt that if Emily was in treatment with somebody whom she liked and found herself, that was better. At least it was a step in the right direction—that is, the move to separate from me, which was a major problem. So I went away."

Twenty-four hours after Rosanne got to the conference, she received a call from Gerald saying that a doctor thought Emily should be hospitalized instantly to get her off very high doses of speed. "I came back to Circlesville and took her to a psychopharmacologist-psychiatrist. He said she *did* need to be hospitalized. It *was* urgent." Rosanne arranged for Emily's hospitalization. Five days later Emily signed herself out against medical advice and returned home in a surly mood.

Angry at Rosanne, and at her father too, Emily looked for an apartment of her own. She was not becoming independent by living with her mother, and Rosanne was encouraged by this sign that her daughter wanted to take greater responsibility for herself. After finding an apartment, however, Emily decided it was burdensome to drive to the psychiatrist's office, which was more than an hour away. She found excuses not to go. Then, when Rosanne left town for a weekend to attend a professional meeting, Emily took a large dose of Seconal. She got the pills from a friend who had made several suicide attempts herself. For whatever reason, after making the pills available and leaving for home, the friend returned and found Emily. She called an ambulance and took her to the hospital. Of the two hospitals in the area, the friend had been in one. "She took Emily to the other," Rosanne said. "I rushed back home and got her transferred out of this excuse for a hospital."

Emily's friend saved her life by returning. Many who attempt suicide, however, succeed. Next to accident and homicide, it is the most common cause of death for people between the ages of fifteen and twenty-four. While national suicide rates changed very little between 1970 and 1976, for two groups in the population there has been an increase in deaths caused by suicide. The United States Center for Health Statistics reports that among the general black population, and among all males between the ages of fifteen and twenty-four, suicide has increased as a cause of death.

For Rosanne, the suicide attempt confirmed how serious the problem was. The difficult years that preceded Emily's attempt on her own life had imposed stress and strain, frustration and irritation, and had involved an army of psychotherapists as her mother tried to manage the situation. She had assumed that whatever problems besieged her daughter, Emily could be helped by getting attention early on. Yet Rosanne now realized that the attention had been insufficient.

At this point Rosanne was advised to consult an internationally known psychiatrist. Dr. Hampster was a man whose reputation was built on working with some of the problems Emily displayed. He had even written textbooks on the subject which are still considered standard references for the field. Determined to leave nothing to chance and to pursue every lead, Rosanne made an appointment to see Dr. Hampster. Both mother and daughter went to the office; Dr. Hampster spoke first with Emily, then with Rosanne. Rosanne told him the story of the several therapists, the drugs, and how Emily "was acting out these horror scenes: burning holes in sheets, taking silver and pawning it, running up big bills. . . . And I was close to the edge myself," she added.

After talking with each of them, Dr. Hampster advised Rosanne to hospitalize Emily. "If there are two people in a lifeboat for one, only one can survive," he said. He added, "You have to survive. You cannot go down with her. You can try, but you have very little to hope for." Dr. Hampster then recommended a particular hospital which emphasized rehabilitation through drug therapy. But he was not encouraging about Emily's future. Rosanne felt there were no alternatives. Clearly Emily had to receive quality treatment, and she must be hospitalized. Taking Dr. Hampster's advice, she arranged for Emily's admission to the hospital which relied primarily on drugs. Four months later doctors were so impressed with Emily's improvement that they concluded there was nothing else to be done for her at their facility. They suggested that Rosanne return to Dr. Hampster for further recommendations.

After seeing Emily again, Dr. Hampster "was impressed with how changed she was. He said that he never would have thought this would happen. And he agreed that she still needed long-term treatment, but because she had a tendency to change therapists and run away from help, he thought she should be in a hospital. That way the therapist would be more effective." Rosanne listened carefully. She was heartened by his current opinion, she was delighted with his first recommendation and its results, and now she would listen again to what he said. He suggested half a dozen hospitals, each of them requiring a minimum of a year for treatment.

With Emily, Rosanne traveled to visit several hospitals, each of which was known for its experienced staff and prominent senior psychiatrists. After visiting these places on Dr. Hampster's list, Emily selected one which was closest to home. In fact, it was only one hour away. She didn't want to be away again, and she didn't want to lose contact with the few friends remaining in the area. Rosanne was more impressed with another but decided the matter was closed. "It was quite far away, however. Emily didn't like it, and because she was the one who was going to be hospitalized, I thought it was her choice." Both knew that Emily would have to be there for at least a year, and Rosanne didn't want the hospitalization to be more traumatic than necessary. Emily would be treated in Circlesville Psychiatric Institute.

After having chosen the institute, Rosanne was reading the newspaper one day and saw an announcement that a new psychiatrist was joining the already illustrious staff. Cited for his contributions in the field and the publication of several books and articles, the new addition was none other than Dr. Hampster. Rosanne's spirits lifted when she knew such a competent man would be joining the staff where her daughter was being treated.

Like the other hospitals they had visited, Circlesville Psychiatric Institute was expensive. The only way Rosanne could afford the $300 a day was through an insurance policy. Yet she could justify what she considered an outrageous charge because of the high repute of the entire staff, a number of whom were recognized as leaders in their fields. For this reason it was somewhat of a shock to her when she discovered that Emily was not being treated by any of the senior staff members for whom the hospital had been chosen. Rather, her daughter's psychiatrist was one of the young residents, new to the specialty and supervised by senior staff during frequent meetings. Rosanne would have preferred the more experienced therapists who had already demonstrated their abilities. But she could not alter hospital policy, and she had to go along with the system.

During the early months of Emily's treatment Circlesville Psychiatric reduced the medication which had worked for her at the other hospital. Gradually the staff took her off it entirely. At this time Emily became depressed again. Rosanne saw her daughter becoming less functional, not more. In addition to a growing lethargy and depression, Emily acquired a passivity which is sometimes called "the patient's role." She learned how to throw up. She cut herself with broken light bulbs. And she began extinguishing cigarettes on her own body. These were things she had never done in the other hospital or when she had lived at home. She learned them from the other patients with whom she spent most of her time, Rosanne lamented.

Rosanne's alarm grew as she saw a decline in every aspect of Emily's personality and character. Rosanne also questioned the therapy her daughter was receiving. For three hours a week Emily was in individual therapy; for five hours a week she was in group therapy. These eight hours, reasoned Rosanne, were less effective "than the rest of the day, when she was learning self-destructive behavior from those on the same floor." When it was clear to her that Emily's treatment had yielded few positive changes after several months' hospitalization, Rosanne asked for a change in therapists. "I said I didn't think she was being helped." The hospital said no. Emily's therapist and the staff disagreed with Rosanne.

"It's just taking a long time," they said, and the staff responded that "the therapist who works with her is quite effective."

Whatever the staff said about Emily's improvement, Rosanne could see for herself that her daughter was gradually withdrawing. She saw Emily stay in the hospital when she could have left on a weekend pass. She saw Emily's cuts and burns and knew they were a bad sign, not one of progress. And she saw that Emily was not acquiring any of the basic skills which would help her become independent when she left. She received no occupational therapy, nor was she learning how to do anything which would afford her greater independence or autonomy when she was discharged. By then Emily had been in the hospital for almost a year, and Rosanne grew more apprehensive about the future, including the fact that her insurance was going to stop paying for the treatment. "That it paid for so long was a miracle," she added.

Unsuccessful in her several efforts to have Emily's therapist changed, Rosanne decided to return to Dr. Hampster, who was now on the staff of Circlesville Psychiatric Institute. His earlier suggestions had been helpful, and he had known Emily long before she entered the institution. "I went to him and said that I thought things were worse, not better. I asked him to do an evaluation," Rosanne remembered. "Dr. Hampster initially replied that Emily was on the best unit in the hospital and that she had the best psychiatrist. He said the doctor was a wonderful person, and so was the social worker." Rosanne thought that was nice, but beside the point. To her it was more important that Emily did not show any signs of improvement than that the unit or the psychiatrist was the best. She told Dr. Hampster so. "She isn't improving; she isn't any better. I think she's actually worse," Rosanne said, and asked again that he do an evaluation.

By the end of the meeting Dr. Hampster had reluctantly agreed to do an evaluation. It was then the middle of the summer, and he would be going on vacation. But when he returned, he assured her, it would be done. Three months later, it was.

In the fall Dr. Hampster proceeded with the evaluation. Rosanne said that if she had known what she was asking for, she never would have done it. The evaluation procedure, which may be different in other hospitals, consisted of interviewing Emily in front of the entire staff. In the presence of the social workers and psychiatrists who worked on Emily's unit, Dr. Hampster questioned the young woman. After listening to her replies, Dr. Hampster gave her his evaluation. In his opinion, Emily was an enormously destructive individual. She was damaging to everybody around her. This included her mother, her therapist, and the other patients on the ward.

"I was undone by this," Rosanne stated. She heard about it first from Emily, then from Emily's social worker. Each of them told her about the same chain of events. "I called to speak with Dr. Hampster and went to his office to see him that evening. I was very upset," she recalled. Reminding him of her requests to change therapists several months earlier and of the reply that her therapist was exceedingly competent, Rosanne asked Dr. Hampster, "How effective could he have been if the results of the evaluation were that Emily was destroying everybody, including this perfectly wonderful person who was so qualified?" Rosanne was enraged. Since Emily was expected to be discharged in three months, she asked that the hospital at least change her therapist for the remainder of the time. Rosanne wanted Emily to have a transition period with a different doctor who she hoped would be more effective and whom Emily would probably see as an outpatient after discharge. Dr. Hampster replied no.

Rosanne remembers driving back home after that meeting. She was so agitated that she had trouble "trying to keep the car from going off the road. And I tried to hold myself together while talking to him." Now it was all rushing in on her. She reworked the conversation she had just had when Dr. Hampster told her not to blame herself. It wasn't her fault that Emily had not gotten better or that she was such a destructive individual. His refusal to change therapists even at this late stage, his efforts to reassure her, and the ultimate reality that Emily Flynn's year had moved her no farther along kept ricocheting through Rosanne's thoughts as she wound her way home. That he "was sympathetic to me, when he hadn't been to Emily the day before" mattered less to Rosanne than her daughter's deteriorated condition.

Rosanne thinks Dr. Hampster was particularly aware of her pain. "He told me that in some instances it is the children who affect their parents. It is not always the parents who damage their children, he said." But this was beside the point as far as Rosanne was concerned. She remembered saying to him, "Okay, Dr. Hampster, maybe that's true, but what about the therapy?" Wasn't that supposed to have helped Emily?

Rosanne found Dr. Hampster's sympathy of little value in the objective situation. Emily had been hospitalized for fifteen months. She was no more functional than when she entered the hospital, and perhaps less so since she had spent so much of her time outside society. In three months, when the insurance ran out, Emily would be discharged. Rosanne could not afford the treatment out of her own pocket, and her life was increasingly problem-ridden. The divorce was under way, her own work was suffering from inattention, and her time was being eaten away by the weekly family therapy sessions and the additional weekly visits with Emily. Exhaustion and frustration engulfed her as she realized that the hospital treatment had been futile. Rosanne's recommendation that they change therapists had been unsuccessful. When she had made the suggestion that the therapist needed changing, "the staff answered that I was an interfering mother. They said that was the reason the therapy wasn't working—because I wasn't supporting it. So I kept my mouth shut. But it still wasn't working."

The insinuation that Emily's treatment was faltering because Rosanne was an "interfering mother" resounds with an insensitivity which many relatives find painful. When Rosanne raised criticisms of Emily's progress, the staff members did not give her an evaluation of the kind of therapy her daughter was receiving or of the hospital's procedures, or even an explanation of why they thought Emily's condition was improving. Instead, they used Rosanne's statement as evidence of her own culpability for Emily's problem. A parallel situation exists for mental patients, as Kenneth Donaldson points out in *Insanity Inside Out.* When complaints of or challenges to the institution are lodged, it is seen as confirmation that the reason someone is not progressing is that he is "resistant" to the therapeutic efforts. When Donaldson refused to take medicine because he said he was not sick, his doctors responded that he was so sick he didn't even realize it. A dilemma is in the making when patients proclaim their health and families challenge professionals. Many people do refuse to take medicine that will help them; some families may undercut the therapies their relatives receive. But without explaining or exploring the merits of a particular situation, assuming that it is the patient or family who is "at fault" creates an unnecessary adversary relationship. Families may err, but so do hospitals!

As Rosanne said, her daughter did not improve when she stopped raising criticisms. But there were additional problems Rosanne had to address, such as arrangements for care after leaving the hospital. Having run into a stone wall when she tried to discuss therapy, Rosanne turned her attention to the issue of discharge planning. And since she was in a therapy group with other parents, she used that as a place to raise the question and see how other parents and the staff viewed the problem.

"I know that you can't just leave a hospital without something to go to," Rosanne began. "And you don't just work out an exit procedure quickly. So I started raising this question." At the time of Emily's discharge Rosanne would have been the primary parent for her daughter. Gerald had moved away from the area long before and left Rosanne with the responsibility. Specific issues had to be resolved: where Emily was to live; how much her mother should contribute to support her; what parental duties would be expected of Rosanne; how Emily's continued reliance on her mother could be reduced in order for each of them to live autonomous lives.

After a few discussions in the family therapy sessions it was clear to Rosanne that this hospital followed no discharge procedures routinely, and that it would do nothing to alleviate the family's task of finding aftercare. As an administrator in her own department and laboratory Rosanne knew that arranging for Emily's aftercare would be a major burden. Added to her weekly schedule of visits to the hospital, the evening therapy session, occasional consultations with the doctors, her own work in the laboratory, such a responsibility would eat away even the few hours remaining during the week when she barely managed necessities such as laundry or shopping.

In the course of speaking with social workers whom she expected to advise her about aftercare, Rosanne found consolation in the family therapy group. Objectively they all had similar problems—teenage children. And they all had similar questions about their respective children's treatment, care, and future health. Furthermore, they all wanted to know how they could help their kids become independent, and each asked what toll it would take on them in the future. The difference, as far as Rosanne could tell, was that she was a single mother and the others were couples. Rosanne asked herself how much of the difficulty was introduced by the instability of her family and by the separations involved in her marriage. One couple whose daughter was on the same ward as Emily helped lessen for Rosanne some of her own doubts about her role as a single parent and her self-abuse as an inadequate one. She remembered that they seemed "so nice and so ordinary. Now for all I know, there were a lot of skeletons in their closet"—she paused—"but it seemed to me that they had been married forever, there had been no tragedies, and no chaos in their home life." The ordinary appearance of this couple served as a reminder that mentally ill children need not be the consequences of extraordinary family crises. The external circumstances allowed her to measure the criteria she had used to judge herself. With some sarcasm Rosanne added, "Mommy hadn't been divorced; nobody had died —all of these superficial things that lead to instability."

Being with other parents who "could talk about their fears and about the hospital" offered some comfort. Each of them had endured some disappointment. And their children were placing them in a stressful situation. They spoke about their feelings and about their kids, "and many of them had angry feelings," Rosanne recalled. "There was a lot of anger. There was a lack of communication between the hospital and the parents," which constituted one experience the group could share. But "because they had different children, they had different complaints." For some it was the quality of care; for others it was the slowness of results; for a few it was the expense, which was measured in money as well as energy. Soon added to all their complaints was the issue of aftercare, which Rosanne helped them appreciate.

Because there were no programmatic arrangements conducted under the hospital's supervision, Rosanne had to work alone trying to guarantee Emily's future. "I had to make some plans. The social worker hadn't made any. I asked the social worker about the future. She agreed that it was reasonable that I be concerned." At that point the total effort the hospital made toward Emily's reintegration had been a program in jewelry making. For Rosanne that was not enough. She was perturbed and thought the hospital should help Emily develop skills which would enable her to function in the outside world. After several private conversations with the social worker it was agreed that Emily would attend typing school.

Enrolling Emily in typing school mildly placated Rosanne's growing ire. She was angry at the paucity of choices but was reassured that in conjunction with the therapist who would see Emily as an outpatient, her daughter would have guidance as she tried to acquire a new skill. It is common for therapists to continue seeing patients with whom they have worked in the hospital on an outpatient basis after they are discharged. In some instances, especially a hospitalization shorter than Emily's, this outpatient treatment may occur in conjunction with a day hospital program to which a person goes while sleeping at home. In other cases the outpatient therapy is the only connection patients maintain with the hospital; in still other cases outpatient care is handled on a private basis with a clinician affiliated with a particular institution. But in all cases continued therapy is designed to ease the transition between the hospital discharge and the return to society. And it is essential to continue the therapy which hospitalization just begins.

With the time of Emily's discharge drawing near, it was apparent to her mother that leaving the hospital would be difficult for each of them. Actually Emily's treatment at Circlesville Psychiatric Institute came to a halt the month before her expected departure; she began burning herself with cigarettes and cutting herself with broken glass. Emily was put on twenty-four-hour observation. It is unclear whether she was punishing herself, or confirming Dr. Hampster's evaluation, or just telling them all how fearful she was to be going home. At different times Rosanne thinks it was all these things. Whatever the purpose for the behavior, it was terrifying. When Emily was placed on round-the-clock observation, Rosanne went to confer with the psychiatrist.

The psychiatrist who had been treating Emily, and who Rosanne assumed would continue to be her doctor after she was discharged, was also alarmed over the self-destructive actions. He viewed Emily's outbursts with disappointment and scorn. In fact, he had such a strong reaction that he informed Rosanne he "could not continue to work with Emily outside the hospital. He could not trust her. This was one week before Emily was to leave!" Rosanne shouted.

Rosanne was furious. She was angry at the hospital, the

therapist, and the treatment, which she considered a failure. The ultimate responsibility was thrust back on her with almost no notice. "As far as they were concerned," she said of Circlesville Psychiatric Institute, where Emily had stayed for eighteen months, "she left the hospital with no therapist! I think it's an outrage," she continued, "in that kind of system. Even if you believe in long-term therapy, you have to have a support system. And the cost . . . three hundred dollars a day. And when you are out, that's it, you're out."

Rosanne considers Circlesville Psychiatric Institute negligent and irresponsible. She has become extremely skeptical of the mental health care system, starting with psychiatrists and psychologists who refused to speak with her, continuing with the failure to be advised in the early stages of Emily's problems how serious the matter really was, and culminating in Circlesville's neglect of continuing therapy and identifying programs that would help. Despite her profound disappointment with the system which discharged her daughter at least as ill and maybe more so than when she entered the hospital, Rosanne Flynn feels that personally she was well treated. As an individual she believes she received respect and consideration. Perhaps it was her professional accomplishment or maybe her advanced degree, which carries a title, but for whatever reason Rosanne knows that she was regarded with respect. This, however, is not sufficient to quiet her protest about the nature of the institution and the organization of mental health care. As far as she is concerned, the chaotic system, which is riddled with contrasting and conflicting theories about mental illness, failed her and her daughter. Rosanne presented her observations this way: "Psychotherapy is like a political ideology. If you believe in psychoanalysis, you don't believe in drugs. That you place confidence in one means you have to exclude the other." In addition, Rosanne is critical of the posture she saw psychotherapists adopt. "It's not that they are malevolent," she said. "They just don't know what to do. They make up a solution which is not a solution. They want to believe it. And there they are . . . maybe they have some successes. It all may be true, but I think the answer is that we just don't know. We simply do not. I am enraged because if they had been able to say to me, 'Look, we really don't know. We are really not sure what would help your daughter . . . but we are willing to try different things,' that would have been better. It would have made me feel better, and they wouldn't have had to be so arrogant."

At one point prior to Emily's discharge Rosanne had a conversation with the ward's chief psychiatrist which symbolizes for her the problematic elements of psychiatric care. Complaining about the lack of progress to this psychiatrist, whom she basically liked and with whom she had a good relationship, Rosanne acknowledged how worried she was. He listened patiently. Then he said to her, "Dr. Flynn, you are a scientist. You want proof." Surprised that a doctor who had a scientific background could actually say this, she shot back: "Doctor! You don't want proof? You don't want to know that what you did was effective?"

When Emily left Circlesville Psychiatric Institute after eighteen months, Rosanne had still not found a suitable program that would bridge the isolation of a hospital and the demands of society. She continued to look—this time in the community.

5

Residential Treatment Centers

Whether the mentally ill person is hospitalized for the national average of less than three weeks or is discharged from a long-term psychiatric center, the problem of where he or she will live after discharge is among the most important questions a family will face. To wrestle with the issue of finding suitable housing after a hospital discharge is a blessed relief to some people. At least they know that their relative is out of the hospital; they are hopeful that a corner has been turned. For others, like Jeanne Adamson, the problem of where her mother will live is just part of the ongoing cycle of coping with mental illness. Jeanne and her sisters have faced this situation before and think they will probably be there again in the future.

After having surveyed the range of choices available for her daughter, Rosanne Flynn was disappointed by the small number of programs that existed. Even though the hospital did not guide her in the weeks before Emily's discharge, Rosanne was looking for a residential therapeutic community for her daughter. Rosanne wanted a treatment program that emphasized personal resources for coping. She also wanted something that would allow Emily to move toward independence and self-sufficiency. Rosanne could not imagine how either of them would survive otherwise.

One example of a therapeutic residential program that Rosanne would have approved for Emily is the Fairweather Lodge.[1] This evolved out of George Fairweather's experience in a Veterans Administration hospital in the 1940s and 1950s, when he was a staff psychologist. Fairweather and his colleagues noticed that the patients who were discharged after more than one year of treatment were readmitted at a high rate. The staff became convinced that part of the difficulty these men faced was simply establishing a community outside the hospital which offered enough support to sustain meaningful living. To see whether it was possible to help veterans stay outside the hospital, Fairweather and his colleagues decided to start while they were still patients. The staff formed patients into groups which worked together, received wages, and had to solve problems collectively. The patients learned to identify responsibilities, work as a team, and become more dependent on each other than on the staff. A natural leadership emerged from the patient groups, and relationships developed as they would in other situations where several people have to become mutually reliant while pursuing a task.

Upon discharge the patients who formed a group within the hospital were moved to a home where, together, they continued the same types of responsibilities they had demonstrated they could already handle. The men were set up in a home type of "lodge," and a coordinator *assisted* the residents in acquiring satisfactory living conditions, employment, and connections to appropriate programs. But the coordinator did not supervise the lodgers. They continued to build on the cohesion, the increased morale, and the independence they had begun to acquire in the hospital. Four years later, when Fairweather studied these men's progress, it appeared that they had achieved greater success than those who were not placed in such groups. One reason may be that one of the barriers to a supportive social system outside the hospital had been eliminated by moving into a lodge together.

The model that Fairweather and his colleagues developed has been adapted to other hospitals. In 1967 they approached 255 psychiatric hospitals to see how many would be interested in establishing the lodge, first within the hospital and then outside, as had been proved successful in the VA experiment. Twenty-five hospitals did, and another nine have joined since. While each of the lodges operates independently, they share the principle of helping the patients form a cohesive community that can be continued when they leave the hospital. In providing a ready-made community the lodge not only offers mutual support but is a buffer between hospitalized dependency and potentially isolating self-sufficiency.

Hospitals that have used the Fairweather lodge system to assist patients after discharge have found it successful. Sometimes arrangements have been made to have the entire residential group employed by one business or industry. In one VA hospital, which has been in the program since 1964, about 550 patients have been moved into the community. Most of them have moved into their own homes, have married, or are living elsewhere. About 100 remain in the same lodge they have lived in since discharge from the hospital. But whether they are living in the lodge or elsewhere, they have been able to sustain a productive working life in the community and not in a hospital.

There exist other examples of programs which help former patients acquire the skills and confidence to live fruitful lives outside a hospital. Many of them are designed as transitional programs, for short periods of time. Others have no limitations on the length of time a person may participate. They vary tremendously. Berkeley House, for example, is a transitional halfway house in which as many as 23 residents can live at any one time. Located in downtown Boston, and affiliated with McLean Hospital in Belmont, Massachusetts, it is staffed with mental health professionals. In its first seven years of operation this psychiatric halfway house served a total of 182 people. It works primarily with young people, like Emily, who have been discharged from a hospital after several months of treatment.

One of the important requirements for living at Berkeley House is that residents participate in some activity off the premises. This activity, which requires people to function in the outside world, is a component of the program's overall objective to help residents develop networks of friends and learn to relate. The staff which runs Berkeley House assumes that people who have had psychotic breaks have a smaller group of friends on whom to rely than do others. Thus, Berkeley House deliberately encourages the formation of networks of association, and it wants one of these clusters of friendships to arise in activities outside the house to supplement the pool of associations formed within.

As with the Fairweather lodges, the emphasis on developing groups of friends who become interdependent rests on a belief that people can negotiate the complexities of life when they have others on whom they can rely for different things. Thus, from one's early days as a resident at Berkeley House activities are directed toward this end. For example, because the home is transitional, residents know that they will need roommates when they leave. With the help and guidance of house managers, residents are encouraged to make friends who might become their roommates when they move away to live independently in their own apartments. Groups of three or four people seem to arise naturally, based on different affinities and interests, and Berkeley House uses these natural clusters to show residents how to solidify the connections which will be important to their independence when they leave. When residents leave to move into their own apartments, parties are given in the new apartments to confirm ritualistically the importance of such an event. The parties also teach the continuing residents how to visit the friends who now live elsewhere, and they validate the act of moving out.

Because ex-residents are considered a permanent part of the community, even when they live in their own apartments, provisions are made for them to drop in casually and to stay for dinner or even for a few nights if they are in a crisis. This policy rests on the philosophy that given the tenuous social relationships of most recently hospitalized patients, the ones made at Berkeley House should offer a model for lifetime acquaintances. Keeping the doors always open allows ex-residents to show current ones that relationships can be sustained even when a person physically moves away.

Berkeley House considers itself successful in helping former patients return to the community. Ninety percent of the seventy-eight residents of the first three years were living independently in the community; close to 60 percent of them continued to remain in contact with other ex-residents; 74 percent were at work or at school. Director Richard D. Budson and Robert E. Jolley wrote: "A direct correlation appeared to exist between the establishment of a psychosocial network and successful community tenure."[2]

Another example of a therapeutic community is Soteria House, in San Francisco, which has been in existence since 1973. Having started this home to meet the social needs of discharged patients, founders Loren R. Mosher, M.D., and Alma S. Menn, A.C.S.W., view Soteria House as a form of surrogate family. It is exclusively for young adults who have not had extensive hospitalization and who are "more likely to be confronting the issues of independence-dependence, separation from family, choosing of a proper vocational and educational career, and choosing a mate."[3]

Like some of the therapeutic communities which are experimenting with rehabilitative housing, Soteria House has a self-consciously non-medical orientation for the six patients who live there at any time. Few structured activities are planned. Rather, a staff of two is available to help them individually on a twenty-four-hour basis, and patients are encouraged to plan and define activities for themselves. Despite the emphasis on having people initiate activities that have not been already programmed, those who live at Soteria House share the domestic chores; cooking, cleaning, and other activities of self-maintenance are part of the rehabilitation program.

The founders of Soteria House feel they have fulfilled one of their goals—helping young people who have had one psychotic break negotiate independence from their parents. They report that 60 percent of the people who have lived in the house were living independently two years after discharge from a hospital, compared to another group with an almost equal number who had not been tutored in Soteria House. Among the other group only 30 percent were living independently two years later.[4]

That Rosanne was shopping for something like the Fairweather Lodge, Soteria House, or Berkeley House reflects one of the current assumptions about treatment for mental illness. The policy of short hospital stays and the emptying of state mental facilities is based on the belief that mental hospitals do not cure. Hospitals can arrest a psychotic episode with drugs; they can supply the staff to keep a watchful eye over a person in crisis. But current theories hold that rehabilitation and readjustment are more likely to occur when someone is actually living in society rather than being prepared to enter it.

Policy planners of the 1960s expected various types of non-hospital housing to shelter the mentally ill who were well enough to live outside medical institutions. Initially these homes were planned to house about a dozen people under the supervision of an elderly couple in a domestic atmosphere. By providing a small, familial, and open setting that was integrated into the community, they were intended to replace the hostile environments found on the huge closed wards of permanent mental institutions that isolated people from society.[5] And they seem to help people adjust to community living. Residents of these homes have a better chance of staying out of hospitals than people who are not cushioned upon their discharge.[6]

The change in policy that resulted in state and national endorsement of halfway houses was made possible by the revolution in chemotherapy after 1962. When the new tranquilizers became part of the arsenal for combatting mental illness, it was possible to think of treating the same people as outpatients, living in the community, who would have been confined in mental hospitals just a few years before. The number of people living in hospitals declined from a peak of 559,000 in 1955 to 193,000 by 1975, despite an increase in admissions each year. This paradox—more people admitted to hospitals, yet fewer living in them—is explained by the prompt discharge of individuals as soon as they have been "stabilized" through drugs in a relatively short time. Thus, in the same twenty-year period the annual number of admissions has grown from 178,000 to 390,000.

The approximate one-third of the mentally disabled who are not living with their families go directly to facilities which have become stations of refuge for the chronically mentally disabled. These are halfway houses, boarding homes, board-and-care facilities, and sheltered residences. They vary in quality and substance. Though the non-hospital halfway house was initially intended as a transitional residence for those on their way back into the community, it has become a semi-permanent facility as a result of the large numbers of people leaving mental institutions.[7] The semi-permanence of the population has produced considerable problems as these homes have grown in size, sometimes with as many as 200 people living in converted hotels. The older couple providing a homelike atmosphere in their own home has given way to entrepreneurs who often manage impersonal facilities for profit. Many halfway houses provide no more than the basic necessities such as food and a bed. Some include laundry service. In those which simply have hotel-type services, residents have no programs for their daytime needs. These conditions have recently come under criticism. A survey of conditions in five states found that many housing programs were "overcrowded, substandard, and [had] dirty facilities without provision being made for needed services. The only service provided to many mentally ill persons released to the community was medication." Conditions such as filthy furniture, walls, and linens and violations of health codes specifying minimum numbers of toilets and showers per person, as well as people sleeping in anterooms or halls, are described also.[8]

In a report on conditions in boardinghouses in Essex County, New Jersey, investigators state that "boarding homes generally evidenced neglect. It was commonplace to find peeling paint, broken windows, weakened and missing banisters, threadworn carpets, broken floors, falling ceilings and plaster, decaying and unattractive furniture, small crowded and sparsely decorated communal areas, inadequate lighting and heat." Few of the boarding homes encouraged activity outside the house, such as a day hospital or other rehabilitation activity.[9]

The conditions in New Jersey were exposed publicly following a fire in a boarding home which took twenty-four lives in August 1980. While investigating the cause of the fire in that particular home, officials came across the non-therapeutic milieu which existed in many of them. According to a report in the *New York Times*, "patients' lives in the boarding homes often consist of little more than eating and sleeping. . . . Visits to several unlicensed boarding homes showed them to have threadbare furniture and few amenities, but they generally appeared clean."[10] On the basis of the investigation following the fire, a law was passed requiring the licensing and inspection of approximately 2,000 boarding homes. The new law holds the homes responsible for the quality of living conditions and for supervising residents more closely.

Critics have noted how profitable it is to run a boarding home for the disabled. The New Jersey investigation, for example, illustrates this. In Asbury Park there were as many as 200 unlicensed facilities compared to only 4 licensed homes. Asbury Park is a resort town on the Atlantic Ocean. Because the large residences go unoccupied during the winter months, proprietors lose money. But when discharged patients become year-round residents, the operators of these homes can more than triple their profits.[11] A similar inquiry in New York, and an audit by the State Attorney General's Office in 1979, revealed the substantial profit —reported to be more than $100,000 a year—by proprietors of some of the homes that are designed as residences for the mentally ill.[12]

Even if the conditions were universally excellent, there are simply not enough community residences to accommodate all the people who need them. Richard D. Budson has studied the problem and estimated that in 1974 an average of 1,500 people per state needed such facilities, adding up to a requirement of 5,000 residential places nationwide.[13] Yet there were only 289 programs in the United States, and in 1975 only 7,000 people were in treatment in halfway houses.[14] Perhaps some of the explanation for the absence of sufficient facilities can be seen in the way federal monies have been allocated. Of the $17 billion spent nationwide on direct costs for the mentally disabled in 1977, slightly more than 19 percent was spent on the following combined programs: residential treatment centers, halfway houses, special programs for children, and outpatient clinics as well as community mental health centers. Though these programs are considered an essential aspect of the commitment to provide alternatives to hospitalization and develop facilities for transitional care, their combined budgets are considerably less than that allocated for large hospitals (23 percent) or nursing homes (29 percent).[15]

. . . FOR ROSANNE FLYNN'S DAUGHTER

When she was looking for a residential program for Emily, Rosanne encountered a number of the inferior ones. She was looking for something like Soteria House or Berkeley House. But in 1978 only fifty to sixty existed nationwide.[16] Locating a therapeutic community was Rosanne's last hope when Emily was discharged from Circlesville Psychiatric Institute. As a single parent she could not offer the companionship or the recreation her twenty-year-old daughter needed. Coming home from a demanding job and needing privacy and a social life to restore her, Rosanne knew that her own inability to meet Emily's needs would generate conflict for both of them at a time when each needed to be free of entanglements and tensions with the other.

The months before Emily was to leave the institute Rosanne was frenziedly looking for facilities which would pick up where the hospital left off. The week before discharge, when the psychiatrist said he could not work with Emily because he could not trust her, Rosanne felt she had to find a place which also had therapists on the staff. Using the same published guides to community residences, halfway houses, and therapeutic communities which are available to social workers, Rosanne looked. She found nothing through these guides, but on the recommendation of a friend, by word of mouth, she located a therapeutic community. For Rosanne this was the first sign of hope in a week punctuated by frantic phone calls, making up long lists of names and places, and appointments with different managers of various homes.

Upon her discharge from Circlesville, Emily went home for several days until the expected opening occurred. Then she went to the therapeutic community. "She stayed there for about two months," Rosanne explained. "The first month was all right. Then she began to deteriorate." Emily became depressed. She went to bed. She stayed by herself and did not engage with others. She did not participate in the activities that were arranged for all. And she started eating binges again—the same pattern that had characterized her behavior prior to her earlier declines.

Rosanne recognized these signs and was alarmed. She wanted to discuss the pattern with the psychiatrist in charge. Also, because Emily was asking for an anti-depressant, Rosanne wanted to raise that question with the doctor. This particular residential community, however, was committed to rehabilitation without drugs. The psychiatrist therefore refused to give Emily an anti-depressant; he argued that therapy needed to take place without the use of artificial or chemical inducements. "I thought the psychiatrist was wrong," Rosanne said, recalling how many times Emily had been through this phase of the cycle. "But he didn't believe in drugs at all. He just wouldn't give her any. Then, in the second month, there was a series of disasters around Emily. They said she would have to leave."

Unlike Soteria House, this residential community was not

committed to helping Emily become separated from Rosanne. Its program had ill-defined objectives, the only unifying element being that all the residents had some form of mental illness. The house provided shelter; it was willing to keep Emily in its program as long as she conformed to its rules. When she became too demanding, it informed Rosanne that she would have to leave.

"I was simply terrified," Rosanne said. "But I decided that it was just as well. I couldn't afford a hundred dollars a day out of my pocket. And she wasn't getting any better." Just as when Emily had been discharged from Circlesville Psychiatric Institute, when she left the therapeutic community she became the exclusive responsibility of her mother. It was a situation that had a fearful familiarity. After each of the four hospitalizations Emily was discharged to her mother. All the while she was in private therapy she was also Rosanne's exclusive charge. Now, once again, as the parent of a young woman with mental illness, Rosanne was the only person available. And she had run out of ideas on how to get Emily help. She had exhausted every possibility she knew, nobody was recommending anything she had not tried already, and she was stumped.

Rosanne has no idea how to help her daughter, who is now living with her. It is not a question of how much she loves her daughter or how many sacrifices she will make. At this point to Rosanne it has become a question of survival. She said, "My God, I work full-time. I live alone. How is she going to manage that? How am I going to manage it? If I don't work, who is going to pay the bills?" While Rosanne is at her office during the day, Emily goes shopping. Rosanne has "had to cancel charge accounts at the department stores. The bills aren't wild. She's not spending five thousand dollars. But I cannot afford what she is spending. And it frightens me! Right now I have to pay a bill at the drugstore for about a hundred twenty-five dollars in cosmetics. That charge will have to be canceled. I know that I'll get home tonight and I'll be exhausted. And she'll be a wreck. And she'll need me. But I can't be a hospital. I don't know what to do. I don't know who to turn to."

Rosanne would have liked to find a place like Berkeley House or Soteria House for Emily. She couldn't. Too few of them exist. Whatever their successes, they have helped small numbers compared to the need. In five years Soteria House has had 50 clients. Berkeley House worked with 182 people the first seven years it was operating. While they have reason to be enthusiastic about their achievements, there are only a handful of such programs around the country, and Emily could not get into one of them.

. . . FOR EVELYN VANN'S HUSBAND

The families of the mentally ill are not equipped to meet the varied and urgent requirements of their relatives who have just been discharged from hospitals. Rosanne Flynn knew this in principle before Emily was returned to live with her again. Evelyn Vann knew it from her previous experience coping with her husband, Tom.

At the time we spoke, Evelyn Vann's husband had just been discharged from another hospital. As she had done in the past, she was again looking for a personal care home where Tom might live. In the preceding years Evelyn had become adept at coping with the cycle of having Tom hospitalized, being called to pick him up, supporting him in his efforts to manage in a day hospital program or a vocational rehabilitation program, and recognizing the signs of his deterioration after he stopped attending his program and left his psychiatrists. In the previous two years she had been through civil commitment proceedings twice. Tom, who has diabetes, refused to eat or take his insulin shots. He was a clear threat to himself. And Evelyn has become knowledgeable about when Tom is well enough for release. She has resisted efforts to have him discharged after two weeks when doctors had "stabilized" him. This time, after eight months of treatment, it appeared that he was ready to leave the hospital. But where he would go was not clear. His family did not want him home this time.

Tom's hostile and belligerent behavior during the past ten years had taken its toll on his wife and three children. "There had been too many fights and too much yelling," Evelyn said. "The children felt estranged from him during the last hospitalization. They were not in a mood for a reconciliation." The teenagers and their mother harbored enormous hostility toward Tom, whose illness held the entire family hostage for a decade. Evelyn described some of the episodes that occurred when Tom was unable to control his bladder. Angry and destructive, he would urinate all over the apartment. "He didn't care where it was," she said. Tom was also prone to angry outbursts when he thought Evelyn was poisoning his food. "Every time I would buy something he would go out and buy his own food. He would take the car out late at night and drive all over creation. There was no income." Tom had not been employed for several years, and his disability stipend was meager support for a family of five. But he "would go out buying bread because he was afraid that I was poisoning his food," and he hid it all over their apartment.

The children felt that his presence provoked more pain and unhappiness than his absence. Tom couldn't tolerate the noise when his teenage children played music. Phone calls to his daughter drove him mad. During eight months of this last hospitalization the children refused to visit their father. On the occasional weekend passes home Evelyn's younger daughter even stayed with neighbors in order not to be in the same house with him. The children still had fright-filled memories of the times he would talk and laugh to himself, and they wanted nothing to do with him. Nor had they overcome their anger for the years when his behavior included loud screaming and abusive language. His inability to do things on time, his gradual personality disintegration, and his ranting and raving after he had stopped attending the day hospital program the last time were more than they could imagine going through again. As far as they were concerned, Tom would have to resume life outside the hospital in a halfway house.

Supplied with a list of residential houses by a social worker, Evelyn Vann visited three different homes. The first was fairly nice, as she recalls, but there were "four old ladies there. He would have been the only man." Evelyn remembered being shown the room available for him. It was quiet and clean, and along with a private bath it would have cost $450 a month. "A lot of money," she said. When Evelyn agreed to do his laundry, the rate dropped almost $200. Despite the pleasant surroundings of this home, Evelyn decided that living with four elderly women would not be appropriate for a man in his late forties. She crossed this home off the list. The second house was even less satisfactory. "He would have shared this little room with two tiny beds, one dresser, and what must have been a one-half-inch closet. His roommate was an eighty-two-year-old man." She also ruled out the third home on the list. The only other person living there was a retired colonel. "None of the houses was acceptable to Tom," Evelyn said. "So we called a private religious agency, and it was able to suggest a place." It recommended a halfway house where he was accepted under the condition that he spend his days elsewhere. Between nine and five the managers expected Tom to be occupied in constructive activity. They never specified what kind, but Tom agreed. He told them that he had a job doing volunteer work in a non-profit agency. The house accepted his explanation. Tom moved in.

While looking for a home for Tom, Evelyn Vann avoided the large facilities that can house as many as 200 people. She did not want to see her husband, just out of a hospital, placed in another institution, which is how the large homes appeared to her. So she confined her search to the smaller board-and-care facilities that house only a few people at a time.

The halfway house in which Tom took up residence charged $380 a month. Evelyn was able to make the payments from her own income and the disability stipend Tom received when he was forced to quit his job. She never knew that as a disabled worker with a history of chronic mental illness Tom was eligible for assistance from the government to help pay the expenses of his lodging and board. None of the social workers had ever mentioned it, and when I asked her why she had never applied for the assistance, Evelyn expressed surprise that it even existed. "Before I went back to work," she said, "it was rough. But when he was hospitalized the first time, I knew I would have to do something. I went back to school to have my nursing degree certified, and then I went to work." And each of her children had been working after school in various jobs. So she never felt that Tom's expenses were greater than her ability to pay for them even when she had to stretch to do it.

The months that Tom remained in the halfway house he never began the volunteer job he described. Instead, he roamed around the local area. He became a fixture at the bus stops and on the park benches. He managed to return to the home in time for dinner, and he was punctual in meeting Evelyn for their occasional visits. But his days were idle, and at first nobody knew. Gradually

Tom began to miss appointments with his psychiatrist. At the boarding home his hours were more erratic. Then he began to wet his bed. He stopped eating. Finally, the halfway house said he would have to leave. The managers called Evelyn to pick him up.

Evelyn feels the same responsibility for her husband that Rosanne feels for her twenty-year-old daughter. That responsibility means that when an institution will no longer help, each of these women steps in to fill the void—sometimes without very much advance notice. As a Roman Catholic, Evelyn does not feel she has the option of divorce. She once seriously considered a legal separation after a psychiatrist recommended it as a way of forcing the social service agencies to take more responsibility. "If I were not his wife, they wouldn't call me the way they do," she explained. She even began separation proceedings. But she cannot bring herself to put a legal and religious end to the marriage which, for all intents and purposes, has ceased to exist. Because she is still married, however, whenever treatment ends or fails to help her husband, Evelyn is called on to step in. And she does.

Evelyn Vann's efforts to find a place for Tom parallel those of Rosanne Flynn. The difficulties they encountered and the failure of the respective institutions to help Emily Flynn and Tom Vann account for the frustration families experience looking for aftercare residences. Whatever frustration there was, Linda Bloomberg did not encounter it in the process of looking for a place. Rather, her acquaintance with a halfway house came after her brother, Mark, was already living there.

. . . FOR LINDA BLOOMBERG'S BROTHER

When Mark Bloomberg was discharged from a hospital in 1978, his social worker had taken great care to place him in a rehabilitation program. She arranged for Mark to live in a halfway house that was affiliated with an outpatient treatment program at the hospital from which he had just been discharged. By the time Linda was brought into the discussions the plans were well under way. "Mark didn't have the hospital call me right away, as he sometimes did. Instead, he waited several days before he told them that he had a sister," Linda said. It was not until after he had been stabilized and his social worker was actively working on his behalf that Linda knew her brother had been hospitalized and was ready for discharge once again.

"After that first conversation with the social worker I was quite encouraged," Linda remembered. "Unlike the other hospitals, it seemed that this one was not just discharging him without any place to go. And this social worker liked Mark very much—that was clear. She told me many times that she was touched by him." Linda was encouraged by the coordination between the halfway house and the day hospital program and their eventual goal of helping Mark find work. And she was enthusiastic about seeing Mark take an interest in something with an orientation toward the future.

The hospital from which Mark had been discharged was affiliated with a federally funded comprehensive community mental health center. Such a facility represents a part of the federal commitment to provide alternatives to hospitalization in 1,500 locales called catchment areas. Each of the catchment areas serves a population of between 75,000 and 200,000, and they were written into the 1963 Mental Retardation Facilities and Community Mental Health Care Centers Construction Act. In order to receive federal funds, a community mental health center must provide five essential services: inpatient, outpatient, emergency, partial hospitalization, and educational programs. In 1975 halfway houses, or other residential homes, were added to the requirements for eligibility in receiving federal funds for the community mental health center.

Upon his discharge from the hospital and his move into the halfway house, Mark was enthusiastic. "He kept telling me that it was his chance for a new start," Linda said. "He was excited because he wanted to begin living independently. He was also nervous because he had had so many failures in the past. We spoke about the program many times, and we went over all his fears. For me it got to be frustrating after a few conversations because he kept coming back to the same set of questions. He was anxious about whether he could manage. He was still quite unsure of himself, and he needed lots of reassurance."

When Mark first moved into the halfway house, he called his sister several times a day. "I think he wanted to just make sure I was still here. He also needed some things. While they gave him a small allowance against his checks from Supplemental Security Income, he didn't have very much when he went into the hospital. So I sent him money to get a few pairs of slacks and a pair of shoes and cigarettes—he chain-smokes," Linda said. "I also spoke to the social worker at the halfway house, who was very nice and explained to me what they had planned for Mark. They were going to have him attend the day hospital program for several weeks. Then they wanted to try him in a vocational rehabilitation program for a while. They would help him locate an entry-level job when he was ready. Their ultimate goal was to have him living independently. But that would take many months," Linda was warned. Still, she was encouraged.

Mark's first reaction to the halfway house was positive; within a few weeks it soured. His initial delight at sharing a room with another former patient from the same hospital turned into criticism of the roommate's personal habits and idiosyncrasies. Mark could not tolerate the sparsely furnished surroundings; he was annoyed by the loud tick of his roommate's alarm clock. The other residents also bothered him. "Mark always thought the others were crazy but he was not," Linda noted. "And growing up in the lap of luxury, he thought the house, the neighborhood, and the other patients were not his caliber." Even the way his meals were prepared became a source of irritation, Linda remembered. "I tried to keep him calm, and I guaranteed him that it was all temporary. Soon he would have the personal resources to live independently, but until he did, he needed to be there," she said.

Mark's social worker was available to Linda at many times during his short stay in the halfway house. As far as Linda is concerned, the major problem lay not with any of the social services but with Mark. He ran away and joined the army. "He just walked out one day and enlisted. I was shocked! I couldn't believe they would take him. But they did," even though he lasted only one week before he was admitted to an army hospital. "I think the frustrations got to be too much for him at the halfway house," Linda continued. "The initial enthusiasm of his 'new start' paled in a week or two. He was disappointed because when he went for a job interview, he thought he would become vice-president of a multinational, and they wanted him to work in the canteen. He couldn't take the humiliation," Linda now reasons.

Linda was furious with Mark for his apparent disregard of the efforts made on his behalf. And she was frightened of the mischief that might befall him. Before she was told that he had enlisted in the army, she was petrified about his safety. "At first I was convinced he would call. Then I kept scolding myself for not having called him the day he ran away. I must have thought about it a million times and told myself that if I had called, maybe I could have convinced him not to run away."

Linda did not hear from Mark for almost a year. By the time she did the call came from another psychiatrist, in a different hospital, at the other end of the country. Mark was being prepared for discharge to a temporary Jewish welfare agency, from which he would be placed in a halfway house. His social worker knew of a board-and-care facility in a community where Mark wanted to live. It was a large facility with almost 250 other discharged patients, and the managers had been in the business for a while. The social worker assured Linda, long distance, that Mark would not get lost in the shuffle because a psychologist, a psychiatrist, and a vocational rehabilitation counselor were affiliated with this facility.

"I didn't know what to think when this started again," Linda said. "Of course, I was delighted that someone was looking after him since he was three thousand miles away. But I was guarding any feelings I had of optimism or success. I wanted to wait and see this time around. I couldn't go through the disappointment again." Over the next few months Linda spoke to Mark each Sunday. He reported that he was taking Prolixin—a new drug for him—and the clouds that formed images and communicated only to him were less plaguing. Gradually Mark expressed an interest in working during the day. He complained that there was nothing to do at the board-and-care. And his Supplemental Security Income (SSI) had not started to come in yet. He had already spent all the money that was due him from his short stint in the army. So Linda sent him $5 at a time and arranged to have the managers of the facility give it to him. "They were giving him about a dollar-twenty-five-a-day allowance against the SSI check, which was forthcoming. But that amount of money didn't go for much. Maybe a package of cigarettes. It wasn't even enough for bus fare if he wanted to go someplace," Linda said.

Supplemental Security Income is a program which dates

from 1972, when Congress authorized the federal government to standardize assistance programs for the disabled. Formerly these programs operated at the discretion of the individual states. Becoming effective in 1974, and replacing the earlier components of welfare, SSI is currently administered by the states. The amount of money to which a disabled individual is entitled depends on his or her living circumstance. For example, a disabled person who lives with his or her family receives premiums of $79.47 per month. If he or she lives independently, outside a family or other designated category of group living, the federal allowance is $238.*

As of July 1, 1980, twenty-five states and the District of Columbia supplemented the federal stipend of $238 for people living independently. The state supplements range from $10 in Maine and Utah to $127 in Massachusetts. The other twenty-five states do not supplement the basic federal allowance. Thus, the entire package of aid amounts to slightly more than $50 a week for all expenses for those mentally disabled who live in states which do not contribute to maintenance. Eligibility for food stamps and Medicaid may be added at the discretion of the state. If the individual has been declared disabled for at least two years, he or she is then also eligible for Medicare.

The categories for payment differentiate between people living alone or with others. If they live with others, there are several groupings which apply and for which different amounts are allocated. For example, Mark was entitled to the extra stipend of $216 for living in a non-medical board-and-care. With the $238 plus $216, his SSI allowance amounted to $454 in 1980, of which the manager of the facility took close to $400. The remainder had to underwrite Mark's additional living expenses.

Mark was growing more despondent as he waited for the Supplemental Security Income to be processed. It didn't matter to him that emergency funds from the state's welfare office guaranteed his keep. He was increasingly fearful that his application would not be approved. Linda decided that she would have to get in touch with Mark's social worker to discuss this. Her own reas-

---

*All figures are based on rates effective July 1, 1980. The federal allocation is geared to the Consumer Price Index and keeps pace with the rate of inflation. Figures are reported in *Summary of State Payment Levels State Supplementation and Medicaid Decisions*, U.S. Department of Health and Human Services.

surances counted for little when Mark's agitation was growing.

"I called the number Mark gave me and said that I wanted to speak with this person. Since she was out of the office, I spoke to the supervisor, who told me that Mark's social worker had been changed and also was out of the office. I made a telephone appointment to have the new social worker call me back." When Mr. Olivetti returned Linda's call, he informed her that Mark had not yet been seen by the psychologist who spent one day a week at the facility. Nor had he had an appointment with the vocational rehabilitation counselor. He was receiving medicine from the psychiatrist, however. Linda was furious. "I had been told that Mark would be connected with these other people shortly." She began to understand why Mark was complaining of the emptiness of the days. "No wonder he was worried," she said. "He had nothing else to do but think about the disappointments in his life."

Linda urged the social worker to act quickly to guarantee that Mark would see the psychologist and the vocational rehabilitation counselor. They arranged another telephone appointment to discuss what materialized. In the meantime, Linda tried to reassure Mark that the wheels would start to roll. Have patience, she told him, knowing full well that if she were in the same situation, hers would have been exhausted long ago.

Telling Mark to have patience was like pulling the stem out of a grenade. He exploded. "How can I have patience?" he screamed into the phone. "There is nothing to do all day long. What do you think my life is like?" he demanded of his sister. "I sit here all day with all of these other crazy people who are sick. I don't get enough to eat in this place. There is nothing for me to do, and every time I say I want to work they tell me not until I see the counselor. When I ask to see the counselor, they tell me my social worker has to arrange for the appointment. I don't even have enough money for toothpaste. I have to get out of here." A long list of complaints followed, including poor teeth and dental needs not covered by the Medicaid allowance, shabby, threadbare clothes, shoes with holes in the heels and soles. Mark was at his wits' end and wondering aloud whether to leave and just go back to the hospital. "At least there I get enough to eat," he told his sister.

Mark presented a convincing argument about the difference in the quality of his life in a hospital compared to living in the board-and-care. He knew that the food was adequate and plentiful in a hospital and that the surroundings were clean. Daily activities gave him something to do. Living in the board-and-care facility, where he had no productive way to spend his time, was too discouraging. "When he said he wanted to return to a hospital because it was the only place where he wasn't worrying about himself, I felt rotten," said Linda.

Linda called the social worker again, reported the urgency of Mark's condition, and pleaded with him to move quickly before her brother disappeared once more. Though Mr. Olivetti expressed understanding, he could not guarantee how quickly he would act. His own caseload was large, and there were others with more pressing needs. "Besides," he told Linda, "there is nothing to worry about. Mark won't go anywhere without his Supplemental Security Income." Linda did not find this reassuring. "It was as if Mark were hostage to this check, which is not adequate to begin with," she said. "And to place Mark on a list of lesser needs because Mr. Olivetti thought he wouldn't 'escape' until it arrived was absurd," Linda concluded.

A few weeks later Mark had an appointment with the psychologist. He was concerned and compassionate and thought he could reach Mark. "Your brother has a lot of gifts," he told Linda in their first conversation. "He's had a rough time, and he is still not out of it—not by a long shot. But I think I can help him." And he did. Over the next two months Mark saw Dr. Sweet in the board-and-care facility. Then Dr. Sweet asked Mark to come to his office. Mark quickly exhausted the $250 maximum from Medicare for outpatient mental health care.* "I told Dr. Sweet that I would pay for Mark's treatment," Linda stated, "but he thought this might be good for Mark to do for himself. By then he had a part-time job earning about fifty dollars a week. If he earned more than sixty-five dollars a week, it would be deducted from his SSI. But he could earn a little and still not worry." Dr. Sweet thought that Mark needed to be responsible about his own treatment and was quick to remind Linda that he charged Mark only a nominal fee. Linda found it hard to disagree with the symbolic importance of Mark's paying $10 a session.

* Task Panel Reports Submitted to the President's Commission on Mental Health recommended increasing this to $750. See vol. 2, p. 503.

Linda spoke with Dr. Sweet every few weeks. "He was encouraging," she remembers. Dr. Sweet reported that Mark was increasing his ability to handle frustration, that he was getting along better with his friends at the board-and-care. He was also gaining some weight and beginning to show an interest in a social life. They liked him at his job, and Dr. Sweet even talked of encouraging Mark to move into a smaller home where the atmosphere was more healthy. "That's really a discouraging place for someone like your brother," he told Linda. "It's just a holding place. I want to see Mark in a situation where he is less susceptible to the bad influences who congregate around these facilities and prey on people like your brother," he concluded.

Everything seemed to be getting better. Then, piece by piece, Mark's new life began to unravel. First his application for SSI was denied. "Mark called to tell me this. He was frightened and hysterical. He didn't know what to do. Well, I didn't either. There was another volley of phone calls to his social worker to find out what the mixup was. Apparently it was a bureaucratic snag, and Mr. Olivetti assured me they would contest it. He said Mark was a good candidate for SSI." Linda tried once again to reassure Mark, telling him that it would turn out all right. But it was not easy. Nor was Mark convinced the second time his application was rejected. At that point, despite Mr. Olivetti's getting a lawyer to take the case to court for a third attempt, Mark felt little hope. Linda didn't know what to feel.

"This system is crazy," Linda said. "I couldn't believe that he would be denied. Dr. Sweet had to write a letter, his social worker went with him to testify, and another psychiatrist wrote too." Linda was so enraged about the entire matter that she showed me the decision rendered in Mark's case. A three-page letter, it noted that each of the people who had contact with Mark—his social worker, psychiatrist, and psychologist—stated that he suffered from schizophrenia. They concurred that he also seemed suicidal. Each noted his constant state of agitation and nervousness and recommended intensive psychotherapy. They agreed that he needed to live in a protective environment. The letter said that Mark was not likely to enter the regular employment market. Linda was shocked, therefore, to read the sentence which said, "In light of the claimant's age, and the fact that with intensive psychotherapy, the claimant's condition is likely to improve, it is recommended that the claimant be re-evaluated in approximately 12 months."

Six and a half months after having applied for his disability, Mark was finally granted the Supplemental Security Income he had been guaranteed would help ease his burdens. In another year, however, he would have to go through the entire process again, a process which requires negotiating a bureaucracy that even the healthy find fraught with frustration and confusion. "I just could not believe all of this happens," Linda said. "It is unreal. What little confidence and comfort he was beginning to find in living in the same place without interruption were undone by his constant need to convince the authorities that he is sick. He has little enough confidence in his ability to simply survive . . . this seemed so unnecessary."

As if it were not bad enough that Mark's confidence was broken by the matter of his SSI, a few months later he lost his job. The small company for which he was working, typing nameplates, went bankrupt. "Dr. Sweet tried to help Mark appreciate that it wasn't his fault. His work was good, and his supervisors thought well of him. But Mark thought it meant that he was not qualified," Linda said. Mark looked for other work, this time as a gardener. He went around the neighborhood, trying to find people who wanted their lawns watered and their gardens weeded. But he found only one job and got discouraged quickly. "Dr. Sweet continued to support Mark through all of this. He really had a liking for him."

One day Linda answered the phone; unexpectedly, it was Dr. Sweet. "My heart almost stopped beating. I knew he wouldn't call unless something bad happened," she said. Dr. Sweet told Linda that the non-medical board-and-care facility that Mark had been living in for the past seven months was closing. "They apparently wrote letters to everybody—about two hundred and fifty people —telling them that in six weeks they were closing their doors. Everybody had to leave and find another place to live. That was it. One day he was there; the next he was out," Linda sighed. Dr. Sweet's concern was mixed. On the one hand, he thought it might be better for Mark to live elsewhere. But there had not been enough time to arrange it, and with only a month to go he wasn't confident that they would find anything better. And Dr. Sweet was apprehensive about how Mark would respond to being returned to the street. Mark already had little confidence in the system's ability to help him, he told Linda.

When the board-and-care facility closed, each of the clients needed relocation. A new apartment was found for Mark, along with several other former residents, in another facility. This one was an apartment building where three people shared an apartment with a small kitchen. "When Mark told me about this move, I was worried," Linda said. Though Mark was pleased to be living elsewhere, his new apartment was an hour-and-a-half bus trip from Dr. Sweet's office. Linda was alarmed when Mark said that it was too inconvenient to continue with his therapy. Though she tried to persuade him that continuing treatment with Dr. Sweet might prove his only salvation, Mark was too dispirited. "He seemed to just give up at that point," Linda said. "He couldn't find a job, he hated the people who were his assigned roommates, and he gave every excuse in the world not to travel. In a short time he stopped taking his medicine. He got crazy again. Our conversations stopped focusing on the problems of the particular day. Instead, he wanted to tell me about messages from ancient spirits again."

Shortly after moving into the new apartment, Mark stopped calling his sister. When she called there, she was told that he was gone. Where he had gone was a mystery. Nobody was even sure when he left. Mark called five months later. He told Linda that he had just been discharged from another hospital, and he wanted his sister to send him money for a sleeping bag so he could sleep in the park. He said he was tired of living in halfway houses.

6

Non-Residential
Treatment Programs

The nationwide reorganization of mental health care in the 1960s and 1970s that spawned halfway houses and therapeutic communities also called into existence a variety of non-residential programs. They suffer from the same financial difficulties. With more monies going to maintain state and county hospitals or funneled into nursing homes which care for the mentally ill over the age of sixty-five, less than 5 percent of the funds allocated for mental health care was channeled into these programs in 1975.[1] Consequently, a similar gap exists between the promise and the reality, and this affects the actual choices available to patients and their families.

The backbone of the non-residential treatment programs is found in the Community Mental Health Care Centers Act, passed in 1963 and amended several times since. This piece of legislation outlined the new emphasis for treating mental illness by proposing 1,500 community mental health centers within each of the nation's geographic catchment areas.* And it specified what services must be provided by each of the centers in order to qualify for federal assistance. Among the several services which a community mental health center must provide are outpatient programs and "partial hospitalization," which often means day hospital facilities.

These two services, along with several rehabilitation treatment centers around the country, constitute the major non-residential treatment programs which the families of the mentally ill might encounter. Sometimes families discover these services as an initial substitute for hospitalizing their relative; other times they find them while looking for a transition between a discharge from a hospital and a return to school, work, and full activity in the community. Though the programs differ in the amount of time a patient spends in them and in the particular services they provide, they all are rooted in the belief that rehabilitation can take place more successfully outside the hospital than within it.

DAY HOSPITAL PROGRAMS

Day hospitals are what the name implies: they are therapeutic programs that patients attend during the daytime. Generally participants sleep elsewhere, most often with their families, but sometimes they come from halfway houses. Patients who participate in day hospitals as a transition sometimes begin attending while they still sleep on the regular wards of the inpatient hospital. Run by a professional staff, day hospital treatment programs may include group therapy, prevocational therapy, and various kinds of recreational as well as individual therapy. Depending on the particular program, patients may be required to attend five full days a week or only a few hours a week. But whatever options programs include, and however often attendance is required, the purpose is to bridge the distance between the isolation imposed by the illness and participation in the community.

---

* *Task Panel Reports Submitted to the President's Commission on Mental Health* noted in 1978 that 590 community mental health centers were operating in whole or in part; another 85 were funded (vol. 2, pp. 314–19).

There is evidence that day hospital treatments might be just as successful as inpatient hospitalization. Though there are very few studies comparing these programs with others (such as inpatient or outpatient programs), one of them indicates that people who were treated in day hospitals managed to return to the community sooner and for longer periods of time than those who were treated as inpatients of psychiatric hospitals. "At every point in time," noted the authors of the study, "it was the inpatients who had a higher readmission rate" to the hospital.[2]

There is also some indication that for people with chronic mental illness—a pattern of many hospitalizations and questionable functioning between them—the day hospital programs are beneficial.[3] Compared to the outpatient program, which requires the patient, and sometimes the entire family, to attend one or more sessions a week with an individual therapist, the day hospital offers greater companionship and structure for the person whose sickness has become chronic. But this is not the only group served by day hospitals. Those who have never been hospitalized are also eligible for the program.

Whether or not one can select a day hospital program depends on availability. Not all hospitals have them. Even if they do, selection may be limited to certain age groups. Grace and Jim Anthony tried to locate a day hospital program for Roger before they had him admitted to Alpha General Hospital, but the only programs that existed in their community did not accept people under sixteen years old. Therefore, the Anthonys were forced to have Roger admitted as an inpatient.

Also, one might not be able to use a day hospital program because of a different kind of problem. Can the family arrange to have the patient attend a program that has specific opening and closing times? If its hours are similar to those of the working day, it may be impossible to arrange to transport a husband or wife. Or the person may not be able to take public transportation because of his or her condition. Or mass transit may not be available in the particular community. So the problem of hours and logistics may prohibit people from selecting this option as a substitute for hospitalization or as a transition.

Even if the person is neither too young nor too old, and even if transportation can be arranged, the day hospital program still must have an opening. And if this obstacle is met, the patient must be willing to participate. Someone who has had one psychotic episode and a hospitalization of only a few months, or who is stabilized on drugs and functions well when taking them, or who has never been hospitalized may think that he or she does not need such a program. Often such patients do not want to be associated with people who appear less able than they are at the moment.

However encouraging the statistics may be about the day hospital program, not all individuals find it a successful experience. Nancy Pollack's daughter, Shelly, is one of them. Shelly has tried everything within the system of mental health care. She has been hospitalized in county facilities for up to a year and has had private treatment in the more prestigious hospitals. She has had private therapy, has been in family therapy with her recently divorced mother, and has had group therapy in different hospitals. The frequency of her hospitalizations—nine in one year—and her several suicide attempts tormented Nancy as she looked for help for her daughter. At times she sacrificed her own privacy and leisure when she was told that the best thing was for Shelly to return home to live with her. At other times she worried alone after she was advised to let Shelly live by herself. And when a day hospital was recommended to her, she followed that suggestion and made certain that Shelly was enrolled in the program that was attached to the hospital from which she was being discharged as an inpatient.

According to Nancy, however, this was no more successful than the other ventures. "It's like a hospital situation," she recounted. "But there's not that much to do all day." Before her series of hospitalizations Shelly had been interested in becoming a professional dancer, having taken years of lessons as a child. She had high expectations for herself, and she had the talent to match them. Even though her self-esteem dropped in the course of her mental illness, her expectations remained high and her ambition was not diminished. But the program did not convey a sufficiently high set of expectations for her, and Shelly was frustrated by the way time passed. She stopped going to the day hospital, and about the same time she stopped seeing the psychiatrist who was attached to it. Within a few months she took another overdose of pills and was admitted to another hospital.

Lorraine Howard, a psychiatric social worker who administers a day hospital program attached to a general hospital, has seen many people like Shelly. "They are bored, or they don't like the idea of attending, or they have difficulty sustaining any single activity," she said. "We used to take it very personally when somebody dropped out. We wanted to know what we were doing wrong. Why were they bored? What could we do to make them more interested?" She discussed these issues with her staff while they worked to improve the quality of the program. They realized that "it is part of the illness. These people cannot make a commitment to something. Or they have a poor attention span. It is not always us," she said.

The program Ms. Howard directs serves those people who have been discharged from her hospital as well as others in the catchment area who have not been hospitalized. When arrangements are made for participation in the program, Ms. Howard tries to remain flexible in meeting the needs of prospective participants. "When I first took over this position, I was convinced that the day hospital should not become a long-term treatment program . . . three months at the most, and then they would be ready to return to a normal schedule," she said. But her experience has taught her that some people need only six weeks of the program while others need six months. She could not specify concrete and rigid guidelines which fit the needs of all. Because of this, she no longer asks prospective clients to agree to come every day. She would prefer that they do because she thinks that the act of getting out of the house, dressing for a day away, and participating with other people is therapeutic. But she also knows that it is difficult for many to make a commitment if it seems too confining. So she no longer asks them to guarantee they will come every day of the week for several months. "I work with six days or eight days at a time. It is more reasonable," she said.

Those who do attend the day hospital program for an entire week will receive three hours of group therapy, one hour of individual therapy, and directed supervision in the recreational or educational aspects of the program. When they leave the program, it is hoped that they have regained some of the confidence, acquired some of the skills, and strengthened some of the mechanisms with which to cope more effectively. "Our favorite outcome is when people go back to school or resume jobs. If they already have school or a job waiting, when they leave the inpatient unit they will come to the day hospital program for a few weeks.

That's the ideal," she noted. But Ms. Howard also said that they do not always attain the ideal. Sometimes people do not have jobs to return to or even the skills to look for one. Then the day hospital will refer those individuals to the division of vocational rehabilitation. But Ms. Howard noted that "it takes forever to go through that process. It depends a lot on the counselor, and a lot of things could happen. But if it works well, the person is given a test to evaluate their strengths and aptitudes, and the counselor tries to figure out if there is a training program for them."

The least favored outcome, according to Ms. Howard, is for the person simply to drop out of the day hospital program. She knows he or she is not going to something, but withdrawing. And while a day hospital may not meet all the patient's needs, she feels that it is better for her or him to be engaged actively with others than to spend the day in idleness.

Day hospital programs do not guarantee that a person will not be hospitalized as an inpatient or will not relapse and develop former symptoms once again. But they do permit people to function in the real world at the same time that they are sheltered from some of the stress which is more than they can handle at the moment. And the programs permit patients to live at home with their families. When the patient is also a parent, this may blunt the shock for a family of having a mother or father hospitalized. But it produces other tensions as the rest of the family members become self-consciously and extremely aware that they are watching for signs of relapse, noting every deviation from the normal routine, fearful of returning symptoms over which they have no control. Some people begin to feel like spies, and others behave with oversolicitous concern as they try to ease burdens for their relative during evenings or weekends.

OUTPATIENT PROGRAMS

When families or patients cannot make use of the day hospital programs, they often rely on the outpatient services of the community mental health centers which many private and community hospitals also have. These programs require that an individual regularly see one of the therapists on the staff: a psychiatrist, a psychiatric social worker, or a clinical psychologist. Sometimes the entire family comes to sessions; at other times only the patient. Some programs require participation of each at separate times. Again, the purpose is to ease the transition between hospitalization and the resumption of regular activities.

One of the more innovative outpatient programs is the Family Therapy Program at the Western Psychiatric Institute and Clinic in Pittsburgh, Pennsylvania. What makes this program unique is the early attempt on the part of the staff to involve the family in each stage of treatment. This is done through a day-long seminar held at the hospital for the families of patients who have been recently discharged from the inpatient unit. Admission to the hospital makes one eligible for the program, which lasts two years and includes family and individual therapies.

The day-long workshop brings together all the new families who have not attended one of the previous sessions. Since the programs occur about every three or four months, it is possible that there will have been several new admissions. The purpose is to provide families with information that is vital to their ability to manage in the future, understanding not only their relatives but also how the illness affects them and forces them to readjust their lives and expectations. One family, for example, might wish to know how to support a spouse or a child who wants employment yet has not acquired the strength to cope with an interview or job. Letting the patient go into the job market too soon might precipitate another crisis, yet keeping her or him at home may promote self-doubt and reduce motivation. The Family Therapy Program helps sort out these knotty problems, and on a continuing basis so that the families' stresses and frustrations are kept under control.

The program begins with a workshop on a Saturday morning, starting around nine. When everybody is there, and after brief introductions have gone around the room, Gerard Hogarty, director of the Community Treatment Evaluation Program, begins. He starts by explaining how the family of schizophrenic disorders is understood by professionals. He discusses the symptoms from the patient's perspective as well as from that of the outsider looking on. Having identified the symptoms—thought disorders, withdrawal, delusions, hallucinations—as a way of realizing that something abnormal is occurring within the brain's processing center, he then describes how neurons and synapses work and explains theories about how new medications affect the brain's chemistry. Hogarty freely cites research and studies and gives statistics on the incidence of mental illness and rates of readmission, and explanations of how medicines can adversely affect someone.

The morning session is interrupted by a coffee break, and the entire group mingles. Participants who have been encouraged to raise questions during the introductory session may have follow-up inquiries. Other people think of new ones. Families casually engage one another in conversations about their respective relatives, and these discussions continue through the rest of the day when an appropriate topic is raised. An informal buffet lunch separates the morning from the afternoon session, when Carol Anderson, director of the Family Therapy Program, discusses family members' reactions to their relative's illness.

During the afternoon session the topic shifts. It moves from the technical aspects of the illness and focuses on the families' needs, reactions, and common problems. While Dr. Anderson was outlining some of the responses families commonly have, such as guilt or frustration, heads bobbed up and down in agreement and signs of recognition marked the faces of those in attendance. The discussion of how people need to guarantee time for themselves, and for their own needs, brought questions from the floor about the tension people feel when their needs conflict with those of their relatives.

While Dr. Anderson was elaborating on the need to set limits for oneself and one's relative, a parent asked about supervising her dauughter's finances. The mother was mindful of not wanting her daughter, a woman in her mid-twenties, to remain too dependent; she was equally aware that the young woman spent money foolishly. "My daughter is going to have to learn how to budget because we are not always going to be around," the mother said. "Given her current behavior, I am worried and do not know what to do." Another woman, whose husband was recently discharged, raised a question about how much time she felt she could be away from him. She worked during the day; he had not yet returned to work. She felt guilty about wanting to spend an evening with a girl friend, and she also resented her husband's wanting to go along. She recognized that he had few outlets for social life, but she feared her concern for him was becoming a trap for her. This woman received concrete guidance, for the moment, just as the mother had. Other participants joined in to share similar experiences and offer suggestions. Both questioners were guaranteed that issues such as these would be discussed more thoroughly with their individual social workers and throughout the two years of their participation in the program.

The day's workshop had a clear impact on one man. He arrived in the morning with a downturned mouth and an air of despair. He did not ask a single question and seemed only peripherally involved as concrete suggestions were made to others about how to negotiate with their relative. At the end of Carol Anderson's presentation he put his arm around his wife and gave her an encouraging hug. A few minutes later, when Dr. Anderson issued the last call for questions or comments, he volunteered his only comment of the day. "I was not looking forward to coming here at all," he began. He looked at the therapist with whom the family had worked and said she could verify it. "But I want to say how wrong I was. This has been the most helpful day I have had since my daughter got sick three years ago. When I was told about this, I thought it was just another hospital like the others. But I was wrong. I want to thank you," he said.

The founders of the Family Therapy Program believe they have succeeded in helping families. First, Hogarty and Anderson provide information which they believe families are entitled to have, but which might take months in the library if they were to search it out for themselves. The kind of information families are given when someone has a heart attack or is struck by another chronic illness, such as diabetes or multiple sclerosis, is what they think should be as available when the illness is mental. But conveying that information to each family on an individual basis would require the same amount of time that a workshop entails. The added advantage of the seminar is that it permits families the opportunity to share with each other in the process. This helps reduce isolation and establishes a support group, if only temporarily.

Another way in which the founders of the Family Therapy Program believe they have helped families is in preventing rehospitalizations. Hogarty mentioned, during the morning session, that as many as 40 percent of those diagnosed as schizophrenic are known to relapse within the first year after a hospital discharge.[4] Therefore, the program can be considered successful in lowering that rate when twenty-two of the twenty-three families involved in it have not had to return to admit their relatives to the hospital.

The Western Psychiatric Institute and Clinic is proud of the effort it makes on behalf of families through its outpatient Family Therapy Program. Most outpatient programs are neither as successful nor as ambitious. What distinguishes this program, and makes it unique, is the aggressive induction of the entire family in the early stages of the patient's treatment and the emphasis on helping everybody readjust expectations and negotiate circumstances which otherwise might become filled with stress and lead to crisis.

In most instances, when a patient is discharged from a hospital and enters treatment as an outpatient, the responsibility for continuing therapy is placed on the shoulders of the family or the patient. The Family Therapy Program, in contrast, aggressively seeks to help families after their relatives have been discharged. Moreover, while it recognizes that patients may show little initiative or even engage in overt provocation, it does not consider that a reason to let them go without helping them or their families.

BERENICE McCOY'S SON: SCOTT

For many of the chronically mentally disabled, outpatient treatment may mean little more than getting prescriptions renewed or having their tests monitored to see if the medicine needs to be changed. This often happens when a person resides in a halfway house or other board-and-care facility. But medicine only stops the overt symptoms. By itself it does not rehabilitate. When drug therapy is not part of a larger package which includes rehabilitation efforts in housing, social activities and recreation, or employment, it does not make a person more functional.

Berenice McCoy, a single mother in her fifties, has seen such treatment efforts extended to her son, Scott. Scott has been hospitalized three times, lived in halfway houses, had his own apartment, and received prescriptions from a psychiatrist at an outpatient program. None of the efforts have benefitted him very much. The hospitalizations served to stabilize him on medicines, and at each discharge there was no effective coordination with social agencies that could help with his rehabilitation. Soon Scott simply would not go to see the psychiatrist who administered the medicine. With the exception of the presence of his mother and an interest in music which he had had since he was a teenager, there were few continuous people or events to occupy his attention between hospitalizations.

After the last discharge from a hospital Scott continued to be medicated for a considerable while. And he wanted to work. In much the same way that Lorraine Howard would recommend the Office of Vocational Rehabilitation (OVR) to a person who had never held a job before a hospitalization, Scott tried this agency.

The Office of Vocational Rehabilitation is a critical link for reintegrating the former patient whose skills are not competitive with those of other job seekers. It is a federally financed program under the jurisdiction of the Rehabilitation Services Administration, currently under the Department of Health and Human Services, and administered by the states. OVR was legislated in 1973 and strengthened through the Rehabilitation Act Amendment of 1974. The act and its amendment were designed to assist disabled individuals, including the mentally ill, who are in need of help locating, preparing for, and acquiring jobs. People like Scott enter the job market at a disadvantage. Their work histories often contain short-term jobs with long stretches of unemployment in between. They may not have experience in a particular area, or they may not have references to submit with an application. So they rely on OVR and hope that something suitable will be found through this agency.

The difficulties Scott encounters searching for work are similar to those experienced by other discharged and chronically mentally disabled individuals. At the time Berenice and I spoke, Scott had taken the test from the Office of Vocational Rehabilitation twice. "That was a real mess," said his mother. Scott made an appointment at the local office. After the interview he took the test, which must be administered before a person can be given a job interview. After the test, OVR had Scott report to another office for subsequent appointments. When Scott got to the second office, he was told that the test wasn't there. He would have to take it again, at the new office. Scott told them that he had taken the exam once, and he didn't understand why it was necessary to take it a second time. Couldn't they just use the original exam? he asked them. To Scott that seemed like a reasonable request; to the Office of Vocational Rehabilitation it did not.

Without checking, the counselor at the second office made Scott return to the first office to speak with the social worker. When Scott got back to the first office, he was told that his social worker was sick and out for the day. "That's understandable," Berenice said. "But why did they make him go to the second office at all? What kind of procedure has people like Scott go running around town to unravel the bureaucracy? Somehow it doesn't seem fair."

Berenice became angry when Scott returned and told her of the two offices, the missing test, and the need to take it again. She called the local office and spoke to the counselor who had seen him. She also called that person's superior in the state office. "I gave it to him. I must have sounded like a hysterical mother," she noted. "But I let him have it. I asked why Scott had to have another exam. I told him that Scott was ready for work. I asked him where all the money went for people like Scott." The person with whom Berenice spoke agreed that it was an irritating situation. He promised to look into it but said that Scott had to take the test again in the second office. "I was told that it was part of the law. Scott had to take the test," Berenice recalled. "I told him that there were other parts of the law, too, such as they were supposed to help him get a placement. The Office of Vocational Rehabilitation was supposed to follow up. They were not doing that."

At the time Scott went to the Office of Vocational Rehabilitation for help, in the middle of the 1970s, according to *Returning the Mentally Disabled to the Community* the Rehabilitation Services Administration did not consider the needs of the mentally disabled a priority issue.[5] Berenice sensed this when she spoke with Scott's counselor. She asked Scott's employment counselor what assistance OVR could offer. "I asked her to level with me. What are his chances of finding work?" She wanted to know. Berenice was grateful that the counselor was honest. It saved her the disappointment that would have resulted from illusory hopes. But she was also disturbed at the reality underlying the response. "The counselor told me that his chances were not very good," Berenice recalled. This led her to ask, "What chances do these people have? When you are faced with not being able to work, and the state doesn't want to support you in a way where you can live decently, how could anybody want to live in these circumstances?" The counselor had no reply. "If they aren't going to help, when they talk of putting these people to work it's like cutting them off and expecting them to find a job," Berenice noted.

The Office of Vocational Rehabilitation is unaccustomed to working with those whose appearance is somewhat unusual or whose social behavior differs from that of the rest of society. Too, it does not understand the slow responses which the mentally disabled sometimes have to the barrage of questions. Because the office is more familiar and has been working for a longer time with the physically disabled, it often overlooks the special needs of individuals with emotional or mental deficiencies.

Berenice reported a heated confrontation with the county Office of Vocational Rehabilitation. The administrator tried to tell her that when an applicant did not call back to inquire about a job, the office thought the person was not demonstrating sufficient interest. To this Berenice responded, "You've got to call the patient." The office said it did not do things that way. It did not have the time. But Berenice reminded the official that the problems in helping the mentally disabled find employment differed from helping people with other kinds of disabilities. "It's not that their legs don't work. It's not that their eyes don't see. The problem which the mentally ill have is that they can't follow through on these things."

Berenice explained that with abundant time on his hands and few things to occupy him, Scott's deficient skills were not replenished by his having to wait several weeks or months for something to develop through the Office of Vocational Rehabilitation. If he had been able to find work without the services of this agency, he would have done so. Because the private sector failed him, he was forced to rely on OVR, and the months of waiting between appointments or interviews seemed like an eternity to someone with a desire to work.

Even if they do find a job through the Office of Vocational Rehabilitation, the prospects for long-term employment seem meager for people like Scott. Only between 10 and 30 percent of the chronically mentally ill can expect to be self-supporting as long as five years after their last hospitalization.[6] Finding openings and then getting hired often prove difficult. Some of this may be due to the negative responses employers have to former mental patients. Studies have shown that when a person with a history of mental illness is being interviewed for a job, "he finds the interviewer is less friendly, the chances of finding a job at the place of interview are described as less good, and there is a trend for jobs to be less frequently offered."[7]

Berenice questioned the use of traditional understandings of employment as an index of recovery. So did the 1978 *Task Panel Reports Submitted to the President's Commission on Mental Health.* They noted:

> An increasing portion of the caseload of vocational rehabilitation agencies is being made up of chronically mentally disabled persons for whom traditional vocational objectives are not always realistic. For this group, the objectives of vocational rehabilitation should be broadened, formally and de facto, to allow for the achievement of daily living and avocational skills without necessarily requiring employability.[8]

After all the paperwork was completed, Scott was sent to jobs that were more stressful than he could tolerate. "Scott is as intelligent as anybody else," his mother said, "but he has difficulty concentrating on tasks. He will go out and have a cigarette break; an extra twenty minutes will lapse, and he doesn't know the difference." Situations like these have caused her son difficulty. And this has led Berenice to question the importance that society and mental health professionals place on work as an index of rehabilitation. "In our society, which cannot fully employ the healthy, why should we be forced to worry about employing the marginal? There is so much concern—an obsession—which forces people to prove themselves," she said. Rather than insist upon employment as proof of recovery, Berenice believes rehabilitation programs should take into account the particular needs of the mentally disabled.

THE TRANSITIONAL EMPLOYMENT PROGRAM

Taking into consideration the particular needs of the mentally ill is what the Transitional Employment Program, designed by Fountain House, has done. Fountain House is a non-profit voluntary organization dedicated to the rehabilitation of former patients within the community. It was founded in the late 1940s by a group of six patients who had been discharged from Rockland State Hospital, New York, and who recognized the need for a support system within the community. Since its establishment in New York City, it has received national recognition for its innovative work with former patients, and one of its endeavors has been the Transitional Employment Program.

The program, started in 1958, helps members locate jobs with business and industry. John Beard, director of Fountain House, believes one of the problems discharged patients face is that they enter communities which disable them as much as the old-style hospitals did. According to Beard, "what the family needs is what the community needs. . . . It's what the neighborhood needs. . . . It's what our society needs. And that is a program which will enable these people to be less disabled." That philosophy underlies all the programs at Fountain House, and it serves to guide their approach to helping members find employment.

Rather than send discharged patients out on a job hunt where they face interviews in an alienating employment office and where they are vulnerable to a highly competitive job market, Fountain House obtains placements for its members in entry-level positions. Before any member is directed to a job, however, someone on the staff has learned it. Training the staff for jobs in which members will later be placed assures that someone has evaluated the stresses and tensions that are likely to arise. The jobs vary. Some require stocking merchandise in stores, operating a Xerox machine for a corporation, delivering mail or messages within a large business, or loading trucks at a warehouse. Knowledge of these tasks helps the Fountain House staff understand what is expected and then to assess what must be tolerated. Beard explains that "the objective is to thoroughly understand the requirements which must be met when the member is on placement."[9] Not only must a staff employee acquire experience in the job in order to train a member who is placed there, but he or she is responsible for the job getting done. If a member who is placed in the position is ill one day or does not come to work for any other reason, the staff must substitute. If a person decides that the job situation is too stressful, the staff member who initiated that job must find a replacement, and do the job until one is found. Therefore, the incentive for seeing that people succeed is high.

One of the goals of the Transitional Employment Program is to arrange for flexible work schedules. Neither the eight-hour workday nor the forty-hour workweek defines the criteria for a job. Members may share a job, perhaps working four-hour shifts on a prearranged schedule. For others, a part-time job is not enough and full-time placements are available. Still others prefer two part-time jobs, and the Transitional Employment Program encourages this as well.

Fountain House collected comments from clients employed through the Transitional Employment Program. Each person described the job he or she was doing and explained why it was satisfactory or not. One of them was written by a man named Douglas who had been in Rockland State Hospital for twenty-one years before going to Fountain House ten years ago. He now works as a messenger for two different firms. He wrote: "I'm capable of doing that kind of work. Not many people like messenger work, but I love it because I know I can do it. And it kills the day. You know you never get bored. You meet interesting people and you take the subways and then you come back. B's our boss. He's a very nice boss. I need these two jobs; I can't work one. I need the money. I have no other income. I was on SSI, but they axed me because I'm working. But I'd rather work. I work eight hours a day."[10]

Lillian, another person in the program, has been affiliated with Fountain House for fourteen years. She described her work in a local department store: "I'm either in refunds, wafering, or the pinning machine, and I like it very much. With wafering, I put little white clips on clothing and use the pinning machine. I also do refunds and putting clothes in different bins. . . . I did work other placements before. . . . We went out with the van from Fountain House. A social worker went with us, and we all put tickets on dresses. I also had a full-time job about six years ago in the Public Library."[11]

Lillian and Douglas each praise Fountain House for helping them find and keep jobs. The successful employment of people like them leads John Beard to scorn the pervasive myth that the mentally disabled are neither able to perform nor interested in work. The program's accomplishments have become the model for others. In 1976, with assistance from a grant from the National Institute of Mental Health, Fountain House became a training center for transitional employment procedures for other mental health professionals. By March 1981, four years after the grant was initiated, the number of programs grew to eighty-eight nationwide—an average of two per month. And the number of former patients who have been employed through these programs grew from 360 to just under 1,000 people earning annual wages of $3,743,000 nationwide.[12]

Despite the huge size of the Fountain House program and the numerous tasks that must be performed simply to maintain it each day, no outside services are contracted. The members do all the work, and this is part of the prevocational training program. With appropriate guidance from the staff, members plan the daily menu, shop in the neighborhood, prepare the meals, serve as cashiers in the buffet line, and clean up. They also learn the clerical and secretarial skills necessary to administer the organization with its daily newspaper, attendance records, numerous reports, and telephone switchboard. All this is part of Fountain House's effort to teach skills which members may use in a productive capacity that helps them overcome their disabilities.

The Transitional Employment Program is only one aspect of Fountain House's diversified rehabilitation program. Dedicated to helping people within the community, Fountain House and the other centers which operate along similar principles provide a place for people to come during the days and evenings. Fountain House members who spend days at the large brownstone in New York City have available to them different recreational rooms, a beauty parlor, a place for quiet conversation, and meals (which are prepared by the members under supervision from the staff). Dinner and evening programs several nights a week are also part of the program. No therapy is offered at Fountain House, though most of the members are receiving at least medication from an outside agency. A "bank" that will cash checks and allow members to open an account from which they can draw each month is also provided.

Fountain House held the lease to sixty-five apartments as of 1981. So did other rehabilitation programs, such as Thresholds, in Chicago. The rationale rests on the difficulty people have renting an apartment when they do not have the cash required for a month's deposit, or because they lack references from previous landlords, employers, or even people who have known them in the community for a year or more. By having the leases in its own name, the rehabilitation center can assist people who need housing and would have few resources to rely on in locating it.

Some of the rehabilitation programs encourage the involvement of a member's family, but most do not. Horizon House in Philadelphia estimates that over 50 percent of its members live alone or in halfway houses. Fountain House, in New York City, also estimates that most of its members are out of touch with their families. But Thresholds, which estimates that 65 percent of its clients live at home when they enter the program, started a program for the parents, or other significant relatives of its clients, in 1973.[13]

The twelve-week program Thresholds offers to families addresses issues of chronic dependence which it believes relatives have not had ample opportunity to discuss. Financial support, daily household tasks, employment, and eventual independent living are among the items on the agenda as Thresholds tries to help families get a clear understanding of how expectations, responsibilities, and obligations are interwoven. The Thresholds staff believes that mentally ill children function better when they are living independently from their parents. Therefore, the focus of their program discusses ways in which parents can facilitate this separation without feeling guilty or that they are rejecting their child. Since part of the rehabilitation program is designed to permit former patients to develop a social network that is not dependent on their families, Thresholds organizes special programs around holidays. This structures an opportunity for the otherwise dependent relative to become more independent from his or her family rather than rely on it for all sustenance.

Part of the difficulty of sustaining enough viable nonresidential treatment programs stems from the chaos within the mental health services. More than eleven separate government agencies administer 135 different programs. And they do it poorly. The *Task Panel Reports Submitted to the President's Commission on Mental Health* noted in 1978 that there was a "lack of clear national policy, legislative dilemmas, professional conflicts, sterotyping and stigma, training biases and funding inconsistencies"[14] in the organization and structure of mental health services. As long as this situation exists, the handful of programs offering real service to the mentally ill and assistance to their families will reach only a fraction of those who need them.

The dilemma confronting families whose relatives require continued help in non-residential settings is the same as that faced whenever a choice must be made about selecting a program. Parents or children, spouses or siblings are asked to consider the particular needs of the sick person and balance them against their own. Families have needs as do patients, and efforts to locate programs that will meet both are sometimes laden with frustration. An appropriate program may not exist, or may be too restrictive even when it sounds ideal on paper, or may have no opening. What is most likely, however, is that the desired form of non-residential rehabilitation is not available. Despite the impressive results of their programs, centers like the Western Psychiatric Institute and Clinic, Thresholds, Fountain House, and Horizon House do not represent a real choice for most families because they are so few in number. Even when all of them are added up, there are more people who need them, in more cities across the nation, than there are spaces available.

And if you close your eyes,
a river fills you from within,
flows forward, darkens you:
its night brings wetness to beaches in your soul.

Octavio Paz—"Water Night"

PART

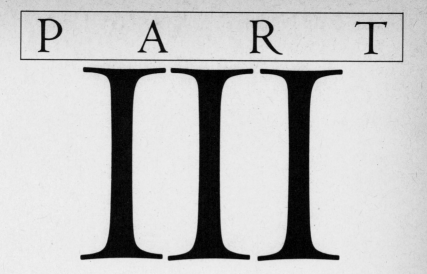

III

SETTLING

7

. . . at Home

Robert Frost once said, "Home is the place where, when you have to go there, / They have to take you in." For many families of the chronically mentally ill, the poet's words ring true. It is estimated that as many as two-thirds of those discharged from psychiatric hospitals return to live with their families.[1] The length of time they stay at home varies, as do the circumstances surrounding their return. Berenice McCoy or Rosanne Flynn, for example, expect their children to become semi-independent one day. Each mother prefers home to be the place that her son or daughter uses as a temporary refuge, a stopping-off place, when necessary. A smaller percentage of those with chronic disabilities live with their families permanently. The parents (mostly) of this group of people may hope for independence for their children, but they would settle happily for some assistance and guidance in the daily burdens of coping with mental illness in their family.

For families who have completed the cycle of rearing children, the presence of a dependent and chronically mentally ill person disrupts the rhythm of events which today's smaller family has come to expect. With women having fewer children than their earlier counterparts, and with couples expecting their offspring to establish an independent life before marriage, parents like Stella and Lloyd Stanwick are having to readjust to their thirty-five-year-old son's living at home in dependency.

STELLA AND LLOYD STANWICK'S SON

Stella Stanwick proudly ushered me outside to sit on the patio that her husband, Lloyd, had added to the house many years ago. The glass walls captured the heat of that early June morning, and potted plants angled toward the sunlight, falling near magazines stacked on reading tables. As Stella began to tell about their efforts to help Christopher, I was faintly aware of movement in the basement, where her grown son spends most of his time in the recreation room that Lloyd finished also. "Don't be unnerved if you see Christopher wandering around upstairs," his mother said to me. "Most of the time he stays in the basement by himself when a new person is here. Every once in a while he does come up and he just stares," she added. "But he is not going to harm you."

Christopher never did appear in the three hours I was there listening to his mother describe how his psychosis has forced the family's reorganization and their current life-style. Regret, mixed with love and the wisdom of hindsight, permeated explanations of how the Stanwicks tried to help their son during his illness. His problem became increasingly apparent during the ten years that he was employed as a shipping clerk. By the first time Christopher was hospitalized his behavior was so bizarre that his job was in jeopardy. After three months of treatment on a psychiatric wing of a general hospital, he returned to his job but was retired from his position and given a work disability within a few months. Since then, with the exception of another two months in the hospital, Christopher has lived at home with his parents.

Stella described how she and Lloyd consulted with doctors prior to Christopher's hospitalization, and she discussed the few conversations they had had with professionals while he was in the hospital. Each hospitalization was relatively short, and neither Stella nor Lloyd is the kind of person who will push professionals. They are practicing Catholics and expect the same kind of order that guides their internal and spiritual lives to guide other events as well, psychiatrists and hospitals being no exception.

Having respect for those with earned degrees and claims to competence, the Stanwicks assumed that whatever they needed to know would be told them. That is one of the reasons they were so excited when they received a phone call during Christopher's last hospitalization, in early 1978, asking them to come to the hospital. "I thought at least we had made a breakthrough," Stella said. "They would tell us what to do, or how to cope, or something useful. But that never materialized."

The phone call requested their participation in the first of what turned into three family therapy sessions. At the time, however, neither parent knew this. When they arrived, "we all just filed into this room. Christopher followed behind." To the Stanwicks it appeared that Christopher just sat, while two therapists along with two unidentified people "picked on him." Mrs. Stanwick thought this strange, but she did not question their approach or purpose or goal. Rather, she tried to figure out what they were trying to do. "I thought, perhaps they are trying to antagonize him so he will blow up and let off some steam," she said. For this reason she went along. "I answered the questions they put to me, but I felt sorry for Christopher all the time," she reported. When the session was over, the Stanwicks were dismissed and told when the next meeting would take place. "I was baffled by all of it," she said, but was willing to do what was necessary to help their son.

After two more sessions the hospital informed Christopher's parents that they were unable to find a medicine which would work for their son. The insurance company informed them that since the psychiatrists doubted that more treatment would help him, the payments on Christopher's behalf would soon stop. The Stanwicks did not see how they could carry the steep expenses by themselves. Both of them are retired—Lloyd is over seventy and Stella is sixty-six—and what funds they had were not going to be replenished by future earnings. "Your life savings can be eaten up in a few months with those rates," Stella lamented. So they told the hospital personnel that they could not afford to keep him there if the insurance payments stopped, and the psychiatrists conveyed a choice to Christopher: either he could be committed or he could go home. He elected to go home.

The hospital called Stella and Lloyd Stanwick the next day and told them to pick Christopher up. "They never summed up anything for us," his mother said. The psychiatrist offered no guidance, provided no outline for continued therapy, presented no alternative for Stella or Lloyd to select. "We felt just as lost after having him there for that length of time as we did before," Stella Stanwick observed.

Before the connection to the hospital was severed, Christopher's mother made an appointment with the psychiatric social worker to ask for specific information about how to draw their son into the family and help shatter the wall that separated him from them. How could she light a spark that might help Christopher engage in the world outside his basement habitat? Were there any concrete suggestions the social worker could make? These were the specific kinds of information Mrs. Stanwick sought as she pondered what the future would be like with Christopher's return to their household.

"The social worker asked me if I had ever invited Christopher to shop for groceries," his mother said. Since Stella Stanwick had not, the social worker thought this might be a good step in involving Christopher in the family—and help him feel greater responsibility for its maintenance while forcing him to be aware of others. Stella Stanwick thought it was worth a try. A few days after Christopher's discharge she asked him if he would help out with the shopping. No reply. But about six weeks later he came home, carrying huge sacks of groceries up the front steps. And there were more out in the car. "He made a practice of going to the store after that," his mother said. The trips, however, were expensive. Christopher bought about $100 worth of food at a time, but it was not what his mother used. There was a lot of junk food, snacks, and none of the staples she needed. She finally told him that there were certain things she needed and asked if he would please buy them. "I gave him a list. I thought that was going to work. He bought my list. But he also bought everything else," she said. "And he wouldn't let up. We had groceries all over the place. Everywhere you looked there was a sack. They were coming out of the refrigerator, spilling out the cupboards. I had to get rid of them. I used to carry groceries out of the back door and over to my daughter's house, to my friends and neighbors . . . any place to get rid of all that extra food."

Other efforts to engage Christopher have been equally futile. When Christopher first came home from the hospital, his mother asked him to read to her while she did the dishes. "I picked something about early American Indians," she said, wanting to select something that would interest him. "Well, he didn't tell me he wouldn't read to me. But he just sat there and kept mumbling. He was saying the words but in such a way that I couldn't take it." Yet she didn't want to discourage him. So she thought, "If I just let this go for a while, he will ease out. He will start to read. But after two or three nights I just had to stop that."

The efforts that Stella and Lloyd are making to reorient their lives to include Christopher's illness, and what appears to be a permanent disability, require flexibility and tolerance in areas which previously required little or no thought. They accept Christopher's peculiar eating habits and no longer expect him to have breakfast with the two of them. "He does eat dinner with us," Stella said, noting that she tries to have the evening meal contain all the essentials people normally acquire throughout the day. "Very often he delays until we are half through, but he comes to the table. The rest of the time he eats crackers, cheese, or he mixes milk and chocolate. And mostly he prefers to eat in the basement, which is sort of his place."

In addition to accepting his peculiar eating habits, the Stanwicks have had to accept Christopher's tendency to slink around the house while his parents are in bed. "He's up most of the night," Stella explained. "You'll hear him running around the house. Lights flash on and off." Occasionally he will pound on the table or give a strange yell. Even when he sleeps, it is not in his bed or his bedroom. The basement recreation room has a couch that Christopher uses. He simply curls up in one of the corners, in the same clothes he has worn during the day.

These kinds of things used to bother both his parents. When he first started sleeping in his clothes several years ago, Mrs. Stanwick would wake him, tell him he had fallen asleep in front of the television, and send him off to his bedroom. But when she awoke in the morning, she would realize that he just went back to sleep without changing. Even as a boy, reminisced Mrs. Stanwick, Christopher did not like to change his trousers. Finally, she had to trick him, and she bought a different pair for each day of the week. This reluctance to change his pants seemed curious to his mother, who remembered how tidy Christopher was as a child. "He never wanted anyone to go into his room after he made it up. He made the bed, and he would run around it measuring the spread. And he kept his toys in drawers, wrapped with towels."

Compared to some people with chronic mental disabilities, Christopher is relatively passive. Yet he has rare explosive moments when he is likely to start yelling. "He has never attacked us, except verbally," Mrs. Stanwick said. "Sometimes he flies off the handle and tells us what rotten parents we are. That really shook me the first time it happened," she recalled. "I remember the first time he said that he hated someone in our family. He picked on our daughter. There is a fourteen-month difference in their ages, and they had always been close." Christopher's married sister and family live about a mile from the house. The childhood closeness kept up through adulthood, and the entire family is linked through easy visits during the week, running errands for one another, and in a pinch Stella baby-sits for her grandchildren. She remembers how upset she was to hear how much Christopher hated his only sister. "When my husband told me about it, I started to tremble all over. I couldn't comprehend that he could do that—hate anybody so much."

Stella and Lloyd have come to accept things in Christopher that they never imagined would be necessary. "I have to remind myself that he is sick, and this is part of his sickness. We have to recognize that these things happen as symptoms of his illness. Yet it's very hard to walk into a room and know he's not going to talk. The only time he says anything is when he has to let off steam. And it's kind of hard to listen to him. But I've learned to," she said. In part, Stella accepts Christopher's mental illness because she thinks it is like the adjustment one is forced to make for a physical illness. "When a person is physically ill, there are adjustments that you have to make," she said. "I think of it in that way rather than that I am sacrificing."

When Stella is home alone with Christopher during the day, she tries to respect his needs. "I try not to vacuum when I think he is asleep." But it is not always easy for her to tell. He spends a lot of time curled up on the couch, even when he is awake. "But I try not to make too much noise or turn on the television." The Stanwicks have found also that it is too much of a strain on them to entertain guests.

With a few friends who understand the situation, Stella and Lloyd can relax. A recent overnight visit from California friends was possible, though Christopher let his displeasure about this be known to his parents and their guests. Understanding on all sides transcended awkward and amusing parts to the visit. But with "people who don't understand or who have not had experience with this sort of thing, it is not possible. The guests feel they are in danger. So there are a lot of people we do not see any more. We just don't invite them into the house," she noted.

Not only have the Stanwicks had to adjust to Christopher's behavior when he is in the house, but they have learned to be relaxed when he leaves for his occasional walks in the neighborhood or to go to the local mall, where he buys food for his fish. "He will leave here when it is getting dark and walk all the way there and back. It's about five miles." A lot of things could happen to Christopher on the trip, and initially the Stanwicks would dwell on them. "But when he leaves, I just turn him over to the Heavenly Father. I ask Him to take care of Christopher and bring him back. Prayer has helped somewhat, and I've gotten to the point that I can actually let him go and not be too concerned. But sometimes he comes home at two o'clock or later."

Stella and Lloyd Stanwick feel that it is best to tell friends and neighbors that Christopher is ill. "In fact, that's one way you cope," she said. When new neighbors moved in next door, Stella and Lloyd decided "to let them know what the situation is. It took awhile. But it was better because we did not have to make a big thing of it," she observed. Then nobody was embarrassed when Christopher's bizarre behavior became apparent.

The Stanwicks were reared in a tradition of large families congregating for holiday gatherings. The current situation with Christopher has put an end to these once joyful festivities. Stella believes that Christopher's illness has "fractured the family." The gatherings which previously took place at their house—the only one large enough to hold the twelve of them (including the grandchildren)—are no longer possible. "We cannot have any of them here . . . birthday dinners, Thanksgiving, Christmas . . . the noise and confusion of the entire family is just too much for him. With five grandchildren ranging from two to thirteen years old, there is a lot of running around," Stella observed. "On two occasions, one was a Christmas dinner, Christopher came upstairs and unexpectedly yelled at the children. It frightened them. It scared one of our granddaughters so much that we have a hard time getting her to come into the house any more." When events like this occur, Stella tries to explain the situation to her grandchildren. She tells them that Christopher is sick and that the noise bothers him and then he becomes irritable. "They seem to understand," she said. "Yet they can't cope with the situation. It just breaks my heart."

Stella and Lloyd Stanwick are regretful of the distance in the family that Christopher's illness has introduced. For the moment, however, they have a life that can be lived with their son's presence. They have adjusted to his hours and to his peculiar behavior. They do not react with anger or alarm but with compassion and frustration when he feeds fruit juice to crickets and other animals, which then invade the basement. And they have learned to accept the limits on their social life. For these people it is not the present or the past that they contemplate so much as the future. "My husband is in his seventies and I am sixty-six," she began. "And we just realize that it is a situation that's got to be taken care of. It worries me. I think I've adjusted to the fact that he might not get well, but I can't adjust to the fact that he won't be taken care of . . . that someday he might be a street person." Referring to articles in their local paper about de-institutionalization, she said, "Since I've heard about it, I realize that Christopher could become one of them if he doesn't have protective care." That frightens both of them.

Their concern about Christopher's future led Stella Stanwick to call the county Office of Mental Health and ask what services might be available. She was informed of a program in which a social worker could visit the house and talk with Christopher. "They have started to come on a weekly basis," Stella said. "We have had three visits, but it's a little too early to tell what's going to happen. The first social worker knew he wouldn't be coming on a regular basis, and now there is a young woman who has come." Mrs. Stanwick is hopeful that this social worker will help them find a place for Christopher to live when the necessity occurs.

DORA AND THOMAS YOUNG'S SON

Dora and Thomas Young are in a similar situation with their thirty-year-old son, James. The big difference between the Stanwick and the Young families is that there are three other children in the Young family with whom Dora is already speaking about how James will be cared for when his parents are no longer able to do so.

James's youngest brother, Matthew, openly and clearly expresses his willingness to accept his share of the responsibility. He and another brother live in their hometown, and his sister lives more than 500 miles away. The whole situation troubles Matthew, who credits his mother with having kept the family together through the last fifteen years, which included not only James's illness but also the presence of their aging grandmother and two heart attacks that Thomas Young suffered. "My mother has done everything," Matthew said. "She's handled it all . . . if there's any problem, she's the one that we all go to. And she's taken care of just about everything we needed." The twenty-three-year-old was quick to say that his mother's example instructed them all. "If I hadn't had somebody like my mother who was so good at coping, I don't know how I'd be right now, or how my brother or sister would be either."

Dora also thinks that her other three children turned out quite well. But she is not sure how they managed, given the uneven attention they had. "So much attention is paid to the sick member that the others are neglected. And your discipline is sometimes biased. James was abusive to his brothers and sister," she said. "That was terrible. But we had to live with it. Elizabeth didn't like taking it from him. And she teased him, too. But she didn't know when to stop—not because he was saying things that were right, but because of his condition. She shouldn't have said those things back to James. And after a while he really had it in for her." Elizabeth reached the point where she was afraid of James. "She used to be scared to go upstairs by herself. I had to sleep with her. It really bothered her. All the time he probably wouldn't have hurt her, but she was afraid that he would." Elizabeth's fear of James, who by then was in his mid-twenties when she was in her late teens, drove her away from home. "Every chance she had, she'd go out of the house," Dora said. Elizabeth "may have wanted to stay home, but it wasn't very pleasant."

Matthew thinks everybody will accept his or her share of the future responsibility, though he quickly adds that he has no idea what that means. Elizabeth's fear has diminished, and since Matthew moved out of the house when he attended college, he has had minimal involvement with his older brother. This has helped because when Matthew lived at home, he was angry with James much of the time. As the youngest brother and child Matthew looked up to James. "I was always looking at him as though he were the one to follow. You have to follow somebody, and usually it is your older brother. But so many things were frustrating to me because I couldn't understand a lot of his actions," Matthew said. When James was sixteen, and Matthew nine, they watched television together. Matthew never understood why his brother laughed at things that were not funny. As James's behavior became more peculiar, Matthew was somewhat embarrassed. "I never mentioned it to my friends," he said. "I would invite them over to watch TV or listen to records, and James would be sitting in a chair, shaking his head or dancing at the door and laughing. It was embarrassing." These kinds of things bothered Matthew when he was a child. As an adult he has become more tolerant. "I realize that you can't blame him for a lot of the things that he does."

Matthew hardly remembers James prior to the time when his mental illness was apparent. But Dora does. She remembers when James first began to behave strangely. He was still a boy at the time. "His grades started dropping. He wasn't working as hard as he usually did." This was unusual since James "never played hooky and always made As and Bs. In fact, he worked hard and did everything that he was expected to do." The lack of interest in school passed, as his math teacher predicted it would, but James was in an automobile accident when he was thirteen and after that began to show considerable confusion. He lost all interest in school, would stay home with stomach aches and diarrhea, and, according to the school officials, became disruptive. "He would walk around the classroom and would laugh out loud and talk to himself. And he was never like that before. They told me that I should withdraw him from school."

Dora called the community hospital and asked for the name

of a psychiatrist. She then took James to the psychiatrist, who thought something was wrong but could not specify what. He gave the boy a sedative and sent him home. It was not until a few days later, when James went on a wild spree, throwing "cups and dishes, breaking picture frames, and breaking in the door," that he was taken to the emergency room, after which he was admitted to the hospital. He stayed for one month.

When the teenager was discharged, already having been dismissed from school, he stayed home. His parents were very concerned about his education and still hoped that he might go to college. So Dora consulted the school counselor, who suggested the names of tutors. For the next two years his parents arranged for him to continue his education at home. "He was taking tranquilizers so much that he couldn't keep his eyes open. I don't know how he ever studied," Dora said. "In fact, I know that he didn't learn very much. But it was an effort that we thought we needed to make. Then, for about a year or two, he went to night school. We took him religiously. He picked up a couple more credits, but again, I don't think he learned very much."

With the exception of a second hospitalization, which lasted about one month, James has lived at home since he left school. Dora admits that it took her about five years to realize how serious his illness was, and before she did, she thought more discipline was what he needed. Then, after a few years, including tutoring and night school, she realized that James's problems were not just a lack of discipline, despite the fact that one of her other sons still insists that it is.

Although James lives at home, Dora has tried to look outside the house for help. In addition to the tutors, she has had him under psychiatric care. Two different doctors have come to the house to work with James. One of the doctors came each week for almost five years. Dora does not think James showed much change under his care, though her son liked the doctor. Matthew, however, renders a different and more critical opinion, leading him to question whether psychiatry is the answer for his brother. The psychiatrist who currently comes to the house to see James prescribes medicine, as did the other one.

Neither psychiatrist has directed Dora toward social services which might help her. She called the one who is currently seeing James and asked to speak with him. He responded, " 'Okay. But it will cost you forty dollars.' So I paid the forty dollars, but I learned nothing," she reported. What did he tell her? " 'It's not easy to live with this,' " Dora replied, and then added, "Of course, I knew that already."

At about the same time that she realized that James's condition was not improving, Dora made an appointment with her minister. As a lifelong member of her church she hoped that someone with pastoral training might offer assistance. The encounter with the minister was no more successful than the one with James's current psychiatrist. The minister "not only did not help," said Dora, "but took James's name off the church roster. He might not have known what to do, but I know that this child's name is no longer on the church roster and the other children's are."

It was not until James became violent toward his mother that she accidentally discovered that he was a candidate for SSI. The doctor to whom she went to look at the bruises James inadvertently inflicted was married to a social worker. He referred Dora to his wife, who informed her of the Supplemental Security Income program which could contribute toward James's expenses. He has now been registered for SSI for several years, and because James lives in his parents' home, in 1980 the monthly amount for which he was eligible amounted to $79.47. But the major financial help on which the Youngs rely has been their private insurance coverage, which pays for the medicine and part of the psychiatry. Dora considers herself lucky that they have not yet exhausted this resource. "I've heard of some people who have used all their insurance, all their assets, everything that they own. And their children are still in the same state," she noted. "We haven't come to that yet, which I'm glad of."

What causes her the most concern, however, is the isolation and dependency of James's life. Dora believes that he will not be able to support himself with work. Several years ago someone found him a job. Working as a shoe salesman, "James didn't sleep for three days and three nights. That was just too much stress for him." So at this point she is not optimistic that he will ever work, but she wants him "to have some kind of life, something that he enjoys doing . . . something that he could get a little pleasure out of." What that will be remains to be seen, but James does like other people, his mother said. "I'm really proud that he's approachable, and he's social to some extent," she added. But there are no programs of which she knows that serve someone like James, who takes almost no initiative and spends most of his life in his room looking at picture books or watching television.

One day, after reading of the formation of an organization of families of the mentally ill in her community, Dora called the office to inquire about its services and programs. Through it she was informed of a county program that reaches out to people like James. Someone from the office arranged for a visit and told of a local hospital that has social centers where James could spend a few hours during the day. The woman who now visits regularly, without charge, shares Dora's concern about James's isolation. "Her objective is to get him out of this house," Dora said. "It might take a year or two to get him to the point where he will go out of the house—now he doesn't go out for anything. And maybe he could meet some other people. I'm kind of hoping for that."

Dora worries that James is so dependent on her and her husband that "if we weren't here, I really don't know but I think he'd probably just go off the deep end." So the goal of getting James comfortable enough so that he will begin to leave the house and interact with other people is not only to relieve his parents of the twenty-four-hour burden but also to anticipate the future. "It's my biggest fear. I worry about what will happen, and I want to get something settled . . . a housing situation," Dora said. "I would like for him to have his own life."

James and Christopher represent an extreme degree of need. Each relies completely on his parents for survival, and each set of parents worries about who will take care of their son when they no longer can. Not all the mentally disabled who live at home are as passive as these two men are.

LOU AND HELEN AMATO'S SON

When a mentally disabled person lives at home and is able to leave the house, different things are required of parents. Perhaps they provide assistance to a child who is looking for a job; maybe they help their daughter or son organize a life in order to keep the job. Other times parents help their son or daughter learn how to manage stress when ambition does not match ability, or they help the person learn to schedule time. And frequently parents just need to rescue their child from some mishap that is hard to anticipate, or to keep a close watch to see if the medication is wearing off.

"At this point we have it down to a science," Lou Amato said. His son, Joseph, lives at home, holds a job, and takes medicine to keep him stable. "Joe gets a shot on Monday, and along about the weekend he needs a pill or two. Otherwise, some of the signs are going to show up." When Joe doesn't take that extra pill over the weekend, he develops irrational fears. He worries that he is going to die, that someone close to him is in danger, that imminent destruction will be unleashed upon the world. These are the things Joseph fears and talks about when his shot begins to wear off. "Tension will also speed up this process," his father said. "But if he's on an even keel and does not have too much pressure or tension, then the shot carries him through five or six days."

When Lou or his wife, Helen, notices that Joseph needs medicine, one of them will ask him whether he wants a pill. Often Joe will agree. "Yeah, I think I do," he says. He'll take his medicine and then a hot bath, which helps him relax. "And then he begins feeling better. So he's kind of manageable as long as he can take the medicine," Lou said. Helen added, "As long as there is not too much stress."

Joseph, who is twenty-eight, has tried different living arrangements. In between his several hospitalizations he has returned home temporarily, with the expectation of later finding something more private for himself. He has tried a counterculture commune, which worked for several months. He also shared an apartment with a cousin; that did not work at all. In between the hospital, back home, the commune, and the apartment, Joseph was in treatment with different doctors, each of whom had a different orientation—psychoanalytic, orthomolecular, behaviorist—none of which worked. And he was an outpatient at a local psychiatric hospital while sleeping at home at night. In short, the Amatos have pursued a variety of treatments for their son.

During those ten years when Lou and Helen were traveling the country looking for hospitals for Joseph, or retrieving him after he ran away from one, or delivering him to the commune, or helping him set up his own apartment, or simply trying to work out a life when he was home, the other two Amato children were also growing to adulthood. The oldest, a daughter, became involved in an Eastern religious sect and tried to persuade her parents that Joseph's problems would be solved if they joined the "movement." Lou thinks that was a "heavy burden for us to bear. To this day she still believes that if we would have just joined her movement, all would have been taken care of." He does not agree.

"And David was the younger one. Poor David just grew up. It fell the hardest of all on him, and he stood it the best. He's a strong one," Helen said with admiration. Lou elaborated on Joseph's mental illness and how it affected David. "He would go places with Joseph where it was terribly embarrassing. Joseph would do something inappropriate, and David, two years his junior, would just move in front of him and put his hand on his shoulder and change the subject. David would calm him down. It was beautiful," said their father, "but, God, was it hard on David." Helen believes these incidents cost David a lot. And they cost her and Lou much, too. "David has turned away from the family. He had to. It was inevitable," Helen said. "To protect himself," Lou added.

David was a popular boy through school, and he had lots of friends. "He's always had friends, and they are always milling around or going someplace. And I'm afraid I would sometimes load things on him by asking him to give more time to Joseph," Lou said. "And it made him guilty because he was doing that already. So it was really hard on him." Today David lives in his own apartment but is available to his family when they need him, as they did recently when his parents went away for ten days.

For the past seven months Joseph has been taking Elavil, which seems to help. During the day he works as an auto mechanic. "He's been on the job now for just under three months," Lou said. "He hasn't missed a day, and he is getting into a pattern of needing more activity. That's what he is like when he is put together." The job, which covers eight hours a day, is sufficient for Joseph, though he sometimes has problems getting up in the morning. "When he was a teenager," his mother said, "I would say that he was old enough to get up in the morning. It was up to him to get his own breakfast and go to work by himself. Well, he would fall flat on his face. He just couldn't do it at that point."

Helen thinks she has learned over the years how to meet Joseph halfway, or at least meet him where his needs are. Today she responds differently to the early-morning routine. "Now that he's got this job, we decided that by golly, the thing that is important is to get him a year of steady work. So we get up at six. I get his lunch and fix breakfast for him. Lou drives him over to work." Lou also noted that the tone of each morning differs. "We don't hound him to get out of bed. We are learning a few things as we go along. We 'report' to him as we go along—in a nice voice, in an 'up' voice," his father said. One of them will say that it's six-fifteen or six-thirty—and they try not to be angry as they once were.

Despite the relative ease of the routine each morning, Lou and Helen live with a constant sense of disruption. Joseph sometimes forgets where he parks the car, and on several occasions he and his parents have spent hours searching for it. Or, when he is out late at night, they are likely to get a phone call asking for directions back home or money for a cab. One time he bicycled to the next city, about sixty miles away. "He went to look for a job —I don't know how he got there," Lou said. "He called and asked me to come get him, and when I got to the place he said he was waiting, he was gone. So we went over to where he applied for the job. They said he left long before. So we came home." Soon after they returned, Joseph called. The police had picked him up riding on the highway. Why had he left the spot where his parents thought he would be? "He was standing near the phone, and the police stopped to see if there was any trouble. But Joseph is inarticulate," his father continued, "and couldn't explain himself very well. So the officer told him to move along." Joseph left the pay phone but returned on his bike to see if his parents were there yet. All he saw was the police officer, and he knew that he couldn't stay. Fearful of being arrested and anxious that his parents would not find him, he decided to return home the fastest way—on the highway where he was arrested for riding his bike.

Lou reported the number of people who advised them to remain uninvolved when Joseph ran into problems like getting home. The county offices of social services, the hospital, the vocational rehabilitation counselors, and the vocational educational offices all told them not to get involved. "Basically they all told us one thing—you caused it, and now the least you can do is stay out of it," Lou said. But Lou and Helen saw that when they were removed and allowed the different offices to work with Joseph, he waited for weeks or months between appointments and had little to occupy his days. Because he was bored and frustrated, his self-esteem fell, and when the different offices returned with an answer, it was often negative.

"This mental illness changes your life so much," Helen said. "We used to do a lot of entertaining and we can't any more. You can't really blame it on Joseph. It's just that your interests change, and you are constantly preoccupied and busy." Lou has a demanding job which requires occasional travel to different parts of the world, and while Joseph was hospitalized for a year, Helen decided to return to school to get a master's degree. She had been a preschool teacher before she decided to get an advanced degree in early childhood education. "Joseph had been diagnosed as learning-disabled when he was in the ninth grade. And I went back to school in early childhood education because I needed to know if there was something that I had done wrong. I really wanted to know," Helen said. She had been told by different doctors and social workers that much of her son's problem was the result of inadequate mothering. "I really didn't believe that I was the reason he was sick, but I wanted to know. The whole time I was in one course, on psychosocial development, I was reading this material which blames the mother. I had to disagree. I wrote a term paper criticizing the theories." When the teacher returned the paper, she told Helen that while she disagreed with the argument, the paper was very well written. "She gave me an A," Helen said proudly.

Helen and Lou Amato would like Joseph one day to be independent enough to take care of himself without their supervision. But they know that the timetable which worked for their other children will not work for him. Simply because their other son and daughter were living in their own apartments when they were in their early twenties is no reason that Joseph should or could. Lou and Helen know that Joseph lives in a cloud much of the time. Where they would get angry or frustrated in the early years of his illness, they now respond with less urgency to the mixups and chaos. They worry, though, because they understand that Joseph is doing the best he can. And they feel they must help structure an environment for him, help him recapture the confidence that he had as a boy, the self-sufficiency that made him class president in his senior year in high school, and the ability to organize his life to find fulfillment from work and leisure. Until he can do that, on whatever time schedule, they have decided they must be available to him even if it imposes unanticipated burdens. One way or another his illness affects them, and they have decided it is better to help their son actively than to seethe with anger because nobody else has.

8

... for an Institution

SELMA: CAROLYN GREENE'S
MOTHER/HAROLD GREENE'S SISTER

The state mental institution became the eventual home for Selma Greene. That is not what anybody expected when her symptoms appeared in the late 1940s. Nor is it what her family expected even after she was admitted to a hospital following a nervous breakdown. But it is what Selma's daughter, Carolyn, and the rest of the family have come to accept as they have reorganized their lives to adjust to Selma's mental illness.

In the late 1940s and the early 1950s, Selma joined an army of people, numbering almost 600,000 by 1955, who entered state or county hospitals. In these years following World War II the field of psychiatry had not changed very much in its practice of exiling the sick to state and county mental institutions. Although new theories had been offered about the causes and the course of mental illness, treatments continued to be hampered by the inability to produce cures. If a psychiatrist's private consultations did not help, and if a short stay in a hospital did not yield success, the only other choice was to remain at home. When that became impossible, the next step was a state or county facility. The embryonic understanding of mental illness offered little hope, and the absence of social supports offered little help.

For those who visited relatives in mental hospitals during the forties and fifties, the experience seemed somewhat like stepping into a prison. That's what Selma's brother Harold thought the first time he visited his sister. "I thought it was like being locked up in solitary confinement—like a prison. That's what it seemed whenever I went there." The locked wards with metal gates, patients in hospital garb that resembled uniforms, and colorless walls and drab furniture for the thousands of hospital inmates even gave Harold the sense that he, too, "was locked up like everybody else."

Before Selma was permanently institutionalized, she lived with her son and daughter and her mother. She had been recently divorced, but it was apparent that Selma had difficulties more extensive than disappointment over a failed marriage and the ensuing financial and emotional disruptions. Gradually Selma's difficulty coping with stress turned into idiosyncratic behavior that was unmistakably irresponsible. There were frequent hospitalizations, and during each one her mother took care of the growing children.

On some occasions, when she was discharged, Selma returned to share the apartment with her children and mother. On other occasions she lived in an apartment of her own, around the corner. Selma's daughter, Carolyn, was only a child at the time, but she remembers these years and her curiosity over her mother's behavior. "My mother had all these clotheslines in her own apartment. She used to hang clothes up in the house, and she also had endless cartons and boxes stacked around the room." The untidy apartment stored with treasures Selma would not let anybody see were only one part of her peculiar behavior. There were other oddities on which Carolyn dwelt as a youngster. Each day, after Selma got up in the morning, she would go out for the day. She never told anybody where she went or what she was doing. For Carolyn her mother's behavior was a mystery to be solved. "One day I decided to see where she went," Carolyn said. "I think I was about nine at the time. I waited by the corner and then followed her for a while." At first she saw Selma just walk, block after block. Then her mother went to a bus stop. "I waited, too," continued Carolyn. "When the bus came, my mother got on, and I snuck on at the back. I just wanted to see where she went," Carolyn said about the maneuver which solved her curiosity. Where did Selma go? "Well, she went to junk stores! My mother bought combs and soap and all sorts of junk. She had this fascination with soap. There must have been fifty boxes stacked with soap in her apartment," Carolyn discovered eventually.

Selma's illness was not discussed with Carolyn or her brother, Marvin, while their mother was in and out of hospitals periodically. "Nobody ever really told me what the problem was," Carolyn recalled. "And my grandmother never told me she was sick. But somehow I just knew it. And I knew how painful it was for my grandmother, too," said Carolyn. She remembers having a few close friends but being unable to bring anybody home after school. "My grandmother would say I couldn't bring anybody into the house with my mother like this. So I couldn't have any friends over. My grandmother would have been very embarrassed."

Carolyn's grandmother cared for her and her brother until they were eleven and fifteen respectively. By then Selma's condition was worsening. The family, which had been supportive of efforts to help Selma get necessary care, had to turn its attention to her children. Selma's two brothers and sister, along with their mother, had to plan living arrangements for their niece and nephew. They no longer held hope that Selma's condition would allow her to become a fully active parent to her children.

When the family met to discuss their niece and nephew's future, it was agreed that the children would have to be separated. Nobody was able to rear the two of them, and Harold had already taken Marvin for extended periods during Selma's hospitalizations. So it was decided that Marvin would continue to stay with his uncle Harold and aunt Eileen, while Carolyn would live with another aunt and uncle.

Carolyn's move into the home of an aunt and uncle was fraught with difficulties, even though it was the solution to other problems. Perhaps some of them started with the strange scene when the family met to discuss her future. She remembers that Harold came over to the apartment where all the other relatives were gathering. Her mother was already in the hospital. She presumes that they told her how much better things were going to be in the future when she would not have to cope with behavior she did not understand or stresses she could not articulate. She would have a family to care for her; she would have a family to care for. And she would have a home with stability. "They probably said I wouldn't have to deal with the interruptions and the chaos," Carolyn said—that is, the chaos caused by frequent hospitalizations, awkwardness when neighbors scorned Carolyn or her mother, pain when she was publicly identified as the child with the "crazy mother." Though nobody ever told Carolyn about her mother's illness, she knew about it nonetheless, and the move to her aunt and uncle's home confirmed her fears.

Whatever material comforts and stability she was supposed to have living with her new family, Carolyn was miserable almost from the day she moved in. "I never felt that I belonged there," she said. Little things reminded her that she was an outsider, that she was living there because of some arrangement over which she had no control, that she was there because of an obligation. She remembers feeling trapped. She rarely voiced an opinion if it was different from what was expected because she feared creating conflict. "It was the only thing that I had. I was afraid to lose it, even though I hated it. I hated living there."

Carolyn thinks a long-standing animosity existed between her mother and her aunt. Maybe the added responsibility of being made to accept a child into the household was too burdensome for her relatives, who already had a son and daughter. Whatever the source of the problem, Carolyn remembers that her mother's illness followed her like a shadow and at times her aunt and uncle used it as a weapon. "One day I must have left some water in the bathtub," Carolyn said. "My aunt told me that my mother was just like that. She was dirty, and she never changed her underwear." Carolyn was told, "You're just like your mother." Her uncle was less vocal than his wife, but he too contributed to Carolyn's unease. "I had temper tantrums," Carolyn remembered. "My uncle would say that I was crazy. That I was going to end up the same way." As a youngster who felt powerless to challenge those who had given her a home, Carolyn had to bear these accusations without protest. And even though she was able to dismiss much of what they said, thinking them ignorant and stupid, another part of her could not ignore it. "I half believed it," she said.

"I could block out only so much of it. Underneath it all I thought, 'Maybe this is going to happen to me.' "

Throughout the six years she lived with her aunt and uncle, it was Harold in whom she invested her affections. He would pick her up once a week, and together they would go visit Selma. By the time she needed braces Harold's business had grown to the point that he was able to pay for them. And when she was ready to go to college, it was Harold, again, who guaranteed that she would have the means to do so. For the constant presence, the weekly visits with her beloved uncle, and his financial support at critical times, Carolyn feels enormous gratitude to and love for Harold.

Despite the warmth she feels for Harold's efforts on behalf of her and her brother, Carolyn feels cheated; she suffered the loss of a family. That is what caused her the most severe pain as a child and still haunts her as an adult. Sitting at my kitchen table, and having just poured herself another cup of coffee, Carolyn held the spoon in midair and looked around. Examining first the utensils hanging from a pegboard, then the bulletin board with pictures and announcements, she surveyed every item. Slowly she said, "It's hard to know what was lost. But here I am sitting down in a kitchen, and thinking about sitting in a kitchen with a real family . . . and talking. That's something I didn't have."

In order to re-create a sense of what her family could have been, Carolyn tried to research her background. That was the only way she could imagine ever understanding herself as an adult. Such a task was not easy, though she thought it was necessary before she could adjust to her mother's institutionalization. She asked aunts and uncles about her life as a child, about the incidents that helped them recognize her mother's illness. She asked for descriptions of places and events, telling them what she remembered and asking them to fill in the details. But they had no answers for her. She asked her brother, Marvin. He did not want to discuss it. So she began to question her mother. Marvin was furious. He did not have the same need to understand the past and did not want to know. Carolyn, by contrast, was not satisfied with just thinking about the pieces that were missing from her background—about the specific circumstances surrounding her mother's sickness, where her father was when she was a child, or how they lived before she can remember. "I don't want to think them; I want to know. But my brother says, 'What good would knowing do? What good? Let it lie.' "

Carolyn felt frustrated because she never got answers to her questions. Then an accidental event cleared some of the haze that clouded her quest. Carolyn needed her birth certificate. She wrote for it, not expecting it to become a magic key. "I opened the letter, and I'll never forget it," she recalled. "It said: 'Mother, 29; housewife. Father, painter.' " Carolyn was overwhelmed. "I thought, 'Gee, I really did have parents.' I knew then that I was really born of people. They were my parents, and I had this incredible feeling of warmth come all over my body because I had touched something that went back to my roots. I'll never forget that feeling. Just from looking at that piece of paper." What did this give Carolyn? "It allowed me not to have those terrible feelings. I knew that I came from somewhere," she said.

Carolyn had come from somewhere—from a large family in which Harold, though not the oldest, was certainly the leader. He began his role of helping Selma and her children when he was a young man in his twenties. Harold was always closer to Selma than his older brother or his sister, who was married by the time Selma's problems began. Yet Harold's wife, Eileen, does not think this basic closeness was sufficient reason for the major family responsibility to fall on him. They disagree about this today as they did when they were first married more than thirty years ago. "Harold always felt that there was nobody else around," Eileen said, "and basically it would be wrong not to step in and help as much as he did." Eileen, however, thought that some of the visiting should have been shared and that others should have taken some initiative once in a while. Whenever something was wrong, Harold should not have been the only person to whom everybody looked to solve the problem, according to his wife. Harold's involvement and role started early in Selma's illness. The others did not volunteer help, and Harold offered to share an apartment with his sister while she recuperated from the hospital ordeal. He knew how stressful the demands of two growing children and a mother in the same house were for Selma. So, while his mother took care of the young children, he kept a watchful eye on his sister for the several months between his army discharge and his wedding.

That was when Eileen thinks Harold's other sister should first have extended herself and with greater charity. Speaking to

Harold, she said, "Your sister felt that she would have been ruining her life. Instead, she wanted to celebrate her life with her husband, and Selma was always in the way." She never mentioned Selma to her friends or acknowledged that family obligations included a sick sister. Harold and Eileen recognized she would do little. "She isn't going to do anything," Harold told Eileen at the time. He was correct.

Despite Eileen's irritation with her older brother-in-law and sister-in-law for not helping share the family burden, she has had no regrets about the decision they made shortly after their honeymoon. Selma's son would live with them. "I came from a very close family where we all helped one another," Eileen said. "There was even a cousins' club to help us all go to college. So I thought that this was the role of a family." Eileen had no doubt or second thoughts whatsoever about opening their home to Marvin. When the social worker came to visit, "I was only twenty-four years old," Eileen said. "The social worker thought it was a big responsibility." With a laugh at the thought of how naïve she must have appeared, Eileen recalled how she argued with the social worker, telling her that young Marvin would be reared by them. The social worker tried to dissuade Eileen and suggested that others might be able to give him a better home. "I don't know what you are talking about," Eileen replied, and asked the social worker, "After all, how could the state, or strangers, be more concerned about this kid than I will be?" In Eileen's mind the case was closed. In fact, it had never been an issue.

Harold and Eileen reared their nephew over the next decade. They added two children to their family. Life was hectic. Though they tried to bring up Marvin as well as they could and provide him with a stable home and a sense of belonging, Harold recognized that probably unforeseen damage was done to him. It was inherent in the situation. "We weren't his parents, and we were bringing up somebody who was almost our age. It was very difficult. And in the meanwhile, we were having our own problems." Harold was working on a newspaper during the day to earn a salary to support his family, and he was attending school at night to finish his education.

Harold also visited Selma twice a week—on Wednesdays and Sundays—and on Saturdays he had to work to make up for the day off during the week. He was always on the move, and

Eileen resented the situation. "The leisure time that he had was spent visiting with his sister. That meant that there was never a day for me or the kids," she observed. Eileen would have liked to spend evenings or weekends with Harold, but his schedule didn't permit that. And she wanted some help with the two babies or some time away for herself. But they couldn't afford any. At the time it seemed "like it went on forever." First she was left alone all weekend with a child in the suburbs. Later she had her own baby; then another. She remembers being miserable, feeling lonely and isolated and having very few choices.

The actual constraints on their time together caused only part of the resentment Eileen remembers. She was also jealous that her sister-in-law claimed more of Harold's attention than she did. This led to arguments, and Eileen felt guiltier with each complaint. "I complained all the time," Eileen said. "Harold told me that it was his responsibility and that I knew it when I married him. I should have accepted it." Eileen did not dispute this. But she did not know how to deal with it, and she found it even more difficult when Harold implied that "I was a very privileged person, but his sister was suffering because she was in the hospital."

With the help of hindsight Eileen now understands how she used her sister-in-law against Harold when she was angry with him. "When Harold and I would get into an argument and I would get mad, I couldn't focus on him as the target of my anger. I would tell him not to treat me like his sister. I would say 'your crazy sister.' " Eileen couldn't find a better barb. "It was the meanest thing I could say," she admitted. And she knew how unfair it was, even at the time. But she did not know how else to punish Harold the way she felt she was being punished. Selma became a crutch for the rest of their lives, and whatever difficulty they were having at the moment, "Selma became the symbol around which arguments took place and we arrived at solutions." Not only did Eileen use Selma to goad Harold, but Selma represented what Eileen feared for herself. During those arguments, when anger flared, "it was very scary for me," Eileen said. "I would bring up Selma, or Harold's time with her, in irrelevant situations. I was also frightened by my own anger. I began to think maybe my anger *was* crazy. Maybe it *was* being out of control to be so upset."

Harold and Eileen managed to overcome the tensions that

were related to Selma as well as those they used her to mask. Gradually things improved. Harold finished school and quit his job at the newspaper. He started a business and had more time to devote to Eileen, Marvin, and the girls. His business flourished, and he was able to send Marvin to the college of his choice, as he was able to help Carolyn later. He cut down his visits to Selma to only once a week.

Visiting Selma started as an obligation; later it turned into a ritual. "When I first started to go out there, there was always the expectation that next year would be different. I stopped that expectation some time ago," he said. "I have no idea when that disappeared," he went on, "but I still see her because she continues to enjoy my company." Sometimes Harold took her to a movie, or to a restaurant, or shopping to buy a new dress. But even if he didn't take her out for an afternoon, he visited the hospital religiously. "I make it a point to see her every week," he said. "And every time I go out there I ask myself about all that time, about all the things that have happened to her in thirty years. And I ask myself what I have been doing all that time. I've visited about fifteen hundred times, and when I think about it, I realize that from her point of view it is so little time."

When Harold said that it was easier for him to accept his sister's condition after such a long period, Eileen asked him why. "What does it mean to you?" she wanted to know. "It means that I don't live in the future or in the past," he said. "I do it without all the emotional baggage. It is based on the reality of the situation."

For Harold the "reality of the situation" warranted that he continue visiting Selma even after he realized that she would not be leaving the institution. Other people, even those in the same family, assess the situation differently. Selma's other sister and brother visit only infrequently; Carolyn sees her mother more often than Marvin does. For different reasons each person decided how often, if at all, he or she can visit. For some the idea of going to a hospital is a reminder of a life they hoped would be different. For others there is the need to stay away. The pain is too overwhelming, and little can be accomplished for themselves or for their relative. Still others carry so much anger that the idea of visiting the person who is its source seems futile.

JONAH: FAY AND STANLEY HARRISON'S SON

Jonah Harrison also lives on the psychiatric ward of a state hospital. He has been there since 1972. Like Selma Greene, he did not begin there. When the symptoms first appeared when he was seventeen, his parents traveled a familiar road. First they encouraged him to get help. When he refused to see a doctor, *they* sought advice from Dr. Macinter, a psychiatrist, about how to deal with their youngest son, who had become increasingly withdrawn over the previous year. He was even refusing to speak. It was not the same type of stage their other children had gone through as teenagers, they explained to Dr. Macinter. It was as if a curtain had been lowered and Jonah was staying behind it, watching the world. On his side of the curtain were aromas and sounds his family could not detect; on their side were conversations and love he would not let in.

After hearing Fay and Stanley Harrison describe the isolation and the long months of absence from school, Dr. Macinter prescribed a liquid medicine that Fay mixed into her son's juice each day. The initial results were impressive. Within two or three days this young man, who had not uttered more than three or four words each day for many months, began conversing with his parents and two brothers. Then, after a few more days, the apparent recovery gave way to considerable agitation. Jonah began running wildly through the house, and his muscles went into uncontrollable spasms.

After one week of this agitated state Dr. Macinter concluded that the household efforts to help Jonah could not be monitored and it would be necessary for him to enter a hospital. Jonah refused to do this on his own, and he was forced into an ambulance, sedated for the trip, and, as a minor, committed to a hospital by his parents. That night began what would be the first of many hospitalizations, numbering more than twenty in the next three years. Fay remembered it this way: "He would be admitted, and they would keep him for five or six weeks, and then he would come home." After he was home for a few weeks, he stopped taking the medicine. First there was an effort to cajole him; then began the pleading, and then the anger. "Take it," his mother would scream at him in frustration, reminding him that it was his only way to stay out of the hospital. But Jonah didn't take his medicine. He returned home, started to smoke marijuana, and in a short time he was back in the hospital. For three years life was spent this way, with Jonah being rushed over to a hospital every few months.

Almost from the beginning of Jonah's illness doctors recommended committing him to a permanent facility. "It was during the first hospitalization. He had only been there a little over a month," Fay said, when "they told us that they had done all they could for Jonah, and they gave us the names of two hospitals where he could be committed." This happened in 1969 before the programs and policies which discouraged permanent hospitalization were in place. Fay and Stanley could not accept the idea of institutionalizing their child. "We couldn't accept it at all. It was unthinkable. We thought he would come home and take his medicine and get better. Or whatever would happen would happen. But we certainly were not ready to put him into an institution."

By the time Jonah was of legal age he had been in several different hospitals. One was an elite psychiatric center from which he checked himself out against medical advice. In another he refused to attend the family therapy group meetings. Fay and Stanley and the other parents attended weekly meetings along with their children who were in the hospital. Jonah did not like the mandatory sessions. After he had missed them for two consecutive weeks of the seven-week stay, the hospital told him that he would have to attend or leave. He chose to leave. "All of a sudden we came into one of the meetings, and they said that Jonah was going to be discharged. My husband was furious!" Fay said. This hospital also recommended institutionalizing Jonah. "We couldn't do it. We weren't ready yet. We had to try whatever we could. So we called a vitamin place we had heard of."

That very night they arranged to have him admitted to another hospital in a distant city. After several weeks of treatment with different vitamins, electric shock was recommended. Jonah refused to have it, and the doctor handling the case felt that no more could be done for him. Jonah was discharged, and his mother remembers that he "was in pretty good shape when he got home—pretty good for him. But he refused to take the vitamins when he came home. He was out of the hospital for two and a half months, which was pretty good for him.

That was the longest period of time in the entire three years."

Fay and Stanley had followed every lead they found about new therapies and different drugs. Yet Jonah's short treatments did nothing more than calm him temporarily, and because he would not continue with the medication or stay under psychiatric care once he was discharged, it was only a matter of weeks until his agitation forced another admission. After Jonah had been in and out of different hospitals for almost three years, he was still no better than after his discharge from the first hospital. Upon being discharged from another hospital, he broke into a neighbor's house and stole something. When Fay and Stanley discovered it the next day, they realized that their son might end up in jail with this kind of behavior. They were terrified, but no more so than when doctors had recommended committing him to a psychiatric institution for life. "We thought about it. We thought that it was better for him to be in a hospital—even the ones they recommended—than it is to be in jail. That helped us understand that he *might* have to be committed. And that is a terrible thing," Fay said. But they were still one short hospitalization away from committing him.

After another six weeks in the hospital Jonah signed himself out. This time, while he was home, he became violent. He was arguing with his father, and for the first time his parents saw a terrifying side of their son's mental illness. It was more than his typical agitation, running in and out of the house; it was not just his verbal abusiveness or the disquieting voices that he heard. This time Jonah tried to kill Stanley, and he and his wife were scared! They decided that he had to be committed.

Fay and Stanley had to go through a court hearing to commit Jonah. It was then that they realized how little hope the doctors held for him. Maybe they should have known since the first hospitalization, when they were told, "We have done all that we can," but somehow it seemed too soon to give up on their son. At the hearing, in 1972, it was made clear to them by the psychiatric testimony that there was no hope, that the family meetings did not make any sense, that the prognosis for Jonah was eventual suicide. It was not until then that it was all spelled out for them and, as Fay said, that they "realized how serious it was."

Jonah was admitted to a state facility about forty-five minutes away from the Harrison home. Fay and Stanley visited their son each week, hoping that even minor changes would signal progress. They saw none, but they continued to visit, to consult with the psychiatrist on Jonah's ward, and to bring him food and money for cigarettes. As they drove home each week, Fay and Stanley compared notes about how their son seemed to each of them. Was he more alert? Less hostile? Did he appear to have more interest in his appearance? They searched for signs of progress; they still hoped that Jonah might be helped to live a different life.

After three years of weekly visits each of them noticed that Jonah was becoming more hostile. He seemed less communicative and in some way out of control. As the Harrisons saw Jonah's mood begin to shift for the worse, they tried to raise the issue with Dr. Ngu, the chief psychiatrist of the ward. On a number of occasions Stanley called to speak with Dr. Ngu. He asked about therapy; he asked about medicine. Yes, Dr. Ngu said, Jonah was getting new medicine. That must be it, Stanley told his wife. The timing seemed to match. The time that they changed Jonah's medicine coincided with his parents' sense of his decline. Would they consider changing the medicine, returning to what he had been taking before? Stanley asked Dr. Ngu. No, they wouldn't, replied the doctor. What about the ward? Stanley suggested. Perhaps he might not be on the right ward. Maybe there was a shift in policy or Jonah's behavior itself warranted a different program now. No, they would not consider changing the ward either, Dr. Ngu replied.

As the weekly visits confirmed their suspicions about Jonah's decline, Stanley called Dr. Ngu more often. He began to press questions about the medicine or the ward with greater urgency. He conveyed his concern and repeated his observations about Jonah's changed behavior. Dr. Ngu was becoming perturbed. Jonah was doing fine, he thought. Jonah was doing as well as could be expected under the circumstances. And he was not manifesting any of the signs of deterioration that Stanley thought. After all, Dr. Ngu was responsible for the entire ward, and it was his business to know about these things. "Couldn't you just consider changing his medicine?" Stanley finally asked, feeling more and more frustrated by reassurances that contradicted his own observations. But Dr. Ngu had begun to feel equally frustrated by this interfering parent. "I think you want Jonah to stay sick," he told Stanley. "Of course, I can discharge him if that's what you want," he added.

Stanley hesitated for barely a minute—just long enough to think of the ugly courtroom experience when he and Fay had committed their son three years before, after Jonah had tried to kill him. But Stanley was also outraged. He responded to the challenge. "Okay. Do that," he said.

Fay and Stanley expected Dr. Ngu to grant Jonah a convalescent leave of absence. That is an administrative procedure which would have allowed them to return him to the hospital if things did not work out without having to seek another commitment order. Dr. Ngu did not do that, though the Harrisons did not know it at the time they picked up their son from the hospital. Three months later, after Jonah hit his mother on the head and they had to abandon hope for their son's existence outside a mental institution, they were back in court for the proceedings to have Jonah returned to the hospital.

When he was readmitted, Fay and Stanley resumed their weekly visits. "I bring him sandwiches and give him seven dollars a week," Fay said. Every once in a while he gets a weekend pass to come home. "If he comes home, we don't visit that week. It takes you a day or two to get over having gone to the hospital and a day or two after he comes home. So maybe you have three days left for yourself out of the week," Fay remarked. And they speak to Jonah during the week. "He calls frequently, and it's traumatic. He's irrational on the phone, and it brings back all those feelings," Fay said. Recently she has been under a physician's treatment for depression, and the doctor recommended that they change their telephone number. "Have an unlisted number," he told Fay. "Move to another house. Then he couldn't reach you." But Fay and Stanley don't feel they are able to do that.

At this point Fay does not expect Jonah ever to be able to leave the hospital. Her expectations for her son have so diminished that "the unthinkable has become thinkable. I wish Jonah were well enough to be wandering around," she said. "I wish he could be able to live in those awful places that people live on the street. Can you imagine," she asked, "that I wish that he could just be out? That you want your son to be well enough to be wandering around with winos? That that is your great ambition for him—to be well enough to be a bum?"

The isolation that mental illness has forced upon Jonah also surrounds his parents. Throughout the first three years when

Jonah was in and out of hospitals, they became estranged from their friends. It started gradually. At first they stopped inviting friends over. "It was too disruptive to them with all that was going on here," Fay said. And then there were periods when they didn't feel comfortable leaving the house. It wasn't fear of what he would do in their absence. Rather, it was a sense that he shouldn't be left alone. When one of the other children came home from school, or if the entire family was home on weekends, Fay or Stanley would go out occasionally. But most of the days were too upsetting for them to be able to enjoy the evenings. After a while it simply became too difficult to explain to people what was happening. Sometimes it was the scorn they sensed in their friends and acquaintances, whose judgmental frowns were hurtful. Other times it was the awkward silences. "I think when people find out that you have a mentally ill person in your family, they can't deal with that," Fay said. "It's too hard. They don't know what to say. They don't know what to do. And on top of that, most people think you are a pretty rotten person to have a son who is mentally ill." Glances and innuendo conveyed the impression to Fay and Stanley that they "must have done something terrible." But Fay said she had difficulty explaining to people "that I didn't have that feeling. I could not accept that. But when you told people about Jonah or that I didn't feel guilty, there was a drawing back on their part."

Fay says they no longer heap self-pity on themselves the way they used to. They have adjusted to a quiet life in which they find companionship with each other and their other three sons. "We have completely withdrawn," Fay noted. "We go to the theater and to the movies, but we go alone. We have become kind of reclusive. But it's all right. We are living. And we don't feel sorry for ourselves any more."

MORRIS: REBECCA KANE'S FATHER

Rebecca Kane does not remember feeling sorry for herself when her father was in a Veterans Administration hospital. She was too young, and if anything, she was confused. She didn't know why he was there, what was wrong with him, why he couldn't come home. But most of all, Rebecca didn't know what to tell her classmates who inquired about him and what to say to people who asked, "Where is your father?" in the 1950s, when she was a young child. "It wasn't that I was embarrassed that he was in a mental hospital," she said. "It's just that it felt so odd to say there was something wrong with him but nobody knew what." So there were times that she told people that he was dead—he had died in World War II in some exotic place. Other times she told people that her parents were divorced, her father lived in a different state, and that was why he didn't visit. She said whatever she could think of at the time, and the inconsistent stories reflected her own lack of clarity.

Morris Kane was hospitalized shortly after World War II. Like thousands of other soldiers returning from battle, he suffered problems that were war-related. Some veterans needed only rest to recuperate from the traumas they had sustained, but Morris's problem was deeper, and it was one that did not correct itself.

When he entered the VA hospital of his own volition, neither he nor his wife, Claire, realized that he would be there for the next five years. And it would have been considerably longer had Claire not happened to read a magazine article discussing the experimental use of Lithium in the fifties. Though the article stressed that Lithium was still in the early stage of experimentation and dispensed in only a few hospitals, Claire took the article to Morris's doctors at the Veterans Administration. She wanted them to try the drug on her husband. Initially they refused, suggesting that she wait until the testing period was over. Then concrete results would be in and they would proceed. But Claire did not accept that. She was dispirited that in the time Morris had been under treatment for what they called reactive depression so little had seemed to help. He had made no progress, and she insisted that they reconsider.

Persistence was Claire's greatest weapon, and finally, the doctors at the Veterans Administration agreed that this new drug, about which they all had heard so much, might help Morris. They agreed to administer it to him and to see if indeed it was as good as reported. Apparently it was; at least it worked for Morris. Within a short time after he was placed on Lithium, plans were being made for his discharge from the hospital and his family was preparing for his return.

Morris's admission to the hospital had been well planned. The increasing difficulty he had functioning as a graduate student attending an eastern college on the GI bill was apparent for quite a while. When he and Claire realized that he might have to be in the hospital for an indefinite length of time, they decided to move to the West, where she would be near her parents, who had settled there recently. It was a fortunate move, for soon other members of the family joined the nationwide caravan toward the Sun Belt, and eventually both sets of Rebecca's grandparents lived nearby.

For the first three years of Morris's hospitalization Rebecca did not see her father. "Children under ten were not allowed in the hospital, but they could visit on the grounds," she said. "But he wasn't well enough for me to see him then." So Rebecca stayed with one set of grandparents on the weekends when Claire visited Morris. When she returned home, she told her daughter that Morris still didn't feel well enough to come home to live with them but that the doctors were trying to help him. "When she went to see him, she came back and said that they talked about me," Rebecca said. "And my mother would bring gifts and other things back from him to me. After a while she brought things that he made in the shop."

Despite the help that Morris's family offered Claire by taking care of Rebecca on occasional weekends or baby-sitting at different times, they were not supportive emotionally. They began telling Claire and Rebecca stories of how Morris was always different from the rest of the family. "He was radical whereas they were middle-class; he was not oriented to material values whereas they placed a premium on earning money," said his daughter. "They always viewed him as the impractical dreamer, and they admired him, at the same time, because he was the intellectual." But they also thought that Claire was simply wasting her time by waiting for this man who was in an institution. "My grandmother [Morris's mother] apparently told my mother that they should get a divorce. She thought it was ridiculous for her to be chained to this guy who was in a mental institution." Rebecca thought this reflected her grandparents' feeling about the entire situation. "I think there was a lot of shame about it on my father's side of the family," she said. Her mother's side of the family was no more helpful. "They never wanted her to marry my father to begin with, and when he got sick, they said it was what she deserved." Rebecca remembered her grandmother saying nasty things to her mother, and then to her, about Morris. "That made me feel bad. And it put my mother in a terrible bind," she said.

Claire resented the intrusions and the suggestions that she divorce her husband. She had no intention of leaving Morris, and whatever pain her family inflicted through the years of his hospitalization, her friends were just the opposite. "A lot of my mother's friends admired her for her behavior. Not that she was like a saint, but they thought it was incredible to live with all the uncertainty, to raise a kid, to visit on weekends, and to have such a demanding job, too," Rebecca said.

After the Lithium showed signs of working and before his final discharge, Morris was transferred to a hospital closer to where his wife and daughter lived. Rebecca was allowed to visit him, and he was given passes to come home on weekends.

Rebecca's fantasies of what life would be like when her father returned grew with the years. As a child she remembers repeating the phrase "Star light, star bright, first star I see tonight . . ." At the end of the jingle she wished for her father's return. "It was a ritualistic thing," she said. "I'm sure at some level I didn't want him to come home. I didn't know what that would be like. But my wish was like magic . . . when he came home, everything would be all right." When he came home, however, she remembered disappointment. "Everything was difficult rather than good. Nothing was perfect as it should have been; in fact, everything was much worse. All the new things were hard and there were fights." At that point, Rebecca confessed, "I started wishing for a piano."

Morris's discharge from the hospital ended the family's wait. Though Claire and Rebecca never expected him to be gone so long, neither did they anticipate the readjustment which would be required when he returned. That meant both of them had to learn to live within confines determined by Morris's illness and hospitalization.

We shall have to accept certain limitations
In future, and abandon some humane dreams; only hard-
    minded, sleepless and realist, can ride this rock-slide
To new fields down the dark mountain; and we shall have to
    perceive that these insanities are normal.

Robinson Jeffers—"May–June, 1940"

PART
IV

THE
CHRONIC CYCLE

9

Families Adjust

Families of the mentally ill are forced to develop new ways of communicating with one another, devise different plans for managing household needs, and learn strategies for dealing with crises. These are adjustments which any illness imposes, but they are particularly necessary to those who must cope with the erratic disruptions or chronic dependence of a mentally ill relative. The interruptions at work because a relative needs immediate attention, the canceled social outing caused by a problem at the last minute, or the extensive planning in order to be away for a period of time forces families to negotiate in ways they never imagined would be necessary.

The specific changes families make in their daily lives to anticipate the needs of a dependent relative have an emotional component. Anger or rage, helplessness or frustration, guilt or remorse are likely to well up at different stages of seeking help and trying to fathom the unknown. Weariness or sadness appear in the course of consultation with health professionals, interaction with social service agencies, or simple conversation with friends or other members of the family. Desperation engulfs us as we wonder how many times it is possible to go through the same traumatic events. Other times it is a painful sense of loss—for our relative and for ourselves—that we experience when we realize that the potential for our brother or daughter, our mother or husband, will not be realized or will take a very different form.

CHILDREN

The response to the new situation depends to some degree on how people are related and where they are in their own life cycles. Children who were youngsters like Rebecca Kane or Carolyn Greene, for example, confronted different problems than did Maggie Connelly and her sisters, who were older and less dependent on their parents. For the young child, confusion can result from physical and emotional absence, immature intellectual understanding, or being forced to rely on the remaining parent or other adults. When that child matures, different questions become prominent, as they do for children who are already adults. One concern which almost all children I spoke with mentioned was that of having inherited a similar predisposition.

Rebecca Kane   "There is this issue in my life," Rebecca Kane said, "that is: To what extent am I like my father? Through my childhood everybody said that I looked like him. And I hated that." When Morris was still at the Veterans Administration hospital, Rebecca resented people's comparing her to her father because he was away. "I wanted to be like my mother. She was on the scene." But once Morris came home, Rebecca could not deny some of the similarities others had observed and called to her attention. And the characteristics they shared were not only physical. Both of them displayed certain intellectual concerns, like grappling with ideas and having a penchant for digging to the root of a problem. There was a similar enthusiasm—a love of life and joy in its expression—and there was a similar empathy with the people around them.

198

It was not only the positive qualities she shared with Morris that Rebecca tried to disown but the quixotic parts of her personality, which struck fear that she too would get sick and become like him. "At some point, when I was in high school, I was snooping and read some of the insurance papers. There were applications to the VA for insurance benefits, and they described his symptoms in terms of anxiety and depression. Later, when I was about to go to college and had my own problems, I had the same kinds of symptoms."

By the time Rebecca was ready for college Morris was functioning fairly well. He had completed his education and, with a newly minted Ph.D., found an excellent job. He resumed contact with his friends, made lots of new ones, and carried on a life which did not betray his five years in a mental institution. Yet the experience of those years at the VA hospital hung over him and the entire family. "My father's attitude was that it had been such a terrible experience that we should not discuss it," Rebecca remembered. That meant he did not want his daughter to consult a psychiatrist if it would require bringing it up. Rebecca said that her father wanted "to turn over a new leaf. It was as if it hadn't happened. Ignore it . . . let's not talk to anybody."

Rebecca eventually did speak with a psychiatrist. She went off to college and later to medical school, and now she is a successful psychiatrist helping families the way she hoped someone would have helped hers. That is one of the issues about which Rebecca still has "a great deal of bitterness—that nothing was done to help us anticipate or deal with the readjustment." She has come to terms with the unpleasant scenes that occurred after her father's return when her parents would argue and she would urge her mother to divorce him. She understands how she inadvertently and deliberately made her father jealous of the special relationship that she and her mother had developed in his absence. She has become reconciled to her mother's commitment to a man whose wonderful qualities she heard about but did not see in the same way. But she has not forgotten that nothing was done to help her or her mother understand what kinds of adjustments would be necessary when Morris returned and that the transition might be rough. According to Rebecca, "it's almost at that point that his treatment should have begun. Rather, it was ended. If we had had some help then, things might have gone more smoothly."

Because Morris Kane died when Rebecca was finishing college, much of her understanding of the impact of his illness had to take place after his death. Maggie Connelly, however, wrestles constantly, trying to understand and deal with the impact of Ruth's illness on the family. She feels that she is succeeding in her efforts, but the process has been slow and at times painful.

Maggie Connelly Of the three Connelly daughters, Maggie missed the presence of her mother the most. By the time Ruth's condition was becoming apparent, she had already stopped "mothering" Maggie. It was hard for Maggie to deal with the void and the anger it caused. "I feel cheated a lot," she said. "I remember in some conversation with my sisters I said that I wanted my mother." They told her that she couldn't have her back again—not the way Maggie wanted. Maggie was hurt and angry at this. "They were older. I remember pointing it out to them," Maggie said. Their being older before Ruth got sick had allowed them to enjoy their mother in the way that Maggie felt she had missed. Yet Maggie's sisters were surprised at her outburst. "Look at yourself," one of them said. But she screamed back, "I feel like having a tantrum. I want to be mothered. Mom didn't do it. Nobody did it. I still need a mother." Maggie did not want to let go of the hope that her mother would re-emerge from years of treatment and hospitalization to make amends for the time lost. "It was a harsh reality for me to realize that she wasn't going to get better. She wasn't going to volunteer to fix a dress. That wasn't going to happen."

Maggie thinks this incident was a turning point in her relationship to her sisters and her expectations of her mother. "My sisters have become very maternal toward me in some ways. They heard my plea and stepped in," she said. Recently one sister gave Maggie a check to help furnish a new apartment. It is the kind of gesture she knows her mother would have made if she had been well. Another sister helped in a different way. When Maggie was still in college, feeling very trapped between her mother's demands and her own desires, this sister taught her that "it was okay to say no. You might suffer under the burden of saying no," she was warned, but Maggie had to learn to do it and to break out of the pattern in which she felt trapped. "They were very protective of me, and I was treated like the youngest in a very nice way," she said. "They also told my mother that it was my chance for college and that she had to back off."

Maggie says her sisters offered the encouragement she needed to draw the necessary boundaries without feeling that she was abandoning her mother. But she also felt guilty. "I began to realize that I was always saying no to her. So one of my sisters asked me to think about when I could say yes. I realized that I could write to her. So I would write letters on a regular basis. That way I felt that I wasn't always negative. That was important for me." Gradually they all learned when they had to say no and when they could say yes. It took a while, but in the process they drew even closer together and learned about one another's strong points. "One of my sisters can do certain things with her, but other things are really hard. So my sister told us and asked if someone else could pick up there. We discovered that one of us can usually do something that the other can't."

The teamwork Maggie and her sisters have developed has been fortunate. "Our family is very close," she said. "I think we are more interested in each other's lives as a result of my mother's illness. And now it has gotten to the place where Mom isn't the focal point of every conversation. Now it is each other." An urgency about Ruth's needs or behavior no longer sends any one of them into a tailspin. Rarely do they call one another, or their father, simply to unload the emotional burden. Instead, they consult about specific problems. Did Ruth have the blood test that registers the amount of Lithium in her system? Who is responsible for taking her to the outpatient clinic that week? When she leaves town to visit one of her daughters, who confirms the travel plans and who follows up to guarantee that the others know she is not in danger? Matters of routine like these occupy Maggie and her sisters because they always expect something to unravel along the way, and they have learned that they must deal with the situation rather than have Ruth conform to a rule.

The events of the previous decade have altered the way each of the Connellys thinks of herself or himself. "I know that I am going to survive—that we are all survivors," Maggie said. "There aren't a lot of bigger things that I can think of to have to deal with. I know that no matter how bad something feels at the time, I will get on with it." The renewed confidence in her ability to cope with other problems in life because she has managed to absorb the impact of her mother's illness sometimes seems strange to her. "I think it is perverse sometimes, but I feel good because of some source of pride in the way I have come through this. I think it's part of that affirmation of our abilities to survive."

Maggie also notes that the quality of the time she spends with her mother has changed. Since they live in different cities, a month or more can pass before they see each other. Each time they visit, Maggie is mindful of the changes she sees. "I didn't realize that mentally ill people can look so blank much of the time." For the daughter who began our interview by discussing the emotional vitality her mother displayed and the striking physical beauty which delighted everybody, it was difficult to accept having her mother sometimes look like a vagabond. And Ruth also shakes and trembles as a side effect of the medicine. "It kills me to see her drink a cup of coffee or eat a doughnut," Maggie said. "Everything goes all over. . . . It just kills me. And yet I know that I'm going to just have to sit here and shut up. I have to let her eat the doughnut and not hassle it the way I used to."

Ruth's poor physical coordination is apparent even to those who do not know her. One of the things that continues to upset Maggie is that people are impatient with or rude to her mother because of it. She remembers an incident when she took her mother shopping and the salesperson behaved badly. Seeing this person treat her mother with disrespect was upsetting. It also made Maggie realize how intolerant people become when a situation is somewhat different from what is expected. The incident in the department store made Maggie realize that "we are all going to have to slow down a bit. If she is shopping, for example, she is going to take a real long time trying on that dress. *We* are going to have to cool it."

Though Maggie has become more tolerant of her mother and more aware of how Ruth's illness affects her, it has not diminished the considerable pain inherent in the situation. For a while she thought that she would always be unhappy "and maybe crazy. That was a terrifying thought to me . . . that things would never change and that they would only get worse. I used to be frightened that I would become crazy like she was. But I know that I'm not. I just know that I never will be the same. I accept that, but it's been recent," Maggie said. "And I don't hate her any more. It's funny.

It's like someone who has died. I'll never recognize her again the way I remember her. And she doesn't really act like my mother. I guess the worst part is that I miss her terribly. I miss her a lot. But I will never know her again—not in the old way. And that is the hardest feeling I have to deal with."

The presence of her father, Art, has been enormously important. Art's continued devotion to Ruth comforts Maggie. He sees his wife frequently, he finances the apartment she has in another city, and while he refuses to live with her again, "my father is incredibly devoted to my mother," Maggie said. This commitment to his wife and his involvement in each of his three daughters' lives strengthen the family and give it a foundation.

Carolyn Greene Carolyn Greene wishes that she had had that kind of support, or loving concern, in her life. Cared for first by her aging grandmother and then by an aunt and uncle who didn't really want her, Carolyn did not have the same emotional backing with which to cope with her mother's illness. And while each of the Connelly daughters remained actively committed to their mother throughout her illness, Carolyn knows only one person who cared—her uncle Harold. The aunt with whom she lived never visited her mother, and another uncle suggested that Selma's pregnancy with Carolyn was one of the reasons for her problems. "Your mother was like a violin," Selma's brother told Carolyn, "and the strings were strung too tight. If she had never had you, she would never have been what she was."

The void she senses when thinking about "family" is powerful for Carolyn. Growing up in the 1950s, when the media's image of family painted domestic perfection, Carolyn has always longed for the stereotype *Ozzie and Harriet* portrayed. But Carolyn is not sure that she grieves for the loss of family because she is not certain that she ever had one. "I lost a promise," she said. "What was lost was an attachment that I couldn't even make."

Carolyn feels that the mystery surrounding her mother's illness while she was still a child has caused her to mistrust others. "Some people say you shouldn't let children see painful things. But I always wanted to know," she said. "Somehow it might have been better. It would have still been painful. But it was very painful not to know." Carolyn finds herself somewhat shy of other people and reticent to enter relationships that might disappoint her. Years of psychotherapy have helped sharpen an understanding of herself, and she concludes that one serious impact of her mother's mental illness has been to keep her from fully relating to others.

Fearing closeness leads Carolyn to live a life "I wouldn't have wanted to have." The fear, sometimes the belief that "I will become crazy too," is so strong that Carolyn hesitates to have a family of her own. "I have always wanted a family," she continued, "but I also thought I was going to be crazy and have crazy kids." So despite her professional success and her promising future, Carolyn does not feel she has yet made a life for herself. She is persuaded that she first has to find a framework for the past that will subdue the pain with which she lives. In this respect she compares herself with her brother, Marvin. "My brother is very different from me. He has already made something of his life. Sure, my mother's situation got to him, but he said, 'Well, it happened. I'm going to shut the door on my feelings.' I can't do that," Carolyn said. "I need to know."

BROTHERS AND SISTERS

It is not only children who wonder whether mental illness will strike them as it did their parent. Brothers and sisters with a mentally disabled sibling ask this question, too. Just like sons and daughters, they are apprehensive about the still unknown elements attributed to heredity. And they think about the similarities in their upbringing—after all, they were reared by the same parents in the same household. So not only do they have genetic similarities, but they also shared an environment.

Janet Goldstein After Natalie Goldstein's break her sister Janet thought, "I'm next." Janet's response drove her to the library, where she spent her lunch hours and weekends reading everything she could find. She started with the prominent psychiatrists and psychoanalysts whose work is well known to lay people. Then she traced out references in the notes of books and articles. "I was living in the library," she said, "just reading all about madness." She remembers becoming knowledgeable as she plowed through reams of reading matter, noting controversies among the specialists, identifying places of disagreement, seeing how little was known about some things and how much about others. "I got into the debate about heredity and environment, about nature versus nurture," Janet said. "And I couldn't help but realize that we were born of the same parents, we grew up in the same house. So was I destined to go cuckoo like Natalie?" she asked herself.

But identifying with her sister's past and empathizing with her present plight, Janet became an ombudswoman on Natalie's behalf. She is the one who picked her up when the police called to say that she had been taken to a hospital for observation. She is the one who brought her home from the hospital to share an apartment while Natalie "got herself together." She is the one who found a typing job for Natalie and ended up doing the work herself when she returned home from her own job. And she is the one who fought her parents' intent to have Natalie placed in an institution. Janet thought they should try every alternative form of treatment before giving up on her. Her parents, on the other hand, were terrified by behavior that was so out of control. For them, the dancing on tabletops in a local diner or the impersonations of Judy Garland were more than they could bear. They could not tolerate the phone calls from Natalie after she was hospitalized, those from Janet to lobby on her sister's behalf, and those from doctors needing information or consent. And they did not think Natalie would change. After two hospitalizations they were convinced she would not be restored and saw no reason to endure further upset waiting for the inevitable step.

Janet's conflict with her parents over what to do with Natalie has forced an estrangement between them. "I really can't forgive them," Janet said. "Not for the way they raised us and not for the things they did." She cannot forgive her parents for wanting to commit Natalie so early. "They wanted to lock her up. That was all they were willing to try." Whatever else they may have done as parents who err or succeed, Janet's idea of their responsibility to her and her sister clashed with their own.

Whether or not the estrangement between Janet and her parents was inevitable remains unclear. The two generations are as different as their upbringings—the parents wounded survivors of the Holocaust, the children knowing nothing of the terror-filled existence of a concentration camp. Janet sees her future as full of unlimited choice, and she is daring and willing to take a chance. Her parents, by contrast, are cautious and circumspect, within the home as well as outside. Could they have sustained an uneasy alliance under any circumstance? It's difficult to tell, but it is certain that when Janet's father assumed conservatorship of Natalie and had her committed to a state mental hospital, Janet not only was despondent but considered it an unpardonable sin.

Why did Janet become so engaged in her sister's plight? Very often children spare themselves major involvement when there are parents on whom the burden falls more naturally. Dora and Thomas Young's children expect to assume their responsibility *after* their parents are gone. Maggie Connelly and her sisters looked to their father when it came to making decisions about treatment for Ruth. And even Harold Greene, who remained involved in Selma's treatment for more than thirty years, deferred to his mother until she died. Janet, however, did not bow to her parents' wishes. "What I did was totally out of a sense that I know what she lived through," she said. "I was there. And Natalie had a terrible life. She never had a chance. I know because I had the same stuff. The same parents . . . I came from the same background."

Linda Bloomberg It is more than a shared background—though that is part of it—which keeps Linda Bloomberg tied to Mark. Because their parents have died, Linda is the only person who is available to Mark. Though a large network of aunts, uncles, and cousins exists, Mark has alienated most of them over the years. The few who remain sympathetic do not seek him out. When he calls on them, mostly during a crisis, they stand by him. But his belligerence when he stops taking his medicine, his unkempt appearance and bodily filth, and the arrogance of his requests do not serve him well with people who would like to help. Also, by the time he seeks these people out he often makes no sense as he speaks of extraterrestrial experiences. Rather than seeing this behavior as a manifestation of his sickness, the few aunts and uncles who are still available are hurt and confused when he appears two or three times a year. He tells them what he expects from them, how they have disappointed him, and why they are rotten people.

Linda is responsible for Mark because there is nobody else. Like many of the chronically mentally ill, he has no friends and no social network. His life exists almost entirely in a vacuum as he wanders from place to place and enters different hospitals. "After the first few hospitalizations I expected him to bounce back —as if he had had an appendix removed. Nobody warned me that this might go on indefinitely," she said. "I was impatient when he didn't get himself reoriented within a month or two." And she often got angry when he acted irresponsibly. "He would call and say that he lost something, maybe his wallet or his watch. I would be furious, yelling at him and telling him that this had happened before. I couldn't understand why he wasn't more careful or why he didn't take better care of himself. It was an awakening to realize that Mark's illness was going to be lifelong," she said. "I don't know when it hit me." Once Linda realized that this was the way Mark was going to be, that he might never change, she was sad. She then understood that he needed support and compassion, not punishment and discipline. She stopped screaming at him and tried to work with him.

After Linda "turned the corner by realizing that no single incident was going to change him," the urgency of a particular happening diminished. She stopped thinking about each episode as a crisis and how she could help him get out of it. "It was naïve," she says, "but in the beginning I kept thinking that without this particular disappointment or that catastrophe, things would improve. Now I realize that it was based on pure hope. So I had to stop seeing every event as a crisis and start thinking of it as a pattern.

"I should make it clear," Linda added, "that there are still times when he is so stubborn that I do get mad at him. But it is the situation I find aggravating, not just his existence." Mark is in three or four hospitals a year, for a couple of weeks at a time. When he is discharged, he feels good because he is still medicated. But fairly soon he stops going to the outpatient psychiatrist, and he begins speaking of ghosts or having wild ideas again. When he calls Linda during those moments, she tries "to convince him that he must return to the doctor for his medicine. When he gives me all the reasons why he doesn't have to, then I get mad," she said. "Mark needs his medicine, but he still doesn't believe it."

Living in another part of the country is both easier and more difficult for Linda. "It is more difficult," she said, "because Mark requires a lot of follow-up. He is not reliable about checking in with his social worker or going to the doctor. When his Supplemental Security Insurance expired, he went to the state office from which the checks are mailed, rather than to his social worker, to find out what the difficulty was. And he can have more than one social worker a year." It all depends on what hospital he is taken to and in what particular catchment area. Because of the bureaucratic snags, Linda is frustrated. She spends many hours on the phone, with Mark as well as with officials, trying to pave the way for her brother. But she is not always successful, and she knows that when two or three months elapse between his calls, he is in a hospital, as he usually confirms the next time they speak.

"The easier part of his being so far away," Linda conceded, "is that I don't have that much contact with him, because every time I speak to him I feel bad." So when Mark doesn't call for long periods of time, Linda feels a sense of relief. It's almost as if the burden didn't exist simply because it is not being felt at the moment. "The time between phone calls allows me to forget."

The last time Mark called Linda was two days before we spoke. He was in another hospital, calling from a pay phone and speaking of devils. If this call had come even two years earlier, Linda would have been beside herself. This time she tried to figure out what was in Mark's best interest. She decided that she should call the doctor to report Mark's medical history. "I spoke to the person who answered the phone. I told them what medicines had worked to stabilize him in the past. I told them that he tends to wander and that I thought he preferred to live in a nearby city. I asked them to make sure the social worker knew that his Supplemental Security Insurance had expired, and I told them that he needs halfway-house living. He cannot cope with the stress of looking for a place to live. He needs a cushion of security. That's how he stayed out of the hospital for eight months at one time," she finished.

The knowledge that Mark will not recover is upsetting. And knowing that there is little she can do materially to change his life disappoints her. "My family always stuck together. They sort of had this code about being loyal to each other and helping one another. But there is nothing I can really do to help him. That hurts. It makes me feel useless. Sometimes I send him a little money," she said, "but that's not what I mean. I mean *real* help, which would allow him to live with some satisfaction and happiness. I wish that he had a life which gave him pleasure, and pleasure to others, too."

Thinking about what will happen to her brother in the future, Linda realized that she needed to include him in her will. "I have to guarantee that if anything happens to me, he is not just cut off and set loose. It was very difficult for me to do this," she said. Linda knows that someone in the family will always give him $5 or $10 in an emergency, but she did not want to rely on that. "It is important for me to know," she said, "that he will not be abandoned, that he will not just starve or have no place to turn if I am not here. It has little to do with passing on my wealth. I don't have that much. It's more a statement to myself that I am responsible for him and to him," she said. Because life expectancy for white males with chronic schizophrenia is lower than for healthy white females, it is unlikely that the trustees will ever be called upon to administer the will for Mark. But if they should, there is an amount set aside for him to be given each month by a trusted cousin.

PARENTS

Grace and Jim Anthony Because she has responsibility for Mark, Linda's situation is similar to that of parents who worry about what will happen to their children after they are gone. In normal situations siblings don't think about it, and parents automatically assume that their children will outlive them. But when a child is mentally ill, what is a normal sequence of events assumes a certain urgency. Dora and Thomas Young, for example, have begun to anticipate the kinds of problems that might arise for James after they are gone. And Stella and Lloyd Stanwick are concerned about Christopher's well-being when they are no longer able to shelter him.

In addition to concern about how their children will be taken care of after they are gone, other issues are significant for parents. As they constantly readjust their expectations, parents may be forced to reassess what it means to be "good" parents. Some, like Grace and Jim Anthony, even find that they have to initiate the separation which children otherwise begin. Grace thinks parents are always in the process of separating from their children. While children are physically and emotionally dependent on adults, parents have invested their kids with equally binding dreams and hopes. Some would not be fulfilled under any circumstance. Others become areas of conflict. But some of the dreams die harder than others, and Grace thinks that part of their struggle was remembering so clearly what they had hoped for Roger. "For parents, even before you separate," she said, "what you have to do is look at what your dreams were. Part of the process of working this out was really letting go of them. It's not having *no* dreams, but at least accepting the fact that you couldn't have any clear-cut dreams. Dreams stand in the way of accepting the moment."

Grace's awareness of the process started with pain. "The suffering of a sick person is your own suffering, too," she said. "It's your inability to do anything to really help. . . . It's terrible. You come to a decision that there's only so much you can do. It's not you; it's not your life. . . . It's him, and it's his life. And suffering through it all isn't going to help." Still, Grace and Jim have not abandoned expectations for Roger. But they view his life in more general terms than they did before he became ill. They accept that he can accomplish only part of what they hoped for him. And they rarely recommend anything that designs his future on their terms. "We hope that he grows up and has a good future. But it's so different. It's all in very general terms," Grace noted. Not knowing whether the psychotic episodes of the previous few years will cease, she said, "We live from day to day. When there is a stretch of ten good days, it's hard to imagine how bad it was before. But you have to shed dreams, and expectations, too. . . ." Shedding dreams and hopes, however, does not mean giving up, to Grace. "It means readjusting to the undreamed-of realities."

It was not only dreams and expectations to which Grace and Jim had to readjust. As with most families, there was a larger group of grandparents, aunts, uncles, and cousins each of whom responded to Roger's illness in his or her own way. For a long time, Grace recalled, the larger family's response was troubling. Jim's family was tentative, and there was a perceptible unease when they spoke on the phone. While the family inquired about Grace and Karee, they rarely asked about Roger. Grace was hurt by this. When she became aware of the pattern, Grace decided that she had to mention it. "We talked about it one day. They didn't know how to ask about Roger, and they didn't know how to bring it up," Grace recalled. "I told them that it hurt me but said I wasn't going to push it on them." In the end Grace felt good about raising the issue. Not only did it clear the air, but it provided guidance in an awkward situation. "It took our helping them to see. I think the family has to help others know how to talk about it."

On another occasion Grace also confronted her sister. When their parents called long distance, Grace's sister never answered questions about how Roger was doing. Instead, she phoned Grace to relay the message that their parents had inquired. Finally, Grace told her sister that anybody who had been at a family picnic the previous weekend could comment. "I think you can tell our parents how he seemed to you," she said. "I don't think that it's only our job." Grace had to teach her and Jim's family that it was okay to get involved. She was not giving them license to interfere, but she was helping them overcome the awkwardness they did not know how to address.

Grace and Jim are aware that what they endured can fracture a family. "The sick person keeps you off balance. It's the unpredictability of behavior, never knowing what to expect," Grace said, describing how they had to meet new situations with Roger while not flailing at one another. "You knew you had to brace yourself for the unknown. And you always had to be prepared for it." This kind of tension raised questions in each of their minds about how they all were going to live together and what the quality of that existence might be. Concerning her relationship with Jim, Grace "was very fearful. It put a terrible strain on the relationship," she said. What might have been a minor problem or a simple disagreement before became fuel for a large explosion; things which would have been quite simple without the tension and stress of Roger's illness became more complicated. Grace remembered that "any little flaw in the relationship became part of the whole picture. Things we were able to overlook when it was just the two of us relating to one another became a terrible problem when it was worked out around the enormous stake of what was best for Roger." The mounting tensions between Jim and Grace evoked criticisms of each other about a particular decision or the way one had handled a situation with Roger or a conversation with a doctor or social worker. Each began to think that he or she was taking more responsibility. "And certainly it was easy to assume the role of critic," Grace said. She noted that "whatever one of us was doing, the other was critical." Therapy helped them identify corrosive issues and cope in the process. But they were able to cope, not "because things had settled with Roger. We just learned how to deal with it," Grace explained.

Part of the strain that Grace and Jim have lived with for the past four years is the issue of blame and guilt. Just as parents are the first to love and nurture a child and to have dreams and hopes, they are the first to be blamed when something as serious as mental illness develops. "We felt blamed even when it turned out we weren't being blamed," Grace said. "And the thought that you could drive somebody crazy is the most horrendous idea." When she went to the library to read about mental illness, Grace discovered theories arguing that parents drive their children crazy. She immersed herself in the literature "first to satisfy my urgent need to understand the illness itself," she said. As she read, she was met "at every turn by the accusations directed against the family."

Grace encountered the scapegoat model, the argument that one member of the family is unconsciously selected to become the scapegoat for the problems everybody has but cannot articulate. She came across the idea of a "schizophrenogenic mother," which was made famous by Frieda Fromm-Reichman in 1948 and contends that an essential failure in early maternal responses to an infant produces schizophrenia. She read about the "double bind" which Gregory Bateson outlined in 1956, in an article titled "Toward a Theory of Schizophrenia," which claims that it is not only the mother's deficiency but that fathers are also culpable.[1] Somehow the communication between the two parents evokes mixed messages that trap children into the double bind. Grace found it all very disturbing. "Gradually I came to see that it was a skewed view. These writers didn't know everything. They were not the parents of somebody who was sick. They were the outsiders, and what they saw wasn't the whole truth," she concluded.

Reading these theories, Grace struggled with the guilt and sense of failure they evoked. "How can you think you've been a good parent when there is this glaring proof of your failure?" she asked. After thinking about it for a long time, she was able to shed some of her doubts, but then another question crossed her mind. "If I hadn't caused it, should I have been able to prevent it? Could we have gone so far wrong?" When she finally let go of this fearsome idea, Grace realized that they had done "everything we could or knew how to do. We tried. We were conscientious parents —not perfect ones. And we had a child whose needs had been hard to meet. Not only by us but by his schools and teachers and now by other institutions."

At the time we spoke, Grace and Jim were in the midst of a quiet period. Roger had been in a new job for almost two weeks, and it was one he had found for himself. He was still living at home, and while things were often turbulent, the focus of his new job seemed to contain some of the energy which was previously dissipated through arguing. Though it is too early to tell whether the new job will work out, the Anthonys hold a guarded optimism. They know that something unexpected could flare in the future as it has in the past. And they know that they must be prepared to deal with it.

The relationship between Grace and Jim has weathered the storm of Roger's illness. They are quite lucky. Many couples divorce when their marriage has been filtered through years of worry and preoccupation with a sick child. Dr. Agnes B. Hatfield, who has studied how families respond to schizophrenic relatives, reports that 20 percent of the respondents in one study "seemed to have troubled marriages."[2] Such trouble was reported by Frank Martins, whose son, Alex, became the vehicle for tension between him and his wife.

Frank and Merle Martins   Frank Martins told about the way he and his wife, Merle, tried to help Alex first through special schools, then through psychiatric counseling, finally through residential treatment centers. For them the tensions grew perceptibly. Alex was excitable, and on occasion he would become verbally abusive. He also fought with his younger sister, Bonnie, and while most brothers and sisters fight, their fights became distorted by Alex's illness. When as a teenager Alex started speaking about violence, Merle was frightened. Frank, on the other hand, thought Alex's ability to talk about his fantasies was a good sign. But "after he started to mention his violent fantasies, things changed," Frank said. Merle feared for herself and their daughter.

Tensions between Frank and Merle existed for the twenty years they tried to help Alex. Each believed a different program of activities was appropriate for him during the vacations or weekends he spent at home. Disagreement, conflict, and argument spilled into their every encounter, crowding out the tender and peaceful moments. While Merle became active in forming consumers' groups and self-help organizations, Frank worked at extra jobs to meet the expense of the special schools and medical treatments. In the evenings, when he returned from his second job, he collapsed with exhaustion. Merle, all the while, resented Frank's long hours and his lethargy when he got home at ten or eleven at night. She felt there was no time for her or Bonnie. And Frank thought he was caring for them both by taking on the burden of earning all the income so that Merle did not have to work for wages and their daughter could have braces and summer-camp excursions.

Through all of it the tensions just mounted, even for Bonnie, who said that her parents "deprived themselves before me. But it was all very tense," she noted. After turning himself inside out, "like a pretzel," Frank said a trivial fight erupted between him and Merle. He knew he could stand no more. The relationship already had dissolved as each justified his or her behavior in terms of how to meet Alex's needs, what was best for him, and how they should sacrifice. Conflicts which had been disguised earlier could no longer be attributed to their concern for their son, and Frank and Merle separated and then divorced.

HUSBANDS AND WIVES

While some parents weather the storm and others stay together only for the sake of the children, for those like Frank and Merle Martins so much tension builds around their child's illness that what otherwise might have been resolved with less drama becomes a major production, replete with guilt, accusations, and misunderstandings. Whatever sense of responsibility and guilt develops when the patient is a child, these issues magnify when he or she is a spouse. Husbands or wives whose hopes for a future were built together confront unique issues. The loss of emotional or sexual intimacy, the erosion of adult companionship which marriage promises, or the abridgment of the social pattern of being part of a couple may haunt the partner of a mentally disabled spouse. When children are involved, it is even more complicated as the healthy spouse has to make decisions alone which may have been shared before. And the task of parenting differs considerably when the children are young, as was Rebecca Kane when Morris was hospitalized, and when children are already leading independent lives, as were Maggie Connelly and her sisters.

Donald Kaplan   The husbands or wives with whom I spoke all have made commitments which spell a long-term responsibility for their spouse. Despite the fact that Donald Kaplan has been divorced from Arlene for three years, he feels he cannot loosen the ties, as would normally happen in a divorce, because he has small children. Arlene first showed signs of mental illness when the children were only two and five. In the course of the next five years Arlene had several bouts with depression. She was medicated and remained at home. Hospitalization was something Donald wanted to avoid, and while they were together, he succeeded. He knew the signs of her manic-depressive cycle, and when she was in one of the high phases, he was aware that a low period would follow. He called whichever doctor she was in treatment with at the time, and the appropriate medicine was generally prescribed.

Donald recalled the times when Arlene rested in bed for what her doctors said was depression. When she was in bed, they managed as if she had the flu. Because the children were young, Donald didn't think he had to explain anything besides "Mommy is sick." "It was easy," he remembered. His mother came over each day to help take care of them, and a housekeeper came twice a week. Since the kids could see Arlene in her own bed, and she was not out of the house for extended periods of time, there were no problems in explaining things until they got older.

Donald always had reservations about his marriage. For whatever reason, it never quite offered what he had hoped for, though he was determined to make it work because of the children. Yet his life became less bearable each year. During her energetic phases Arlene was demanding, and she involved Donald in the various schemes she had brewing. She would interview for jobs for which she was not qualified, or on the basis of a shred of evidence she would assume that a commitment had been made and proceed accordingly with all the energy she could summon. These escapades made Donald nervous, knowing that Arlene was on the brink of another collapse, yet he was not sure how to handle the situation. "When she speaks, she makes people stop and listen," Donald said. "Yet I knew that she was on this 'high.' " He didn't know whether to stop his wife or let her continue with unrealistic plans that fooled others. Hopeful that one success might turn things around, he often let her continue. But he was always doubtful about the various schemes, and now he feels guilty. "Was it my own wish that she not succeed?" he asked. "Was I trying to stop her from achieving? I have a real guilt problem!"

But for the sense of duty and guilt he felt at the thought of leaving, Donald might have separated from Arlene earlier. He stayed and tolerated many things that caused him pain. Doctors would speak with him only during a crisis, and he never managed to find a psychiatrist who regarded him as an ally. "When she was not functioning at all or irrationally, they were willing to talk to me," he said. "I would call them up and give them progress reports. As soon as she turned the corner, they refused to talk with me. I felt that I had been rejected."

Feeling rejected by his wife's doctors, who did not include him in the process of her treatment, and ultimately by his wife, who kicked him out of the bedroom, Donald was still "willing to endure it." Though he knew that the marriage was not meeting his expectations or needs, he "had children, and they were still young. And I didn't think that Arlene could take the rejection of my leaving. But then I realized that the kids were suffering more than if I were not there," he said. Donald asked for a divorce. But he continues to be actively involved in Arlene's world. He is often called to take her to the hospital or to keep a watchful eye when she appears troubled. A neighbor called recently in the middle of the night and said that Arlene was behaving strangely. He urged Donald to come over, so he did. After seeing Arlene, he decided that he should spend the night there. When the children found him on the couch in the morning, they were delighted. But he was pained. He knew that he had to take Arlene to a hospital in what had become part of her routine since the divorce.

"I feel very responsible for her," Donald said. "She has only one good friend. The friend has been quite helpful. She came to visit in the hospital and has been very nice. Yet I still feel very responsible for Arlene. She has no parents. She has one brother, but he does not have a very good track record at helping. She has no other family around. I feel I have to be there—for the kids."

Now that Arlene has become accustomed to going to the hospital, where she stays for a week or two, Donald is torn about what role to play. The last time she was in the hospital, the psychiatrists wanted the family to attend therapy sessions. Donald and the psychiatrist each thought it wise for the sessions to occur without him. So they did, but Donald had to take the children and pick them up afterward. And he took them to additional sessions with a social worker.

While Donald feels responsible for Arlene, it is the children who concern him the most. He worries about what effect this is having on them and where they will draw the resources to cope. He is concerned about the disruptions and about the emotional pressures which their mother's illness might cause. "My ten-year-old has a best friend in her class. This little girl also lives next door. The girl friend knew that Arlene wasn't doing well and that things were going on," Donald reported. Despite the agreement not to tell neighbors about Arlene's hospitalization, Donald's older child is still perplexed. She said to her father, "Joannie is my best friend. I don't mind her knowing because she is my best friend. But she has a big mouth and will tell one of her friends, like Sarah. And Sarah will tell others."

Donald was distressed by his daughter's dilemma. He had no answer but said she should raise it in the upcoming session with the social worker. "I took them to the social worker, who said he wanted to talk to them. He asked the kids if they had any questions. My daughter asked him what to tell her friends." Donald was proud of her ability to raise this question, which lay at the root of how she would publicly cope with her mother's hospitalization. The social worker with whom they spoke, however, was not helpful. He told her, "It *is* a very difficult problem." But he had no suggestions. In the meantime, his son "sat and cried and kept asking why is this happening to us again." He didn't understand any of it and wanted to know if it was because his father "left Mommy." Donald felt helpless.

Despite being fed up with the havoc Arlene's illness has wrought in his life, Donald expects to be responsible until his wife remarries or until the children are older. He doesn't see any other choice, especially because Arlene fought for and won custody of the children. He is prepared to be available to take his former wife to the hospital when psychiatrists or police beckon, he assumes that he will have little help from friends or family, but he hopes the toll this disruption takes will not be more than his children can handle.

Evelyn Vann Like Donald Kaplan, Evelyn Vann cannot bring herself to break the tie that prevents her complete freedom. Though Evelyn's commitment to Tom is not bound up with the children, who are in their early twenties, she feels responsible for the man she married more than twenty years ago. Even if religious principle did not stand in her way, she does not see any social agency that would step in and help Tom when he needs to be rescued. "It's very hard to turn someone out," she said. "Even though this person is mentally ill, he is still a human being with his own desires and ways of doing things."

Though Tom's behavior continues to complicate her life, Evelyn has worked out a solution because her expectations have changed to meet the situation. At one time she tried to hide the clear signs of Tom's behavior. "We didn't want anybody to know that this man had a problem. I'm not sure why, but there was a stigma attached to mental illness. I guess I also didn't want anybody to know how lousy my marriage was with him. And, for my kids' sake, that their father was any different from anybody else's." Now Evelyn does not feel that she has to hide Tom's problem from her neighbors or her friends. And she no longer hides it from herself. She has no expectation that her marriage will improve or offer what she once hoped. Evelyn has also learned to enjoy social outings, which she denied herself earlier. "So much of the time Tom didn't want to do things that I did," Evelyn said. "When he did go, he caused so many problems that I was sorry that he went. So now I'm rather independent and just do things by myself." Evelyn still showed traces of suntan from the recent cruise she took through the Caribbean. Proud of her newfound independence, she said, "His mental illness has been good for me in some respects."

Tom's illness and financial needs also forced Evelyn to return to school to update her nursing license. "It got me to go back to work, and that has opened up a whole new world to me," Evelyn said. After her license was updated, she looked for jobs and decided to accept one at a psychiatric nursing home. It is a small facility, with thirty-six beds for people who are not sick enough for hospitalization but who need care that their families cannot provide. Through her work she has met other people and now counts two of her colleagues as good friends.

Evelyn's commitment to Tom and her choice of occupation have altered her life. She thinks that the experience of finally accepting her husband's illness has made her a different person. "I want you to say," she told me, "that I have this situation at home and I have it at work. Somehow it has made me a better person for all of it—having to deal with mental illness all the time." And even in her hours away from home or the hospital, Evelyn has become active on behalf of the mentally ill. She was recently appointed to the Community Mental Health Advisory Committee in her county, and she uses her insights from firsthand experience to effect policy for those in a similar situation. So, despite the profound regret she feels for what her life could have been without Tom's demanding illness, Evelyn has settled some of the disquieting features in her own mind and remains responsible for a man from whom she has become independent. After more than a decade of responding to Tom's needs, on his time schedule and with his well-being in mind, she is beginning to reclaim some of her energy for herself. And she is defining herself within a context that takes for granted Tom's limitations and requires her to make sacrifices on specific issues but does not claim her vitality as the price for assuming this responsibility.

Each of these families has adjusted to its relative's mental illness in different ways. Their experiences make it clear that some people need years to resolve the accumulated pain and disappointment before they can adjust their expectations to the current reality. For others acceptance comes more quickly yet offers little help in reorganizing their lives, even though they know it is necessary. Whether they are sons or daughters, brothers or sisters, husbands or wives, mothers or fathers, all have confronted a range of issues which ultimately forced them to deal with themselves. And to a large degree, the issues each has been forced to face are part of the cultural and social texture of contemporary life.

10

Families Organize

To view families like the Connellys, the Anthonys, the Greenes, or the Stanwicks only as particular instances of heroism or tragedy is to overlook the social fabric that shaped their experience. No matter how they have coped, whether it generated turbulence and despair or promoted compassion and growth, none of these families lives in a vacuum. A system of health care, social supports, fiscal policy, and cultural values has created a context within which their experiences have unfolded. Prodded by their own frustrations, some, like Evelyn Vann, have deliberately chosen careers in the field of mental health in order to help others alleviate some of the difficulty she encountered. Others, like Jeanne Adamson and Rebecca Kane, have also selected careers in the field, though their decisions may have been less deliberate. Still others have joined the burgeoning movement of self-help groups which are beginning to tackle some of the thorny problems that had been ignored or unresolved because the mentally ill had no constituency. Helen and Lou Amato, Berenice McCoy, Stella Stanwick, and Dora Young have each become active in local groups that work to improve the delivery of services.

In the early 1970s those who realized that the existing system of mental health care failed not only their relatives but themselves as well began to organize. They challenged the professionals and the politicians who decided to close facilities without opening the promised alternative treatment programs. They objected to the priorities which placed mental illness low on the social agenda and led to the fragmentation of services that affected their relatives' ability to get sustained help. Encountering the theories that blame the family for the illness, they pointed out that nobody was helped when spouses and parents were assaulted by professionals who expected them to take charge when all else failed.

Families who had searched for programs in vain, and retrieved their relatives from the doorsteps of hospitals or halfway houses, became angry. If the programs and services did not exist in sufficient quality or number, then it was time, they thought, to find out why. They realized there was a difference between the way they envisioned their problems and the way health care professionals did. Part of that difference led them to band together. From California to Maine, thousands of people across the nation began to organize community-based consumer advocacy groups. Some of the groups were designed for the mutual support and encouragement of those who were in similar situations. Others were formed to lobby for political change and speak on behalf of the mentally ill, who had no representation. Many combined these functions.

Parents of Adult Schizophrenics (PAS) of San Mateo County, California, which began in 1974, was one of the first. The group, like the approximately 125 in existence by 1981, had a modest beginning with a handful of people. One person, Eve Oliphant, sent letters to individuals who were on a list that she obtained from the American Schizophrenia Association in San Francisco. She invited them to a meeting in her home, and ten parents arrived. They continued to meet there weekly until the group expanded and outgrew Mrs. Oliphant's living room.

Initially the participants whom Eve Oliphant brought together shared their experiences and received support and empathy from one another. "The first months of those early meetings," according to Fran Hoffman, a charter member, "all we could do was discuss our problems. And cry a little bit. Then we realized we had to do more." It was apparent that besides the particular problems of their relatives or households, there were enough common concerns that they formed a natural coalition to try to change some of the circumstances which troubled them.

Effective advocacy for the consumer of mental health services requires grass-roots organizations like PAS to monitor public agencies. PAS members knew this and attended county Mental Health Advisory Board meetings to become familiar with the process through which decisions were made about services and programs in the four regions under the board's jurisdiction. When they left the first meeting, they were angry at what they had witnessed. It appeared that a psychiatrist from one hospital, which was in the smallest and wealthiest region of the four, had convinced the Mental Health Advisory Board to allocate a disproportionate amount of the available public monies to his facility.

In one of its first public statements this young organization objected to what it had seen. PAS members criticized the psychiatrist who claimed that the additional funds which had been made available should be allocated to his facility, and they challenged his participation on the board. Members noted that the other regions under the board's jurisdiction were losing between five and nine people, each of whom worked with the chronically ill. In addition, a health center that served a poor minority population was cut entirely. And the vocational rehabilitation program was scheduled to receive a severe reduction in funds.

Many inequities such as these have been observed by consumer groups that advocate on behalf of the mentally disabled. And changes have been made because of the vigilance of community-based organizations. In the situation involving the San Mateo Mental Health Advisory Board, after PAS started objecting to the inequitable distribution of resources, the psychiatrist from that hospital was removed from the board. Whether this would have been done anyway is unclear. What is clear is that after PAS had become involved, and its members been alerted to the ways in which monies were allocated, they let their feelings be known.

"We decided that something had to be done about these boards," said Tony Hoffman, another charter member of the group. Over the next two years the organization succeeded in changing the existing law in California. Through lobbying, letter writing, visiting, and calling state legislators, they were able to effect the passage of a new law requiring that 25 percent of the members of each county mental health advisory board be either former mental patients or members of families of mental patients.

Securing a voice for the consumer often requires attending countless local meetings, alerting members to new bills which are before various legislative bodies, and identifying the agencies responsible for particular programs. Such activities use up many hours for members of Threshold, an advocacy group in Montgomery County, Maryland. Founded in 1978, it has several standing committees organized around specific issues such as housing, employment, recreation, legal concerns, or emergency services. Whenever a proposed bill comes before the Maryland House of Delegates, for example, Threshold discusses it at the monthly meeting or in its newsletter. Members are asked to respond so that the appropriate committee can plan a strategy to address the bill with the constituency in mind. Another example comes from the time Threshold's housing committee members attended a meeting with the Montgomery County Housing Opportunity Committee to apprise them of the housing needs of the mentally disabled. And when the City Council held public meetings on the proposed Health Systems Agency, Threshold told its membership whom to call in order to testify at the appropriate time.

Self-help advocacy groups recognize that the power they wield as organizations is greater than if they acted as individuals. Since it was founded, Threshold's reputation and credibility have grown along with its membership. By the end of the first year it had grown from the 35 people who attended the first public meeting called by a few to more than 100 who were regular members. In September 1980, its newsletter was sent to more than 600 people around the country. The growth of this organization has not escaped Montgomery County officials, and many public agencies now recognize that it is better to consult with Threshold in the process of making changes rather than run the risk of a confrontation because the needs of the mentally disabled have been overlooked. Three members of Threshold, for example, were on the advisory committee when plans were being made to open a psychosocial rehabilitation center in Montgomery County. The plan for the center was developed jointly by three agencies: the Mental Health Association, the Community Mental Health Center, and

Family Services. Threshold was asked to participate in the initial stage when the grant was developed. Within the terms of the grant, which was submitted to state and federal agencies, Threshold would receive money to act as ombudsman on behalf of resident members of the rehabilitation center and their families.

Threshold was initially reluctant to become involved in such a venture, which appeared to blur the lines between an advocacy group and an organization that provides services. Many advocacy groups believe they should not provide services because it lessens their credibility.* Though gratified that the needs of the chronically mentally ill are finally being recognized and that their perspective as consumers is being requested, Threshold wants to maintain its autonomy in order to be able to monitor and criticize when it is necessary. So, while it had reservations about accepting part of the grant for the ombudsman's role at the psychosocial rehabilitation center, and with the distinction clearly in mind between the providers and the consumers of these services, Threshold agreed. It also agreed to allow one of its members to serve on the executive committee of the center. How long the relationship will continue is under debate within the organization.

The lack of alternative housing programs and psychosocial rehabilitation centers is often noted by grass-roots organizations. As one woman said when she spoke at a session on residential alternatives at the second annual conference of the National Alliance for the Mentally Ill (held in Chicago in September 1980), "We are worried about what will happen to our children after we die." Along with the other participants in the workshop, she discussed in detail how her organization was attempting to facilitate the building of these needed homes.

Expanding the number of community residential programs is part of the agenda for community advocacy groups. This speaks to the frustration parents have experienced finding adequate alternatives for their children, as well as to the nationwide shortage. The *Task Panel Reports Submitted to the President's Commission on Mental Health* noted that "the range of alternative community residences and residential programs with a rehabilitation component is an essential need for the chronically mentally disabled population."[1]

*Not all groups share this belief. See below: Families and Friends of the Mentally Ill, Charleston, South Carolina.

And families know only too well that they are essential, for which reason advocacy groups like PAS or Threshold work to promote their growth. One group, Families and Friends of the Mentally Ill, of Charleston, South Carolina, surveyed its membership and discovered that 99 percent favored a group home. Soon thereafter members began to survey other programs around the nation in order to identify potential sources of funding, meet with local and state officials, select an appropriate building (which would be located near a bus line and close to a mental health center), and lobby with political and social leaders whose support would be important in the community. Two and a half years after the idea was conceived, the first person moved into the house, which can accommodate sixteen to eighteen people. Though Palmetto Pathway Homes, Inc., is run by Families and Friends of the Mentally Ill, membership in this organization is not a prerequisite for a relative's living there.

Families and Friends of the Mentally Ill met with only slight hostility from the community when it founded Palmetto Pathway Homes, Inc. This was extremely fortunate, because many groups have come up against virulent opposition from potential neighbors. With the fear of mental illness still rampant in America, and given zoning laws that permit discriminatory practices, many who have tried to set up these programs have encountered the "not on my block" response. PAS met such opposition when it joined the fight in San Mateo County to have therapeutic residences and a skilled nursing home approved. Homeowners' associations protested, claiming that each of the dwellings, which would house between six and twelve people, would incur excessive expenses for city-required fire and safety inspection. They also expressed fear for their own safety and for their children's. Charges were hurled that the mentally disabled were "outsiders." These statements, and others, were challenged by articulate spokespersons, who reminded the various groups that the residential homes would serve members of the community who had grown up there or were long-term residents. And PAS explained that rather than being violent or lawless, the chronically mentally disabled are often the targets of senseless crime. They are vulnerable both physically and emotionally, and are victimized not only by the pervasive notion that they are potentially dangerous but by those who actually are.

The difficulty that groups like PAS have encountered trying to facilitate the founding of therapeutic residences (PAS does not operate these programs) relates to the lingering stigma attached to mental illness. A stigma is based on a culture's consensus that a certain attribute is inherently unworthy. It is often a physical trait or deformity, but it may be any other characteristic that is used to differentiate those who are socially acceptable from those who are not. Each of the charges PAS addressed illustrates how the mentally ill are characterized by a stigma because the culture is unable to accept this illness with so many unknowns, including the cause and the cure. Because a mythology engulfs its victims, the idea of introducing the mentally ill into a neighborhood strikes fear into those who have never been exposed to them. The overall tendency has been to quarantine the disabled. Mental illness carries a stigma which the *Task Panel Reports Submitted to the President's Commission on Mental Health* identified as "a primary barrier in every phase of the provision of mental health services in this country." It goes on to say that "it brands any person seeking professional services with a mark of shame. . . . Stigma is society's means of protecting itself against falsely conceived dangers. In doing so, it legitimizes ridicule, humiliation and dehumanization of persons with emotional problems."[2]

Stigma serves to isolate because everybody, even the one who carries it, accepts the designation until some person or group boldly challenges it. Thus, those who rally "not on my block" campaigns can stop or delay the opening of therapeutic residences because so few people disagree. And complicit in promoting the stigma, whether they realize it or not, are the media, professional educators, and legal experts. In fact, each has contributed to the continuation of erroneous beliefs about the mentally ill. This is so overriding a problem that the National Alliance for the Mentally Ill is launching an educational campaign.

NAMI is an umbrella organization for more than 100 self-help advocacy groups. It consists of diverse local affiliates who do not necessarily share political or social values and who come from different economic and ethnic backgrounds. The single experience that unites them is their concern for the future of the mentally ill. Organized in 1979, by February 1981 NAMI had moved into an office in Washington, D.C., from which it works on issues of national scope. One of the most pressing of these issues, according to president Shirley Starr, is the "anti-stigma campaign," which was mounted in 1981.

Inaccurate and misleading depictions of the mentally ill in the media have been conveyed through regular television serials as well as news reports which perpetuate an image of moral and psychological defects. Police and detective heroes are often shown tracking villains portrayed as mentally unbalanced, violent, or sadistic. The villains are "shown typically as sinister people lurking in the shadows to do bodily harm to innocent people, particularly women."[3] The news feeds these prejudicial images in its reporting. Stories of sensational nature, such as that of the "Son of Sam," dominate headlines and reinforce the myth that all mentally ill people are prone to similar violence. Or the words "former patient" will be used to modify and describe the suspect of a crime. This designation is as discriminatory as were earlier references to race before the civil rights movement waged battles against stereotyping and prejudicial reporting.

The media's current role in perpetuating stigmas and their enormous potential for re-educating the public have led different local groups to work on this problem at the same time as the National Alliance for the Mentally Ill. For example, the Illinois Alliance for the Mentally Ill announced the formation of a committee which will prepare guidelines for media coverage in order to encourage greater journalistic accuracy.

Another target of NAMI's anti-stigma campaign is the mental health profession. Despite their professional commitment to working with the mentally ill, psychiatrists, psychologists, and social workers have promoted stigmatization through their writing, teaching, and treatment. Because a stigma is likely to remain in place when people are uninformed about the illness, the profession's reluctance to share information with the families promotes a sense of shame. Therefore, the stigma that isolates the patient works on the family with equal force. In addition to the pejorative use of diagnosis, theories that blame the family for the patients' ills, despite the contradictory and inconclusive ideas about the origins of mental illness, contribute to the family and the patient's isolation.

Finally, legal labels such as "insanity" are used to explain and excuse those who might be guilty of a crime. Insanity is not a medical term; its only significance is legal. Circumstances have made it acceptable for lawyers to build a defense strategy which claims a person was "insane" at the time of a crime, reinforcing the misperception that the mentally ill are violent. A perverse irony results, indeed, when a claim of insanity is accepted and the criminal is forced into treatment at the same time that the mentally ill are denied it because programs are insufficient.

In addition to its anti-stigma campaign, NAMI is actively forming coalitions with groups of other disabled people. President Shirley Starr feels it is important to remind the public constantly that people with schizophrenia or manic-depressive illness are disabled in the same sense as the physically disabled who are without sight or who have lost limbs. Forming coalitions with health-defined associations, such as those concerned with cerebral palsy, epilepsy, or muscular dystrophy, will further efforts to reduce or eliminate the stigma. According to Starr, it is important to win acceptance for mental illness as a medical problem to remove the stigma that is attached when it is labeled a form of social pathology.

All groups, national and local, are concerned with the quality of services that now exist to treat chronic mental illness. And others have joined the advocates in this area. Professional concern was evident in the testimony on the Mental Health Systems Act in 1980, which would expand the provisions of the Community Mental Health Care Centers Act of 1963. Speaking before House or Senate subcommittees, representatives of mental health associations and professional groups recommended securing the existing programs and expanding them to enable greater use by the underserved populations, including the *chronically* mentally ill.

With the election of Ronald Reagan, and his administration's emphasis on transferring funds from social programs to embellish the military, many fear that the services and programs available to the mentally ill are in jeopardy. Budget trimming will reduce and lump together major health programs, including those for mental health. And the Mental Health Systems Act will be consolidated into block grants, which will be administered by the states. In addition to the Mental Health Systems Act, programs such as Medicaid, Vocational Rehabilitation Grants, and Developmental Disabilities State Grants are among those which will be reduced and then administered in block grants. Because of the new responsibility that states will have in allocating funds, NAMI's president,

Shirley Starr, believes it is more important than ever that local grass-roots organizations become visible and aggressive. In order to help them, NAMI has spent considerable time responding to inquiries of those who are interested in forming new groups, in addition to being supportive of the existing groups.

Perhaps the kinds of battles which will be required of local groups in this area can be seen in a situation which exists in California. Governor Edmund G. Brown, Jr., has proposed reducing the state hospitals by another 200 beds, a proposal which local groups in California oppose. "It is not that we are intrigued with the state hospitals," said Fran Hoffman of San Mateo County's PAS. "But they seem to be the last resort for a lot of people." Without them the shameful "dumping" of the mentally ill will prevail if an equal number of places is not found in other treatment centers. "If they close two hundred beds," Tony Hoffman said, "the people who would have filled them will be dumped out onto the streets."

The California Association, which is the umbrella organization for the thirty-seven different local advocacy groups in the state, is fighting to retain the 200 beds. In order to achieve this, the members of various chapters are in frequent communication with one another, passing along information through a telephone tree, writing to appropriate legislators and public officials. The spirit of the California Association, like that of the local groups, rests on the assumption that everybody must learn to become politically involved and experienced. Tony Hoffman, the first president of the California Association, thinks it is important to have responsibility rotate. This enhances the development of skills in all the members. Too, when members share the responsibility, the organization can be self-sustaining because no single person becomes indispensable or cripples the group when exhaustion sets in. As Marie Hibler, from Parents of the Adult Mentally Ill (Santa Clara County, San Jose, California) said when she described her organization, *"Everyone* has something to contribute. . . . We have found that leadership, duties, and responsibilities must be rotated and shared in order to maintain a strong, active and interested organization. Most of our success can be attributed to having such an active and involved group."[4] Agnes B. Hatfield, founding member of Threshold, concurs. She believes one of the reasons her organization grew so strong, and so quickly, is that it is committed to spreading responsibilities in order to develop leadership. This, she thinks, is a way of guaranteeing that the organization is larger than any single leader at its helm.

Families organized because they realized that the problems they were dealing with were larger than any single person or situation. As they drew on their own personal resources to negotiate with a confused system of mental health care, they experienced futility and despair. Might it not be more fruitful, many asked themselves, to join with others whose understanding of the problems and commitment to seeing them resolved were as deeply rooted as their own? Because so many people answered yes, local organizations that advocate on behalf of the mentally ill and their families have mushroomed around the country since the middle of the 1970s.

Because so many obstacles remain to a truly judicious social program and an effective medical one, some people are painfully aware that their efforts may not help their son or husband, daughter or mother. Shirley Starr's column in the NAMI newsletter recently said:

> The only way in which I can continue my efforts is to accept the reality that benefits for my son may have to be deferred, or even worse, never received. It is the future that we direct our efforts toward—the young children growing up and the ones not yet born. If we can in the meantime even make a small difference in our children's lives, we can consider ourselves fortunate.

Those who have joined to lobby on behalf of their mentally disabled relatives have begun a process which points toward a different future for families. They are overcoming a sense of powerlessness by participating with others and holding policy makers and professionals accountable. Mobilizing networks of self-help groups advocating change, they are forcing public awareness of the needs and rights of the mentally disabled and transcending their isolated and personal suffering.

APPENDIXES

Glossary

AFFECTIVE DISORDERS: Disturbances in emotions and mood. Depression is the most common affective disorder.

BORDERLINE DISORDER: A relatively new diagnostic category of disorders, this refers to a syndrome in which people often have extreme feelings of loneliness, isolation, or emptiness. It is sometimes called a personality disorder.

CATCHMENT AREA: In 1963, when the nation became committed to providing services and programs in the community, 1,500 geographic areas in which community mental health services would be available were designated. A catchment area serves a population of between 75,000 and 200,000 people.

COMMUNITY MENTAL HEALTH CENTER: A community service set up in order to move mental health care away from the state hospitals. Each community mental health center must provide the following services in order to qualify for federal assistance: inpatient services, emergency services, partial hospitalization (such as day hospitals), outpatient services, and consultation and educational services. It must also assist courts and other public agencies in screening people who are being considered for admission to state hospitals and follow-up care for those discharged from them. Halfway houses are included as a program for those discharged from mental institutions.

DE-INSTITUTIONALIZATION: The effort to move people out of state and county mental institutions. Adopted in the mid-1960s as a result of confidence in new medicines that can be used outside a hospital, this policy was accelerated by fiscal considerations and legal changes. De-institutionalization has been called "dumping" by those who argue that former patients, as well as those who need hospitalization, are discharged prematurely or without adequate planning for their social and medical needs.

DELUSION: A belief that has no basis in reality. Those suffering from this kind of disturbed thinking are often convinced they are famous people, are being persecuted, or are capable of extraordinary accomplishments.

DENIAL: A psychiatric explanation which suggests that in order to protect themselves, people refuse to appreciate the significance of events or situations. This means they sometimes overlook symptoms that those who are not as close to the situation might see.

DOUBLE BIND: This theory was first articulated by anthropologist Gregory Bateson. It argues that schizophrenia is a result of family interactions in which two or more people send contradictory messages—by words or behavior—to another person. The person (usually a child) who has to interpret these messages is caught in the middle—in a double bind.

DYSLEXIA: A learning disorder generally detected in children when they are in grade school. People with dyslexia often perceive and write letters and numerals incompletely or backwards. Because this disorder causes frustration in a learning situation, youngsters who have not been diagnosed are often thought to be poorly motivated or to have behavior problems.

HALLUCINATION: The perception of external sensory stimuli that are not actually present. These may be sights, smells, or sounds.

INPATIENT: A patient who receives treatment in a hospital twenty-four hours a day.

INTAKE INTERVIEW: An interview conducted when a patient is admitted to a hospital, its purpose being to obtain information that will help the staff diagnose and treat him or her. In most instances, when the admission is for psychiatric problems, members of the family are asked to provide information about the patient's symptoms and behavior as well as previous hospitalizations.

INTERN: A doctor who has completed four years of medical school and received an M.D. degree. This doctor will spend the year following graduation working in a hospital. Some hospitals place interns on a rotation through units, with time devoted in turn to obstetrics, gynecology, surgery, psychiatry, pediatrics, internal medicine, and other specialities. Other hospitals place interns in one specialty for the entire year.

MANIC-DEPRESSIVE ILLNESS: A form of depression characterized by extreme swings in mood ranging from enormous amounts of energy to complete exhaustion and withdrawal. Sometimes called bipolar depression, it is an affective disorder. It is estimated that 0.3 percent of the population suffers from it.

MAO INHIBITOR: A group of anti-depressant drugs which block other chemicals the body produces naturally in response to emotion, fear, or exercise.

NEUROSIS: An unconscious emotional conflict that leads someone to perform less satisfactorily in an area of life than he or she would like. The symptoms are broad-ranging, including extreme anxiety in a particular situation, repetitious or compulsive behavior, or a general dissatisfaction with life. People with neurotic difficulties have a greater ability to control their environment than do people with psychotic problems.

ORTHOMOLECULAR TREATMENT: An approach to treating schizophrenic disorders which relies primarily on vitamin and diet therapy. It is sometimes turned to by those who have found traditional medicine disappointing.

OUTPATIENT: Someone who receives treatment outside a twenty-four-hour-a-day hospital. This could include treatment through a day hospital or private therapy.

PARANOIA: A tendency toward unwarranted suspicion of people and situations. Those with paranoia may think that others are plotting against them or ridiculing them. It falls within the category of delusional thinking; one subtype of schizophrenia is paranoid schizophrenia.

PSYCHIATRIST: A person who has received a medical degree and completed additional training as a resident in psychiatry. Psychiatrists have the authority to prescribe drugs and to discharge people from hospitals. Many psychiatrists are in private practice and do not have privileges to treat someone in a hospital. This is a matter of choice, not of professional qualification.

PSYCHOANALYST: A therapist who is generally a psychologist with a Ph.D. or a medical doctor who has completed a residency in psychiatry. Psychoanalysts receive additional training in institutes that focus on unconscious processes and symptoms as relating to underlying conflicts.

PSYCHOLOGIST: A person who has done graduate study in psychology and has earned a Ph.D. There are many subspecialties, and not all psychologists practice therapy. Those who do may be trained in one of several different kinds, including psychoanalytic, behavioral, or milieu therapy.

GLOSSARY

PSYCHOTIC EPISODE: Psychosis is a break with reality and an inability to function. A psychotic episode is that time during which a person's behavior indicates such a loss of touch with reality. It may last anywhere from a few minutes to several days.

PSYCHOTROPIC DRUGS: Drugs that affect mood. They include sedatives, tranquilizers, and anti-depressants.

REACTIVE DEPRESSION: Depression in response to a particular trauma or crisis. This was a common diagnosis among soldiers of both World Wars who had been in battle or had witnessed shocking events. While most people are affected by a traumatic event, in reactive depression the state of despair and despondency has become chronic.

RESIDENT: A doctor who has completed medical school and an internship and then spends additional years training in one area of medicine. The training goes on within a hospital, and every field of medicine has a different length of time for its completion. A residency in psychiatry generally lasts three years.

SCHIZOPHRENIA: A family of thought disorders with several different subcategories, such as paranoid, schizophreniform, and schizoaffective. Its symptoms may include delusions, hallucinations, paranoid ideas, inappropriate affect, and a general impairment of daily functioning. It may be called chronic, which indicates that it is a recurring illness over years; or it may be called acute, which suggests a somewhat sudden onset in a person who has previously been functioning well. Important information in diagnosing schizophrenia is age of onset, duration of symptoms, and length of time between healthy functioning and the particular symptoms a patient displays. It is estimated that between 0.5 and 3 percent of the population has this disease.

SCHIZOPHRENOGENIC MOTHER: According to psychoanalyst Frieda Fromm-Reichman, a mother who causes schizophrenia in her child by inadequate or deficient mothering. As a way to protect itself, the infant is forced to develop unique ways of thinking and responding to its mother. She is thought to be the toxic agent.

SOCIAL WORKER: Someone with at least two years of postgraduate work in a school of social work. There are many specialties within this profession, each requiring training with a slightly different emphasis. A psychiatric social worker, for example, is trained to practice therapy in a clinical situation. Other social workers do not do therapy but help families find appropriate programs or services.

STABILIZATION: The use of medicines to calm a patient's agitation, reduce hallucinations or delusions, or elevate a mood. Stabilization is one of the purposes of hospitalizing a patient.

STIGMA: A negative attribute that discredits a person. Every culture identifies characteristics that disqualify people from social acceptance, though they are not necessarily the same ones.

SUICIDAL IDEATION: Ideas and expressions on the part of a patient which indicate to a therapist that self-destructive tendencies may be reaching a level that is dangerous to the patient.

TARDIVE DYSKINESIA: Muscular weakness or contractions caused by certain medicines.

Statutes Concerning Emergency Involuntary Hospitalization and Civil Commitment *

State	Who Can Initiate an Emergency Involuntary Hospital Admission Without a Court Order†	Length of Time a Person May Be Held Before a Court Hearing	Maximum Duration of a Civil Commitment Order
Alabama	No state law	—	Unspecified
Alaska	Interested party or police officer	48 hours	Indeterminate
Arkansas	Law enforcement official or interested citizen	72 hours	Initially 45 days (an additional 120 days may be ordered)
Arizona	Anybody can make a written application	24 hours	60–360 days

California	Police or designated professional or member of a mobile crisis team	72 hours	90 days
Colorado	A police officer or professional person	72 hours	6 months
Connecticut	A physician	15–30 days‡	"For the period of duration of such mental illness." Patient has a right to an annual hearing in court
Delaware	Any person or police	72 hours	Initially 6 months; mandatory report to the court every 6 months
District of Columbia	Police, health officer, or doctor	48 hours	Indeterminate (right to hearing every 6 months)
Florida	Police and doctor	48 hours	6 months
Georgia	Police and one doctor	24 hours	6 months
Hawaii	Police officer	48 hours	90–180 days
Idaho	Peace officer	24 hours –5 days‡	Unspecified (mandatory report to court every 4 months)
Illinois	A doctor and any person. If doctor cannot be found, person must have petition signed by physician or clinical psychologist	24 hours	60 days (an additional 180 days may be sought)

State	Who Can Initiate an Emergency Involuntary Hospital Admission Without a Court Order†	Length of Time a Person May Be Held Before a Court Hearing	Maximum Duration of a Civil Commitment Order
Indiana	Written application of health or police officer, or other individual *plus* physician's statement to probate court	72 hours	Unspecified (mandatory annual court review)
Iowa	Any interested person can file an application with the court	48 hours	Unspecified (mandatory report to court every 60 days)
Kansas	One doctor or police and hospital superintendent	72 hours —close of first day when court in session	Unspecified (mandatory report to court every 90 days)
Kentucky	Two authorized *staff* physicians or one physician and one mental health professional	72 hours —21 days‡	360 days
Louisiana	Police, doctor, or any person	72 hours	Indeterminate
Maine	Law enforcement officer	18 hours	Indeterminate (initially 4 months; subsequent hearings annually)
Maryland	Any interested person may file petition with peace officer	96 hours	Unspecified

242

Massachusetts	One doctor or police	10 days	1 year
Michigan	Police officer or mental health emergency service unit	24 hours	Unspecified
Minnesota	Peace or health officer	72 hours	60 days
Mississippi	Any person	7 days	Unspecified (commitment order not appealable)
Missouri	Health or police officer	10 days	Indeterminate
Montana	One doctor or peace officer	Next regular business day	6 months
Nebraska	Peace officer	36 hours	Unspecified
Nevada	Peace officer, physician, psychologist, social worker, or public health nurse	2–7 days‡	6 months
New Hampshire	One doctor; justice of the peace (after receiving a petition)	3–10 days‡	2 years
New Jersey	Police, relative, or two physicians	15 days	Indeterminate (review 3 months later; subsequent reviews annually)
New Mexico	Police	5–30 days‡	6 months (with a new hearing every 6 months)
New York	Any person and hospital physician	15 days	Initially 60 days (subsequent hearings may be held for orders up to 6 months and 2 years)

State	Who Can Initiate an Emergency Involuntary Hospital Admission Without a Court Order†	Length of Time a Person May Be Held Before a Court Hearing	Maximum Duration of a Civil Commitment Order
North Carolina	Law enforcement officer	10 days	90 days (subsequent hearing may be held for hearing up to 120 days; thereafter, annually)
North Dakota	Police, doctor, or mental health professional	72 hours	"Continuing hospitalization order" (status reports required every 6 months)
Ohio	Police, psychologist, or psychiatrist	7–30 days‡	Initially 90 days (subsequent hearings for up to 180 days; 2 years)
Oklahoma	Police	48 hours	Unspecified
Oregon	Two doctors	5 days	180 days
Pennsylvania	Physician's certificate or written application of other responsible party	120 hours	90 days (an additional 1 year may be ordered)
Rhode Island	Physician, qualified mental health professional, or police	10 days	6 months
South Carolina	Any person and one doctor	24 hours	Unspecified
South Dakota	Peace officer	24 hours	Unspecified

Tennessee	Licensed physician or psychologist, or officer authorized to make arrests	15 days	Unspecified
Texas	Court order required	24 hours	Indefinite
Utah	Health officer or police	24 hours	6 months or indeterminate
Vermont	Written application accompanied by physician's certificate	72 hours	Initially 90 days (application may be made for continued treatment)
Virginia	Sworn petition from any responsible person	48 hours	180 days
Washington	One doctor	72 hours	180 days
West Virginia	Any adult can apply for court order	Not specified	6 months or indeterminate
Wisconsin	Law enforcement officer	72 hours	Initially 6 months; subsequent orders may be for 1 year
Wyoming	Law enforcement officer	36 hours	An examination every 6 months to determine if "the conditions justifying hospitalization" continue to exist

*Because the law is subject to change, for the most up-to-date statutes consult the state's appropriate reference.
†There are additional proceedings for most states to have somebody admitted in an emergency through a court order. This table refers to those individuals who may initiate an emergency involuntary hospitalization *without* such an order.
‡When two lengths of time are indicated, it means that official court proceedings have been initiated and the longer time period is the maximum length of time which is permitted to follow through that process.

Drug Tables

TABLE A / ANTI-PSYCHOTIC DRUGS

Anti-Psychotic Drugs[1]
(Major Tranquilizers or
Neuroleptics)

Total Daily
Dosage
(mg.)[2]

Generic Name	Brand Name	Outpatient	Hospital
PHENOTHIAZINES*			
A. Aliphatic Series			
Chlorpromazine	Thorazine	50–100	200–1600
Triflupromazine	Vesprin	50–150	75–200
B. Piperidine Series			
Thioridazine	Mellaril	50–400	200–800
Mesoridazine	Serentil	25–200	100–400
Piperacetazine	Quide	10–80	40–160
C. Piperazine Series			
Prochlorperazine	Compazine	15–60	30–150
Trifluoperazine	Stelazine	4–10	6–30

Butaperazine	Repoise	5–50	25–100
Perphenazine	Trilafon	8–24	12–64
Fluphenazine	Permitil	1–3	2–20
	Prolixin	1–3	2–20
Acetophenazine	Tindal	40–60	60–80
Carphenazine	Proketazine	25–100	50–400
BUTYROPHENONES			
Haloperidol	Haldol	2–10	4–100
THIOXANTHENES			
Chlorprothixene	Taractan	30–60	75–600
Thiothixene	Navane	6–15	10–60
DIBENZOXAZEPINES			
Loxapine	Loxitane	20–125	60–250
DIHYDROINDOLONES			
Molindone	Moban	15–100	100–225
	Lidone	15–100	100–225

[1]Source: Adapted with permission from Richard I. Shader, M.D., ed., *Manual of Psychiatric Therapeutics: Practical Psychopharmacology and Psychiatry*, copyright 1975 by Little, Brown & Company, Boston.

[2]Source: Adapted from Aaron S. Mason and Robert P. Granacher, *Clinical Handbook of Antipsychotic Drug Therapy*, 1980, with permission from BRUNNER/MAZEL, Publisher, New York, p. 38.

*Anti-psychotic drugs may have short-term and long-term side effects. The side effects for phenothiazines appear below. According to Goodman and Gilman's *The Pharmacological Basis of Therapeutics*: "Therapeutic doses of phenothiazines may cause faintness, palpitation, nasal stuffiness, dry mouth, and some slight constipation. The patient may complain of being cold, drowsy, or weak. The most troublesome side effect is *orthostatic hypotension*, which may result in syncope [fainting]. A fall in blood pressure is most likely to occur from administration of the phenothiazines with aliphatic side chains." There are also a variety of nuerological side effects, among them "a slowing of involutional movement . . . rigidity and tremors." These are signs of Parkinsonism and develop early. Tardive dyskinesia, a late-appearing neurological syndrome, has caused concern because it may be irreversible. It includes "involuntary movements consisting in sucking and smacking of the lips, lateral jaw movements, and fly-catching dartings of the tongue." Other side effects reported include jaundice, retinal pigmentation, and breast engorgement. For detailed discussions of these and other side effects, consult Ross J. Baldessarini, "Drugs and the Treatment of Psychiatric Disorders," in Alfred Goodman Gilman, M.D., Ph.D.; Louis S. Goodman, M.A., M.D., D.Sc. (Hon.); and Alfred Gilman, Ph.D., D.Sc. (Hon.), eds., *The Pharmacological Basis of Therapeutics*, 6th ed. (New York: Macmillan Co., 1980), pp. 391–448; also see Richard I. Shader, M.D.; Alberto DiMascio, Ph.D; et al., *Psychotropic Drug Side Effects: Clinical and Theoretical Perspectives* (Baltimore, Md.: Williams & Wilkins, 1970).

TABLE B / ESTIMATED EQUIVALENCY OF ANTI-PSYCHOTIC DRUGS

Drug Classification	Estimated Equivalent Dose (mg.)	Conversion Factor*
PHENOTHIAZINES (classified by side chain)		
Aliphatic		
Chlorpromazine (Thorazine)	100	1:1
Triflupromazine (Vesprin)	25	1:4
Piperidine		
Thioridazine (Mellaril)	100	1:1
Mesoridazine (Serentil)	50	1:2
Piperacetazine (Quide)	10	1:10
Piperazine		
Actophenazine (Tindal)	20	1:5
Carphenazine (Proketazine)	25	1:4
Prochlorperazine (Compazine)	15	1:6
Perphenazine (Trilafon)	10	1:10
Trifluoperazine (Stelazine)	5	1:20
Fluphenazine (Prolixin, Permitil)	2	1:50
Butaperazine (Repoise)	10	1:10
BUTYROPHENONES		
Haloperidol (Haldol)	2	1:50
THIOXANTHENE DERIVATIVES		
Chlorprothixene (Taractan)	100	1:1
Thiothixene (Navane)	5	1:20
DIHYDROINDOLONE		
Molindone (Moban, Lidone)	25	1:4
DIBENZOXAZEPINES		
Loxapine (Loxitane)	15	1:6

*Estimated dosage ratio in relation to chlorpromazine. For example, a dose of 10 mg. of perphenazine (Trilafon) is equivalent to 100 mg. of chlorpromazine (Thorazine) since it is ten times as potent.

SOURCE: Reprinted from Aaron S. Mason and Robert P. Grenacher, *Clinical Handbook of Antipsychotic Drug Therapy*, 1980, with permission from BRUNNER/MAZEL, Publisher, New York, p. 33.

TABLE C / ANTI-DEPRESSANT DRUGS

Generic Name	Brand Name
TRYCYCLICS	
Imipramine	Tofranil, Imavate, SK-Pramine, Presamine, Antipres, Jamimine, Ropramine
Amitriptyline	Elavil, Amitril, Endep, Rolavil
Nortriptyline	Aventyl, Pamelor
Protriptyline	Vivactil
Doxepin	Sinequan, Adapin
Desipramine	Norpramin, Pertofrane
MAO INHIBITORS	
Isocarboxazid	Marplan
Pargyline	Eutonyl
Phenelzine	Nardil
Tranylcypromine	Parnate

SOURCE: Adapted with permission from Richard I. Shader, M.D., ed., *Manual of Psychiatric Therapeutics: Practical Psychopharmacology and Psychiatry*, copyright 1975 by Little, Brown & Company, Boston.

TABLE D / SIDE EFFECTS OF SELECTED ANTI-DEPRESSANTS*

Side Effect	Imipramine or Amitriptyline	Nortriptyline	Phenelzine	Isocarboxazid	Tranylcypromine
Dry mouth	20–40*	15–25	30	10–30	10
Constipation	10–30	0–5	5–20	5–20	5
Urinary retention	5–10	—†	5–10	5–10	—
Disturbed vision	10–20	0–10	10–20	10–20	10
Sweating	20–30	0–5	10–20	10–20	—

Side Effect	Imipramine or Amitriptyline	Nortriptyline	Phenelzine	Isocarboxazid	Tranylcypromine
Dizziness	15–30	0–15	0–25	10–25	5–20
Increased sexual desire	0–20	—	0–20	0–20	—
Decreased sexual desire	0–5	—	0–10	0–10	—
Nausea	0–10	0–5	0–10	0–10	0–5
Tremor or twitching	5–25	0–5	0–10	0–10	—
Drowsiness	0–20	0–15	0–20	0–20	0–10
Confusion	0–5	0–5	0–5	0–5	—
Palpitation	0–10	—	0–10	0–10	0–10
Hyperactivity	5–15	5–15	5–20	5–20	—
Edema	0–2	—	0–15	0–15	—

*Results are given as percentages of patients having side effects. Data are taken from several representative studies.
†No data available.
SOURCE: Reprinted from Donald F. Klein, M.D., Rachel Gittelman, Ph.D., Frederic Quitkin, M.D., and Arthur Rifkind, M.D., *Diagnosis and Drug Treatment of Psychiatric Disorders: Adults and Children,* 2nd ed. (Baltimore, Md.: Williams & Wilkins, 1980), p. 450.

TABLE E / SPECIAL CONCERNS OF PATIENTS ON MAO INHIBITORS (NARDIL, PARNATE, EUTONYL, MARPLAN)

1. FOODS AND BEVERAGES TO AVOID

—Matured or aged cheeses, such as blue, Swiss, Cheddar, American, and processed cheeses and spreads. However, cottage, cream, or farmer cheese may be eaten
—Red wines (Chianti in particular) and rosés
—Sherry, vermouth
—Beer
—Marmite, Bovril, and similar yeast or meat extracts (beware of drinks, soups, or stews made with these products)

—Yogurt not made by a reliable manufacturer
—Broad beans, fava beans, or Chinese pea pods
—Banana skins and overripe bananas
—Any meat, fish, poultry, or other protein food that is not fresh, freshly canned, or freshly frozen (this includes game meats, offal, lox, salami, sausage, corned beef, and liver, including pâté)
—Meat prepared with tenderizers
—Pickled herring and pickled lox
—Any food that previously produced unpleasant symptoms

2. THE FOLLOWING FOODS AND BEVERAGES SHOULD BE USED WITH MODERATION, AS THEY ARE OCCASIONALLY ASSOCIATED WITH ADVERSE REACTION.

—Caffeinated beverages, such as coffee, tea, cola
—Chocolate
—Alcoholic beverages of any kind (distilled liquors [vodka, gin, rye, scotch]) will not produce a hypertensive reaction but will interact with a MAO inhibitor to produce more rapid intoxication)
—Avocados
—Soy sauce

3. MEDICATIONS TO AVOID

—Cold tablets or drops, nasal decongestants (tablets or drops)
—Hay fever medication
—Sinus tablets
—Weight-reducing preparations, pep pills
—Anti-appetite medicine
—Asthma inhalants
—Demerol
—Other anti-depressants
—Epinephrine in local anesthesia (includes dental)

4. DO NOT TAKE ANY MEDICINES, DRUGS, PROPRIETARY PREPARATIONS (INCLUDING COUGH AND COLD CURES), OR ANY OTHER MEDICATION OF ANY SOURCE WHATEVER WITHOUT CONSULTING YOUR DOCTOR.

SOURCE: Adapted from Donald F. Klein, M.D., Rachel Gittelman, Ph.D., Frederic Quitkin, M.D., and Arthur Rifkind, M.D., *Diagnosis and Drug Treatment of Psychiatric Disorders: Adults and Children,* 2nd ed. (Baltimore, Md.: Williams & Wilkins, 1980), p. 484.

TABLE F / CLINICAL LITHIUM SIDE EFFECTS

Degree	Symptoms
Very mild	Nausea (particularly during first few days of treatment) Fine tremor of hands
Mild to moderate	Anorexia Vomiting Diarrhea "Upset stomach" or "abdominal pain" Thirst and/or excessive urination Muscular weakness Muscle twitching or chronic movements Sedation, sluggishness, languidness, drowsiness, giddiness Coarse tremor
Moderate to severe	Hyperactive deep tendon reflexes Hyperextension of arms and legs with grunts and gasping Impairment of consciousness Confusion, stupor, sleepiness Seizures

SOURCE: Adapted from Donald F. Klein, M.D., Rachel Gittelman, Ph.D., Frederic Quitkin, M.D., and Arthur Rifkind, M.D., *Diagnosis and Drug Treatment of Psychiatric Disorders: Adults and Children,* 2nd ed. (Baltimore, Md.: Williams & Wilkins, 1980), p. 471.

Resources and References

1 / Organizations

(The following are national organization headquarters which may be consulted for information about what exists in your local area.)

National Alliance for the Mentally Ill
1234 Massachusetts Avenue, N.W.
Washington, D.C. 20005
This is an umbrella for local chapters of self-help or advocacy groups. It is composed of families and friends of the mentally ill. Newsletter and annual conference.

Mental Health Association
National Headquarters
1800 North Kent Street
Arlington, Virginia 22209
Voluntary mental health associations made up of citizens working through community services.

Mental Health Law Project
2021 L Street, N.W.
Suite 800
Washington, D.C. 20036
A public-service legal firm which litigates on behalf of the mentally retarded and the mentally ill. Quarterly newsletter about mental health and the law.

American Civil Liberties Union
132 West Forty-third Street
New York, New York 10036
A non-profit organization which provides legal service on matters dealing with threats to civil rights or civil liberties.

American Schizophrenia Association
1114 First Avenue
New York, New York 10021
An association concerned with orthomolecular treatment and research.

National Association of Mental Health Directors
1001 Third Street, S.W.
Washington, D.C. 20024
Each state has an office or division which concerns itself with mental health. This association can put you in touch with the government official in your state.

Recovery, Inc.
116 South Michigan Avenue
Chicago, Illinois 60603
An association of former patients that provides self-help.

Network Against Psychiatric Assault
2150 Market Street
San Francisco, California 94114
An organization that publishes exposés of poor treatment of patients. Newsletter.

2 / GUIDES TO SERVICES AND PROGRAMS

*Directory of Halfway Houses
and Community Residences for the Mentally Ill—1977*
U.S. Department of Health and Human Services
National Institute of Mental Health
5600 Fishers Lane
Rockville, Maryland 20857
Lists halfway houses and community residences by state; thirty-eight pages.

Directory of Psychosocial Rehabilitation Facilities
International Association of Psycho-Social Rehabilitation Services
2700 North Lakeview Avenue
Chicago, Illinois 60614
Provides information about groups served, services provided, and requirements for admission. Is updated constantly.

Mental Health Directory—1977
National Institute of Mental Health
5600 Fishers Lane
Rockville, Maryland 20857
A state-by-state list of public and private psychiatric hospitals, psychiatric services in general hospitals, residential treatment centers for emotionally disturbed children, outpatient psychiatric clinics, mental health day and night facilities, federally funded comprehensive community mental health centers, and other multiservice mental health facilities not classified elsewhere.

National Directory
The National Training Program of Fountain House
Community Rehabilitation of the Mentally Ill
March 1981

Mental Health Services Information and Referral Directory
100 East Thousand Oaks Boulevard
Suite 224
Thousand Oaks, California 91360
There are four regional editions to this volume, listing mental health services by state, statistics about mental health, and resource services. The states within each regional edition are:

Eastern Edition: Maine, New Hampshire, Vermont, Massachusetts, Rhode Island, Connecticut, New Jersey, New York, Pennsylvania, Maryland, Delaware (also Washington, D.C.).

Central Edition: Ohio, Michigan, Indiana, Illinois, Wisconsin, Iowa, Minnesota, North Dakota, South Dakota, Nebraska, Kansas.

Southern Edition: Virginia, West Virginia, North Carolina, South Carolina, Georgia, Florida, Alabama, Mississippi, Louisiana, Arkansas, Missouri, Kentucky, Tennessee.

Western Edition: California, Nevada, Utah, Arizona, New Mexico, Texas, Oklahoma, Colorado, Wyoming, Montana, Idaho, Oregon, Washington, Alaska, Hawaii.

Thomas Malamud, Director
Fountain House
425 West Forty-seventh Street
New York, New York 10036
Lists the facilities participating in the Transitional Employment Program.

---

3 / Printed Materials

Reference Works *(also consult Notes)*

American Psychiatric Association. *Diagnostic and Statistical Manual, III.* American Psychiatric Association, 1980.

Bernheim, Kayla F. and Richard R. J. Levine. *Schizophrenia: Symptoms, Causes, Treatments.* New York: W. W. Norton & Co., 1979.

Ennis, Bruce J. and Richard D. Emery. *The Rights of Mental Patients.* New York: Avon Books, 1978.

Friedman, Paul R. *The Rights of Mentally Retarded Persons.* New York: Avon Books, 1976.

Kovel, Joel. *A Complete Guide to Therapy from Psychoanalysis to Behavior Modification.* New York: Pantheon Books, 1976.

Mishara, Brian L., Ph.D., and Robert D. Patterson, M.D. *Consumer's Guide to Mental Health.* New York: New American Library, 1977.

Parish, Peter, M.D. *The Doctors and Patients Handbook of Medicines and Drugs.* New York: Alfred A. Knopf, 1980.

Park, Clara Claiborn, and Leon N. Shapiro, M.D. *You Are Not Alone.* Boston: Little, Brown & Co., 1976.

Silverstone, Barbara, and Helen Kandel Hyman. *You and Your Aging Parent.* Rev. ed. New York: Pantheon Books, 1981.

Snyder, Solomon H., M.D. *Madness and the Brain.* New York: McGraw-Hill Book Co., 1974.

Reports and Proceedings

Advocacy for Persons with Chronic Mental Illness: Building a Nationwide Network, edited by Roger T. Williams and Harriet M. Shetler, University of Wisconsin—Extension, 432 North Lake Street, Madison, Wisconsin 53706.

A Special Kind of Help: A Study of the Needs of People Discharged from Psychiatric Hospitals, Mental Health Association of Essex County, 424 Main Street, East Orange, New Jersey 07018.

From Back Wards to Back Streets, Mental Health Association of Essex County, 424 Main Street, East Orange, New Jersey 07018.

Returning the Mentally Disabled to the Community: Government Needs to Do More. Report to the Congress by the Comptroller General of the United States, 1977. Requests should be sent to U.S. General Accounting Office, Distribution Section, Room 18, 441 G Street, N.W., Washington, D.C. 20548.

Task Panel Reports Submitted to the President's Commission on Mental Health. Washington, D.C.: U.S. Government Printing Office, 1978. 4 vols.

The Following Publications Regularly Have Articles of Interest:

Schizophrenia Bulletin

The Mental Disability Law Reporter

Current Population Reports, U.S. Bureau of the Census

Mental Health Statistical Notes, National Institute of Mental Health, Division of Biometry and Epidemiology

Closer Look, A Project of the Parents Campaign for Handicapped Children and Youth, Box 1492, Washington, D.C. 20013

Rehab Brief, National Institute of Handicapped Research, Office of Human Development Services, Department of Health and Human Services, Washington, D.C. 20201

Notes

2
ENTERING THE SYSTEM

1. Bruce J. Ennis and Richard D. Emery, *The Rights of Mental Patients* (New York: Avon Books, 1978), p. 38. Also, consult Donaldson's autobiographical account in *Insanity Inside Out* (New York: Crown Publishers, 1976). The Mental Health Law Project, *Summary of Activities,* March 1975, September 1975; Patricia M. Wald and Paul R. Friedman, "The Politics of Mental Health Advocacy in the United States," *International Journal of Law and Psychiatry,* vol. 1 (1978), pp. 137–52.

3
THE DILEMMA OF DIAGNOSIS

1. Four articles discuss the role of stressful life events and schizophrenia in *Schizophrenia Bulletin,* vol. 7, no. 1 (1981).
2. Harry Stack Sullivan, *Conceptions of Modern Psychiatry* (New York: W. W. Norton & Co., 1953), p. x.

3.   Dr. Richard Wyatt, "Frontiers of Research," paper delivered at the Second Annual Conference, National Alliance for the Mentally Ill, Chicago, Illinois, September 1980.

4.   *Ibid.* Also see Richard Jedd Wyatt, M.D., et al., "The Schizophrenia Syndrome: Examples of Biological Tools for Subclassification," *Journal of Nervous and Mental Disease,* vol. 69, no. 2 (February 1981), pp. 100–12.

5.   Heinz E. Lehmann, "Psychopharmacological Treatment of Schizophrenia," *Schizophrenia Bulletin,* no. 13 (1975), pp. 27–45.

6.   *Schizophrenia Bulletin,* vol. 6, no. 1. (1980), pp. 1–4.

7.   Eric Gopelrud and Richard Depue ask whether 25 percent of the patients who have depression after acute psychotic episodes are diagnosed accurately as schizophrenic. See "The Diagnostic Ambiguity of Postpsychotic Depression," *Schizophrenia Bulletin,* vol. 4., no. 4 (1978), pp. 477–80. Also see a subsequent article by the same authors, "Affective Symptoms, Schizophrenia, and the Conceptual Ambiguity of Postpsychotic Depression," in *ibid.,* vol. 5, no. 4 (1979), pp. 555–59.

8.   A 1972 study confirmed this difference, which was first reported in 1959. See Barry J. Gurland, et al., "Use of Diagnosis for Comparing Psychiatric Populations," *Psychiatric Quarterly,* vol. 46 (1972), pp. 461–73.

9.   Loren Mosher, M.D., "Can Diagnosis Be Nonpejorative?" in Lyman C. Wynn, M.D., Ph.D., *The Nature of Schizophrenia* (New York: John Wiley & Sons, 1978), pp. 690–95.

10. Thomas McGlashan and William T. Carpenter, Jr., "Affective Symptoms and the Diagnosis of Schizophrenia," *Schizophrenia Bulletin,* vol. 5, no. 4 (1979), pp. 547–53.

11. John Neary, *Whom the Gods Destroy* (New York: Atheneum Publishers, 1975).

12. Mosher, "Can Diagnosis be Nonpejorative?"

13. William S. Appleton, M.D., "Mistreatment of Patients' Families by Psychiatrists," *American Journal of Psychiatry,* vol. 131, no. 6 (June 1974), pp. 655–57. Also see Carol M. Anderson, "Family Intervention with Severely Disturbed Inpatients," *Archives of General Psychiatry,* vol. 34 (June 1979), pp. 697–702.

4
PSYCHIATRIC HOSPITALS

1.   Mildred S. Cannon and Richard W. Redick, "Differential Utilization of Psychiatric Facilities by Men and Women, United States, 1970," Statistical Note 81, National Institute of Mental Health, June 1973.

2.   Richard Almond, "Issues in Milieu Treatment," *Schizophrenia Bulletin,* no. 13 (1972), pp. 12–26.

3.   "Additions and Resident Patients at End of Year, State and County Mental Hospitals by Age and Diagnosis, by State, United States,

1976," National Institute of Mental Health, September 1978.

4. Joan Jenkins and Michael Watkin, "Foreign Medical Graduates Employed in State and County Mental Hospitals," Statistical Note 131, National Institute of Mental Health, 1976.

5
RESIDENTIAL TREATMENT CENTERS

1. The discussion of the Fairweather Lodge is based on George Fairweather, ed., "The Fairweather Lodge: A Twenty-Five Year Retrospective," *New Direction for Mental Health Services,* no. 7 (1980).
2. Richard D. Budson and Robert E. Jolley, "A Crucial Factor in Community Program Success: The Extended Psychosocial Kinship System," *Schizophrenia Bulletin,* vol. 4, no. 4 (1978), p. 612.
3. Loren R. Mosher, M.D., and Alma S. Menn, A.C.S.W., "Extended Surrogate Family Treatment of Schizophrenia: An Alternative to Hospitalization," in J. C. Shersow, ed., *Schizophrenia: Science and Practice* (Cambridge: Harvard University Press, 1978), pp. 223–39.
4. *Ibid.*
5. Richard D. Budson, *The Psychiatric Halfway House* (Pittsburgh, Pa.: University of Pittsburgh Press, 1978), pp. 10–15.
6. Dennis J. Rog, M.Ed., and Harold Rausch, Ph.D., "The Psychiatric Halfway House: How Is It Measuring Up?" *Community Mental Health Journal,* vol. 11, no. 2 (1975), pp. 155–62.
7. Budson, *Psychiatric Halfway House,* p. 8.
8. Comptroller General, *Returning the Mentally Disabled to the Community: Government Needs to Do More* (Washington, D.C.: U.S. Government Printing Office, 1977), p. 17.
9. The Discharged Patient Advocacy Project, *From Back Wards to Back Streets* (East Orange, N.J.: Mental Health Association of Essex County, 1978), pp. 44–45.
10. *New York Times,* September 2, 1980.
11. *Ibid.*
12. *Ibid.,* November 18, 1979.
13. Budson, *Psychiatric Halfway House,* p. 10.
14. *Task Panel Reports Submitted to the President's Commission on Mental Health* (Washington, D.C.: U.S. Government Printing Office, 1978), vol. 1, p. 52.
15. *Ibid.,* vol. 2, p. 531.
16. *Ibid.,* vol. 2, p. 388.

6
NON-RESIDENTIAL TREATMENT PROGRAMS

1. *Task Panel Reports Submitted to the President's Commission on Mental Health* (Washington, D.C.: U.S. Government Printing Office, 1978), vol. 1, p. 17.

2. Marvin I. Herz, M.D., et al., "Day Versus Inpatient Hospitalization: A Controlled Study," *American Journal of Psychiatry,* vol. 127, no. 10 (April 1971), pp. 1371–81.
3. Elaine Weldon, Ph.D., et al., "Day Hospital Versus Out-Patient Treatment: A Controlled Study," *Psychiatric Quarterly,* vol. 51, no. 2 (Summer 1979), pp. 144–50.
4. Gerard E. Hogarty, M.S.W., and Richard F. Ulrich, "Temporal Effects of Drugs and Placebos in Delaying Relapse in Schizophrenic Outpatients," *Archives of General Psychiatry,* vol. 34 (March 1977), pp. 297–301.
5. In April 1975, the assistant commissioner for program development said there would be an attempt to specify the needs which corresponded to the de-institutionalization policy as part of its future priorities. By April 1976, the Rehabilitation Services Administration established a task force to redefine the qualification of severe handicap for the vocational rehabilitation program. See Comptroller General, *Returning the Mentally Disabled to the Community: Government Needs to Do More* (Washington, D.C.: U.S. Government Printing Office, 1977), pp. 151, 153.
6. William A. Anthony et al., "The Measurement of Rehabilitation Outcome," *Schizophrenia Bulletin,* vol. 4, no. 3 (1978), p. 368.
7. Amerigo Farina and Robert D. Felner, "Employment Interviewer Reactions to Former Patients," *Journal of Abnormal Psychology,* vol. 82 (1973), pp. 268–72. Also see "Enhancing Employer Receptivity to Hiring Disabled Workers," *Rehab Brief,* vol. 2, no. 8 (September 24, 1979).
8. *Task Panel Reports,* vol. 2, p. 369.
9. John Beard, "Psychiatric Rehabilitation at Fountain House," in Jack Meislin, M.D., ed., *Rehabilitation Medicine and Psychiatry* (Springfield, Ill.: Charles C. Thomas Publishing Co., 1976), pp. 393–413.
10. Client Comments Concerning Transitional Employment, Fountain House, January 1980, no. 1.
11. *Ibid.,* no. 26.
12. Personal communication from John Beard.
13. Raymond M. Glasscote et al., *Rehabilitating the Mentally Ill in the Community* (Washington, D.C.: Joint Information Service of the American Psychiatric Association and the National Association for Mental Health, 1971), p. 103.
14. *Task Panel Reports,* vol. 2, p. 277.

7
SETTLING . . . AT HOME

1. Kenneth Minkoff, M.D., "A Map of Chronic Mental Patients," in John A. Talbott, M.D., ed., *The Chronic Mental Patient* (Washington, D.C.: American Psychiatric Association, 1978), pp. 11–39.

9

FAMILIES ADJUST

1. Frieda Fromm-Reichman, "Notes on the Development of Treatment of Schizophrenics by Psychoanalytic Psychotherapy," *Psychiatry,* vol. 11 (1948), pp. 263–73; Gregory Bateson et al., "Toward a Theory of Schizophrenia," *Behavioral Science,* vol. 1 (1965), pp. 251–64. Discussions of more recent studies about the patient's family may be found in Eugene B. Brady, M.D., "Can Mother-Infant Interaction Produce Vulnerability to Schizophrenia?" *Journal of Nervous and Mental Disease,* vol. 169, no. 2 (February 1981), pp. 72–81; Leslie Y. Rabkin, Ph.D., "The Patient's Family: Research Methods," *Family Process,* vol. 4, no. 1 (March 1965), pp. 105–32; T. Jacob, "Family Interaction in Disturbed and Normal Families: A Methodological and Substantive Review," *Psychological Bulletin,* vol. 82, no. 1 (1975), pp. 33–65; Lyman C. Wynne, M.D., Ph.D., "Current Concepts About Schizophrenics and Family Relationships," *Journal of Nervous and Mental Disease,* vol. 169, no. 2 (February 1981), pp. 82–89.
2. Agnes B. Hatfield, Ph.D., "Psychological Costs of Schizophrenia in the Family," *Social Work,* vol. 23, no. 5 (September 1978), p. 357.

10

FAMILIES ORGANIZE

1. *Task Panel Reports Submitted to the President's Commission on Mental Illness* (Washington, D.C.: U.S. Government Printing Office, 1978), vol. 2, p. 367.
2. *Task Panel Reports,* vol. 2, p. 345. On stigma, see Erving Goffman, *Stigma: Notes on the Management of Spoiled Identity* (Englewood Cliffs, N.J.: Prentice-Hall, 1963).
3. "Mental Illness and the Media: An Unhealthy Condition," *Disability USA,* vol. 2, no. 2 (1978), pp. 23–24.
4. Roger T. Williams and Harriet M. Shetler, eds., *Proceedings of a Conference: Advocacy for Persons with Chronic Mental Illness* (Madison, Wis., September 1979), p. 18.

Index

adolescents, 30–6, 48–53, 71–83, 94–111. *See also* children; siblings

affective disorders, 58. *See also* manic-depressive psychoses

aftercare, 90–3; residential treatment centers, 112–34. *See also* hospital discharge; non-residential treatment; outpatient programs

alcoholism, 84, 92

Almond, Richard, 260

American Civil Liberties Union, 254

American Psychiatric Association, 62, 256

American Schizophrenia Association, 222, 254

Anderson, Carol M., xv, 142–3, 260

Anthony, William A., 262

anti-depressant drugs, *see* medication

anti-psychotic drugs, *see* medication

Appleton, William S., 260

Asbury Park, N.J., 118–19

at-home care, 160–74, 184–6; costs of, 168; effects on family life, 160–74; medication for, 170; requirements of, 169–70

Austen Riggs Center, 51

bag ladies, 8. *See also* de-institutionalization

Bateson, Gregory, 212, 263

Beard, John, xv, 149, 151, 262

Beels, C. Christian, xv, xix–xxiii

behavioral therapies, 73–4, 170

INDEX

Berkeley House, 114, 119, 121–2
Bernheim, Kayla F., 256
Bleuler, Eugen, 58
block grants, 229
board-and-care facilities, *see* housing
Brady, Eugene B., 263
Brown, Edmund G., Jr., 230
Budson, Richard D., 115, 119, 261

California: Parents of the Adult Mentally Ill, 230; Parents of Adult Schizophrenics (PAS), 222–4; state hospitals, 230
California Association, 230
Cannon, Mildred S., 260
Carpenter, William T., Jr., 260
catchment areas, 136, 235
Charleston, S.C., 226
Chestnut Lodge, 51
Chicago, 152, 225
children: institutionalized, 184–8; mentally ill, 22, 23–4, 26, 30–6, 48–53, 71–83, 94–111, 119–22, 138, 144–8, 152, 157–74, 209; of the mentally ill, 12–13, 18, 19–21, 37–8, 83–93, 112, 122–3, 140, 175–80, 181, 189–92, 198–204, 217, 218. *See also* adolescents
chronically ill, *see* mental illness; mentally ill
civil liberties, 39–40
clergy, 168
Colorado, 41
commitment proceedings, 38–41, 48, 84, 122, 186; statutes on, 240–5
Community Mental Health Care Centers Act, 126, 135–6, 229
Community Mental Health Centers, 119, 126, 135–6, 224, 235–6; obligatory services, 136; outpatient programs, 136, 140–4

community residences, 92, 120; directory of, 254. *See also* housing
counseling services, 91
counterculture, 28, 170
county mental health offices, 164

day hospital program, 71–2, 109, 122, 127, 136–40; compared with outpatient programs, 137; components of, 136, 139; families and, 140; functions of, 140; length of, 139; obstacles to choosing, 137–8
de-institutionalization, xxi, 8, 164, 236, 262. *See also* hospital discharge
delusions and hallucinations, 24, 28–30, 40, 47, 57, 60–1, 236. *See also* schizophrenia and schizophrenics
dementia praecox, 58. *See also* schizophrenia and schizophrenics
denial, 50, 236
Depue, Richard, 260
diagnosis, xxii, 9, 50, 51–3, 54, 55–66; cultural and subjective criteria, 61; drugs and, 58, 59–60; emergency room, 45; family and, 21, 51–3, 56–8, 61–2; hospital staff involved in, 56; importance of, 62; as pejorative label, 50, 62–4, 228
discharge, *see* de-institutionalization *and* hospital discharge
District of Columbia, 129
divorce, 191–2, 216–17
Dix, Dorothea, 8
Donaldson, Kenneth: *Insanity Inside Out,* 39–40, 106, 259
double bind, 236
drugs, 73; illegal, 95, 96, 97–8; LSD, 34; marijuana, 36, 95, 185; "speed," 98, 100. *See also* medication
dyslexia, 33, 236

Other Pantheon Titles of Interest